LIFETIME CONVERSATION GUIDE

James K. Van Fleet

PRENTICE HALL

Library of Congress Cataloging-in-Publication Data

Van Fleet, James K.
    Lifetime conversation guide.

    Includes index.
    1. Conversation.   2. Success.   I. Title.
    BJ2121.V36   1984   84-4718
    153.6—dc20   CIP

Printed in the United States of America

30 31 32 33 34 35 36 37 38 39 40

ISBN 0-13-536400-0

PRENTICE HALL
Paramus, NJ 07652

On the World Wide Web at http://www.phdirect.com

To my dear wife, Belva, who has been the light of my life for more than forty years.

Other Books by the Author

Guide to Managing People
How to Use the Dynamics of Motivation
Power with People
How to Put Yourself Across with People
Miracle People Power
The 22 Biggest Mistakes Managers Make and How to Correct Them
Van Fleet's Master Guide for Managers
25 Steps to Power and Mastery over People

What This Book Will Do for You

After more than 30 years as a consultant in business management and human relations, I have found that a person's success depends as much on the ability to talk as it does on the professional and technical know-how to do the job.

All other things being equal, advancement and promotion will invariably go to the person who has mastered the art of self-expression, both in speaking and writing, while his colleague, who attaches little or no importance to what can be achieved with the use of language, will be marked for mediocrity or failure. The famous British statesman of the 19th century, Disraeli, summed up this idea succinctly when he said, "Men govern with words."

This book will show you exactly how to do that. It will give you the tools and techniques you need to gain power with people and win mastery over them through the art of conversation. You will be shown how to influence and control specific key individuals in your life by what you say, so you can achieve your goals and become highly successful.

Why You Should First Master the Language

If you want to become successful and get to the top, you should first master the language. Language is ever so important, for if you will analyze your day, you'll find that no less than 75 to 80 percent of it is spent in oral communication with someone: explaining, persuading, advising, ordering, influencing, asking and answering questions. In short, you'll spend most of your time putting your proposals across to others—including your own family—so you can gain power and mastery over people and get them to do what you want them to do.

The more capable you become in expressing yourself clearly and precisely to others so there will be absolutely no chance of misunderstanding, the more successful you will become in mastering people and controlling their actions.

Why Language Is the Magic Key to Success

I am not alone in recognizing that language is the magic key to getting ahead and becoming successful. A famous and well-known psychologist made a detailed study of hundreds of successful men and women to determine the main reasons for their success. She found that all these people had one specific thing in common: *their skill in using words*.

She also discovered that *their earning power was closely linked to their word skills*. You, too, can expect your earning power to increase when you improve your own language skills. This is just one of the many benefits you'll gain from the *Lifetime Conversation Guide*.

Some of the Other Benefits You'll Gain from This Book

When you learn how to govern and control people with words, you'll be at home in any social environment. You can walk into any group and be as much at ease as if you were with your own family. Master the art of self-expression and you can become the recognized leader in all the social, business, political, and community affairs in which you participate. You can easily be elected to the presidency or chairmanship of clubs and groups if that's what you want. In fact, wherever you go, you'll be hailed as a leader; you'll be treated with dignity and respect; people will listen to you and do as you want them to do.

Aside from these benefits I've just given you, here are seven more valuable dividends that will be yours:

1. You'll develop a winning, positive, and powerful outgoing personality.
2. You'll have greater self-confidence, emotional security, and peace of mind.
3. You'll gain the ability to think clearly and to express yourself precisely.
4. People will listen to you and get the job done right the first time.
5. Your boss will take notice of you and recognize your talents.
6. Promotion and advancement will come your way as a matter of course.
7. You'll develop the power to influence and control others so they will do what you want them to do.

How This Book Is Organized

Your *Lifetime Conversation Guide* is divided into six parts for your convenience and ready reference. This organization is not arbitrary. It is based on the fact that there are basically two general types of conversation with which we are mainly concerned: social and business. Business conversations can be further subdivided into those that order, command, or direct; those that exchange information; and those that use persuasion.

Part I covers social conversations, although many of the techniques presented are also useful in business situations. In Chapter One, you'll learn how to take advantage of the 14 secret motivators all people have; how to use a person's greed to get what you want from him; 5 guaranteed ways to find out what a person really wants.

In Chapter Two, you'll discover the tactful way to strike up a conversation with a complete stranger; how to take control of the conversation immediately; getting superior service from a waitress or a clerk—even a haughty government bureaucrat; how to get a total stranger to go out of his way to help you; 3 sure-fire ways to make friends with a complete stranger; controlling the attitudes and emotions of strangers.

In Chapter Three, I'll show you how to build your friendships on a strong and enduring basis. You'll learn specific techniques you can use to gain a person's friendship, avoid arguments and disagreements, mix friendship and business successfully, and finally, 15 ways to keep your friendships warm and cordial.

In Chapter Four, you'll be given the techniques you can use to be well-liked and highly popular wherever you go. For instance, you'll learn the first big secret of how to be liked, not only by your friends, but also by your spouse and your children. You'll also learn 5 techniques you can use that will cause people to consider you a "whiz" at conversation. I'll show you how to practice the 5 big secrets of being popular and well-liked. Finally, I'll give you a 12-point checklist to follow to insure your own popularity.

Chapter Five will give you the magic methods that can make your marriage and your home life much happier. Use them, and you'll enjoy a peaceful and pleasant atmosphere in your home. You'll be shown how to get in the habit of saying the cheerful thing; a technique that will work for you if you're a newlywed; how to have a family love feast; how to guide, direct, and control your children without effort; how a wife can help her husband become highly successful.

In Part II, I discuss business conversations that order, command, or direct people to do something. Chapter Six will give you the techniques you can use to get immediate compliance with your commands. You'll also learn the 3 basic requirements for issuing orders. I'll give you the techniques you can use to get the person "in the mood" to follow your orders; you'll find 6 specific guidelines to help you issue clear, concise, and positive orders that are easy to understand and 3 methods you can use to check for understanding; I'll show you how to get the maximum from your orders. Finally, you'll be given 6 guidelines to help you develop your own *aura of command*.

Chapter Seven offers a 16-step program you can use to correct a person's mistakes so subtly that your criticism will sound like a compliment. You'll also receive an 8-point checklist to help you determine the effectiveness of your criticism.

In Part III, I discuss business conversations that are used to exchange information. In Chapter Eight, you'll see how to make the average employee a superior one by what you say to him. You'll learn how to let a person know exactly where he stands without injuring his pride. I'll give you an 18-point checklist you can use to evaluate a person's performance. You'll discover the correct way to tell an employee when his work is not up to par. I'll show you how to use praise to make an employee feel like a very important person.

Chapter Nine gives you 8 specific techniques to use for gaining information from employees that will benefit you. You'll learn how to stop spending money on efficiency experts and management consultants; you'll see how a company was saved from financial ruin by employee suggestions; I'll show you how to encourage employee initiative and how to keep the employer-employee communication lines open and working.

Chapter Ten will show you how to find out what's *really* going on in your own organization. I'll give you a 6-point checklist you can use to get accurate and reliable information from your employees. You'll find 10 techniques that will vastly improve your listening abilities. You'll learn to watch for the 7 telltale body language signs that often reveal more than the spoken word. I'll give you 12 guidelines for handling employee gripes and complaints.

Chapter Eleven discusses a fascinating subject: how to use body language to project your personal power. I'll show you how to develop a powerful and commanding personality. You'll learn the *steepling technique* to project your power without ever saying a single word.

You'll see how to create your own *space bubble* to establish your turf, how to use body gestures to your advantage, how to use your eyes to invade another person's territory, how to stop trouble without ever saying a single word, how to project your power in telephone conversations, and finally, 6 tips on how to project your power with body language alone.

Part IV covers business conversations that use persuasion. Chapter Twelve shows you how to get people to do what you want them to do. You'll learn the important precept that is the foundation for all persuasive techniques. I'll give you a method that forces people to pay immediate attention to you. You'll learn the 9 benefits that will be yours when you use the *leading question technique.* You'll discover a 5-step procedure to persuade a person to your point of view.

Chapter Thirteen reveals the secret of dealing with your listener's resistance. You'll be shown how to keep digging for the hidden reason behind his objection. I'll give you a technique to overcome resistance by shooting for the heart instead of the head. Finally, I'll show you a 6-step technique you can use to win every argument.

Chapter Fourteen reveals the 10 secrets of persuasion that super salespeople use to become successful. When you use them, you too will become a master in the art of persuasion. I'll show you how to get your prospect saying "Yes" immediately. You'll see how to concentrate on a single point and not scatter your fire so you can make your sale. You'll learn the secrets of selling benefits instead of features. You'll discover the best way to clinch a sale and how to keep from losing your sale after it's made.

In Chapter Fifteen, you'll see how to gain people's complete cooperation and full support. You'll learn 5 techniques to win and hold the confidence of others, a simple sure-fire method to gain a person's trust, how to use the *participatory management technique,* using the *buffer technique* to get cooperation and support from your subordinates, and 3 magic words that will always get people to back you to the hilt.

Part V covers special conversational situations; it includes Chapters Sixteen through Nineteen, and shows you how to use your conversational expertise in certain specific circumstances.

For example, in Chapter Sixteen, I'll show you how to give a talk or make a speech like a professional. You'll learn how to overcome your fear of speaking in public. You'll see how to organize your talk or speech for maximum effectiveness. I'll give you the 5 major parts of a talk or speech along with 12 methods to make your talk forceful and convincing, and 5 ways to develop confidence in your abilities to speak to an audience.

In Chapter Seventeen, you'll learn the 9 important trade secrets of professional platform speakers. I'll show you how to develop your own distinctive speaking style, the master methods you can use to control the emotions of your audience, 5 ways to control and overcome your nervousness, 4 ways to physically project your personality while speaking, 7 irritating mannerisms to avoid as well as 7 important don'ts to remember. You'll also learn 8 professional guidelines for using visual aids.

Chapter Eighteen offers you a seven-step program that shows you how to use your conversational expertise to succeed in business. You'll be shown how to talk your way to success, how to sound like a top-level executive, how to make that first good impression in an important job interview, 7 guidelines to getting that raise you deserve so much, 7 techniques you can use to talk your way to the top in the big company, how to attract the favorable attention of the upper hierarchy, and 8 ways to let your business do your talking for you.

Chapter Nineteen will show you how to make your conversation count with the most important people in your life. You'll learn the best ways of getting along with your own boss; I'll give you 5 specific guidelines you can use to put your ideas across to your superior; you'll learn how to talk at employees' affairs; I'll show you how to give a briefing for a group of VIPs. I've also included 5 guidelines you can use for a VIP briefing as well as 5 specific don'ts to keep in mind while you're giving it. You'll be given 4 simple guidelines to help you relax and talk with your fellow workers and associates, as well as with members of the opposite sex, no matter what the age or the position of those persons might be.

In Part VI, I discuss the major conversational problems you can encounter in both your oral and written relationships with people. The written language almost always causes trouble, so in Chapter Twenty I've given you the master formula that shows you how to write as you talk. You'll learn 6 techniques you can use to make sure you're understood. I'll give you a fail-safe way to chop the deadwood out of your writing. You'll see how to use *power words* to get your reader to take action. I've also shown you the 6 basic rules for writing powerful and masterful letters. I've given you a 5-point format for a persuasive letter using the *hook technique*. You'll also learn the best way to use fear in a persuasive letter to stir your reader to take action.

Chapter Twenty-One covers the 7 cardinal sins of conversation. It shows you how to correct them, or better yet, how to avoid them. When you avoid these seven cardinal sins, you'll be regarded as the person with the *golden tongue*. You'll prevent misunderstandings and disagreements. You'll improve your ability to get along well with others and be well thought of by your friends and neighbors. Everyone will have a good word for you.

Finally, in Chapter Twenty-Two, I'll give you a magic list of techniques you can use to successfully open and close a conversation, a talk, or a speech. You'll be shown how you can make a good first impression and a good final one so you can leave your listeners with a good feeling toward you.

You'll learn how to open a conversation gracefully with a woman if you're a man, and how to talk to a man if you're a woman. I'll give you a magic method you can use to open and close a telephone conversation. You'll also find 7 ways to open a talk or a speech. You'll learn the advantages of using leading questions to start off a business conversation. Finally, I'll show you how to know when to stop talking.

That, in brief, is what your *Lifetime Conversation Guide* is all about. But it is even more than that. It will also answer all your questions about conversation, for you will have a conversational problem-solver right at your fingertips. For instance, your *Lifetime Conversation Guide* will show you specifically how to:

- Avoid deadly "conversation killers"
- Turn off a nonstop speaker
- Add zing, sparkle, and punch to your conversation
- Develop your timing instinct
- Listen between the lines to find out what the other person really means.
- Find out if other people are actually listening to you
- Salvage a dying conversation
- Sidestep and avoid deadly conversational mistakes
- Project the power of your personality

As you can see, the *Lifetime Conversation Guide* is an organized, cohesive, and sure-fire program for getting ahead and gaining both your social and professional goals. It will stand you in good stead for the rest of your life.

But your *Lifetime Conversation Guide* is not meant to be read only once and then placed on a bookshelf to gather dust. After you've finished reading it the first time, you will want to refer to it again and again for the instant benefits you can gain, and the help it will give you in developing your conversational expertise and sharpening your verbal techniques. Whenever you have a communication problem of some sort, all you need do is turn to the appropriate section or chapter to find your answer.

If you will use your *Lifetime Conversation Guide* as a ready reference book, you will become a much better speaker as well as a much better writer. You will never be at a loss for words, no matter what the situation might be. You'll always know what to say, and when and how to say it. That, I guarantee.

James K. Van Fleet

Contents

What This Book Will Do for You .... *vii*

PART I:
LETTING YOUR CONVERSATION
TAKE CHARGE OF YOUR SOCIAL LIFE *1*

Chapter 1:
Using a Person's 14 Secret Motivators
to Your Own Advantage in Conversations *3*

How George Rogers does it *4* Three major points to
remember from this one example *5* You'll gain these major
benefits for yourself *5* Techniques you can use to gain these
marvelous benefits *6* The 14 deep secret motivators that
turn people on *7* Using these 14 secret motivators to your
advantage *9* Five sure-fire guaranteed methods you can
use to draw a person out *9* How to ask questions that get
honest answers *10* Specific subjects people like to talk
about *10* Why accurate information about what people want
is so important *11* Two examples of how to use a person's
secret needs and desires for your own benefit *13*

Chapter 2:
Six Guaranteed Ways to Strike Up
a Conversation and Feel Completely at Ease
with a Total Stranger *17*

Make a good first impression *18* You'll gain these 6 highly
significant benefits *19* The 6 techniques you can use to gain
these benefits *20* The tactful way to strike up a conversation with a complete stranger *20* How to take control of
the conversation immediately *21* How to get superior service from a waitress or a clerk *22* How you can get a complete stranger to go out of his way to help you *23* Three
sure-fire ways to make friends with a total stranger *24* How
you can control the attitudes and emotions of complete
strangers *26*

Chapter 3:
How to Use the Psychology of Conversation
to Build Strong and Enduring Friendships **29**

You'll gain these 6 terrific benefits *30* Eight potent guidelines you can use to gain these magnificent benefits *31* How
to put the first guideline to work *31* How to build your
friendships on a solid foundation *32* Specific ways you can
praise a person to gain his friendship *33* Finding a common
denominator for your friendship *35* Why you should accept
a person exactly as he or she is *36* Avoiding arguments and
disagreements at all costs *37* How you can mix friendship
and business successfully *39* Fifteen ways to keep your
friendships warm and cordial *39*

Chapter 4:
How to be Well-Liked and Highly Popular
Wherever You Go **43**

Seven fabulous benefits that will be yours *44* Five big secrets
of being well-liked and highly popular *45* How to practice
the first big secret of popularity *47* How to put the second
big secret of popularity to work *47* How to use the third
big secret of popularity *49* How to put the fourth big secret
of popularity into action *51* Practicing the fifth big secret
of how to be popular and well-liked *52* How Max W. prac-
tices these techniques to be popular *53* Six ways to become
a loner and not be invited anywhere *54* How to win a popularity contest: A 12-point checklist *54*

Chapter 5:
Magic Methods That Will Make Your Marriage
and Your Home Life Much Happier **57**

You'll gain these 6 huge benefits *58* Nine magic methods
you can use to gain these benefits *58* How to create a happy
family atmosphere by what you say *58* How to get up on
the right side of the bed *60* How to get in the habit of saying
the cheerful, pleasant thing *60* A technique that will work
magic in your marriage for you *61* How to work this technique if you are newly married *62* How to have a family
love feast *63* How to guide, direct, and control your children without effort *65* How a wife can help her husband
become highly successful *66* How to make your spouse the
most important person in your life by what you say *66*

PART II:
BUSINESS CONVERSATIONS THAT ORDER,
COMMAND, OR DIRECT *71*

Chapter 6:
How to Give Orders and Commands That Will
Always Be Obeyed Without Fail *73*

The 5 outstanding benefits you'll gain *74* Nine techniques
you can use to gain these benefits *75* How to give orders
that will always be followed without question: The first
requirement *75* How to give commands that will always
be obeyed: The second requirement *76* How to issue orders
that will always be carried out: The third requirement *77* How to get him in the mood to follow your
orders *78* Six guidelines for issuing clear, concise, and positive orders that are easy to understand *79* Three methods
you can use to check for understanding *82* How to get the
maximum for your orders *83* Developing the *aura of command*: Six guidelines *84* You'll gain these 4 valuable
benefits *85* How to project your aura of command to
others *85*

Chapter 7:
How to Correct a Person's Mistakes so
It Sounds Like a Compliment:
A 16-Step Program *87*

The enormous benefits you'll gain when you learn how to
say it with flowers *88* Sixteen techniques you can use to
gain these benefits *89* How to call attention to a person's
mistakes indirectly *89* Why you need to get all the pertinent
facts first *90* How to decide whether a formal counseling
session is necessary or not *91* How to pick the right time
and place *91* Why you must never lose your temper when
counseling an employee *92* Why this is the only way to
begin *92* How to take your own inventory *93* Why you
should let him tell his side of the story first *94* How to
weigh all the evidence and facts carefully *94* Why you should
discuss only one mistake per interview *95* Why you must
be specific about how to correct the mistake *95* Why you
should fit the penalty to the offense *96* How to close your
counseling session on an up-beat note *96* How to get your

employee to constantly improve *96* How to give your
employees a good reputation to live up to *97* How to follow
up with further action if necessary *97* A final checklist for
you *98*

PART III:
BUSINESS CONVERSATIONS THAT
ARE USED TO EXCHANGE INFORMATION *99*

Chapter 8:
How to Make the Average Employee
a Superior One by What You Say to Him *101*

You'll gain these four extraordinary benefits *102* The well-
informed employee is always the best employee *102* Keep
your people informed to encourage their initiative and
enthusiasm—Their teamwork and morale *103* Keeping
people well-informed will eliminate rumors *103* Keep your
people well-informed to gain their respect, confidence, willing obedience, loyal cooperation, and full support *103* Ten
techniques you can use to gain these benefits *104* How to
let people know exactly where they stand with you *104* How
to rate a person's performance: An 18-point checklist *105* How to tell a person when his work is not satisfactory *106* Why you should always praise a person for a
job well done *106* How to praise a person properly *107* How
you can make an employee feel like a VIP *107* Why you
should brief your assistants at an early stage on planned
changes *108* How to prevent or eliminate misunderstandings *108* If a planned company change affects a person, let him know *109* If a planned change does *not* affect
a person, let him know that, too *109* Have your people tell
you what you have to hear *111*

Chapter 9:
Eight Techniques for Gaining Information
from Employees That Will Benefit You *113*

You can gain these 4 fantastic benefits *114* They'll feel as
though they're really part of the team *114* You can identify
people of above-average ability *114* Your employees will

put their imagination, initiative, and ingenuity to work for you *115* You'll give people a feeling of importance *115* Eight techniques you can use to gain these superb benefits *115* How to get yourself in the right frame of mind *115* How you can stop wasting money on efficiency experts and management consultants *116* How to make your subordinate feel it's his problem, too *118* How a company was saved from financial ruin by its employees' suggestions and recommendations *119* How asking for help will encourage individual initiative *121* How to keep the lines of communication open *122* How to follow through on a person's idea or suggestion *123* How to reward a person for his suggestion or his idea *123*

Chapter 10:
The Only Reliable Way to Find Out
What's Going on in Your Own Organization *125*

You'll gain these 4 big benefits *126* 1. You'll get to know and understand each employee better *126* 2. Even though you're in management, your employees will like you when you listen to them *126* 3. Listen to your employees; they'll know you're really interested in them *127* 4. You'll find out what your employees really want when you listen to them *127* Techniques you can use to gain these wonderful benefits *128* Why listening to employee complaints is your responsibility *128* The only way to get accurate and reliable information from your employees *129* A 6-point checklist for asking questions that get answers *129* Why you must make the first move yourself *130* How you can become a better listener *131* Ten techniques to help improve your listening abilities *131* Seven tell-tale body language signs to watch for *133* How to calm down an angry person just by listening *133* Twelve guidelines for handling employee gripes and complaints *135*

Chapter 11:
How to Use Body Language to Project
the Power of Your Personality *137*

The immense benefits you'll gain from this chapter *138* The powerful techniques you can use to gain these benefits *139* Why nonverbal communication is so important to understand *139* How to look the part of a commanding and powerful personality *139* How to use the *steepling technique* to project your power *140* How to create your own *space bubble* to establish your turf *141* How you can use body gestures to your advantage *141* How to use your eyes to invade another person's territory *142* How body language can clearly reveal a person's inner thoughts and feelings *142* How a schoolteacher stops trouble without saying a word *143* How to project the power of your personality on the phone *144* Why you should eliminate these words from your vocabulary *145* How to interpret body language in social activities *145* Six final tips on how to project the power of your personality with body language *146*

PART IV:
BUSINESS CONVERSATIONS THAT
USE PERSUASION *149*

Chapter 12:
Using Persuasion to Get People
to Do What You Want *151*

The head never hears 'til the heart has listened *152* You'll gain these 4 extremely worthwhile benefits *153* Techniques you can use to gain these desirable benefits *153* How to find out what people want before you start *153* A technique you can use to persuade people to pay immediate attention to you *154* Nine benefits you can use by using the leading question technique *155* Why you should start with questions that are easy to answer *157* A 5-step procedure you can use to persuade a person to your point of view *158* How to overcome your listener's objections *160*

Chapter 13:
The Secret of Dealing with Resistance
and Overcoming Objections *163*

You'll gain these 6 splendid benefits *164* Techniques you can use to gain these sensational benefits *165* How to overcome your listener's objections: The first technique *166*

How to overcome your listener's objections: The second technique *167* How to overcome your listener's objections: The third technique *168* How to overcome a person's objections by asking him questions *169* A guaranteed 6-step technique for winning every argument *170*

Chapter 14:
The 10 Secrets of Persuasion That
Successful Super Salespeople Use *175*

You'll gain these phenomenal benefits for yourself *176* Ten techniques you can use to gain these amazing benefits *177* How you can get your prospect to say "Yes" immediately *177* Discovering the real reason behind the person's objection *178* How you can use this important salessecret yourself *179* How to sell benefits instead of features *180* How to concentrate on a single point and not scatter your fire *181* How to keep from losing the sale after it's made *182* Selling the right person on the right product *183* Use this technique: You will always succeed *184* The best way to clinch a sale *184* Why you should always leave the person with a good taste in his mouth *185*

Chapter 15:
How You Can Use Persuasion to Gain
People's Complete Cooperation and Full Support *187*

Benefits you'll gain when you cooperate with people *first 188* Techniques you can use to gain these great benefits *189* A method of persuasion you can use to gain cooperation *189* Five ways to win and hold the confidence of others *189* Here's a sure-fire method to gain a person's trust *190* Why this method of persuasion is so highly effective *191* How to get people to support you even when you're the boss *192* Why the participatory management technique is so effective *193* A specific example of how to use the participatory management technique in business *194* Other places you can use participatory management *194* How to use the buffer technique to get cooperation and support *196* Three magic words that will get people to support you *196*

PART V:
SPECIAL CONVERSATIONAL SITUATIONS *199*

Chapter 16:
How to Give a Talk or Make a Speech
Like a Professional:
A 7-Point Checklist *201*

Six spectacular benefits that you'll gain *202* Techniques
you can use to gain these marvelous benefits *203* How to
overcome your fear of giving a talk or making a
speech *203* Understanding the difference between nervousness and fear *204* Why you should know the purpose of
your talk or speech *205* How to identify and pinpoint your
main ideas *205* Organizing your talk or speech *206* Twelve
ways to make your talk sound forceful and
convincing *207* Five ways to develop confidence in your
ability to speak to an audience *209*

Chapter 17:
Eight Important Trade Secrets
of Professional Platform Speakers *213*

You can gain the following magnificent benefits for
yourself *214* Techniques you can use to gain these valuable
benefits *215* How to develop your own distinctive speaking
style *215* How to control the emotions of your
audience *216* Five methods you can use to overcome your
nervousness *217* Four ways to physically project your personality while speaking *217* How to be the final authority
on your subject *218* Seven irritating mannerisms to
avoid *219* Seven important don'ts to remember *220* The
professional way to use visual aids: Eight guidelines *221*

Chapter 18:
Using Your Conversational Expertise
to Succeed in Business:
A Seven-Step Program 227

The fabulous benefits you can gain *230* Techniques you can
use to gain these tremendous benefits *228* How you can

talk your way to success *228* How to sound like a top-level executive *229* Making that first good impression in a job interview *230* How to get that raise you deserve so much: Seven guidelines *231* Seven techniques you can use to talk your way to the top in the big company *233* How to attract the favorable attention of the upper hierarchy *235* Eight ways to let your business do your talking for you *235*

Chapter 19:
Making Your Conversation Count with
the Most Important People in Your Life *239*

The huge benefits you can gain from this chapter *240* The 6 techniques you can use to gain these benefits *241* How to get along with your boss *241* How to put your ideas across to your boss *242* How to talk at employees' affairs *243* How to give a briefing for a group of VIPs *245* Guidelines for a VIP briefing *245* Five don'ts to keep in mind when giving a VIP briefing *247* How to talk with your associates and fellow workers *247* How to talk successfully with members of the opposite sex *249*

PART VI:
CONVERSATIONAL PROBLEM AREAS *253*

Chapter 20:
How to Write as You Talk:
The Master Formula for Powerful
and Persuasive Writing *255*

You'll gain these 6 outstanding benefits *256* Eight techniques you can use to achieve these benefits *257* Six ways to make sure you're understood *257* What to do about big words *259* The best way to get rid of big and useless words *260* How using small words can improve your writing style 100 percent *261* What to do about your grammar *261* How to use power words to get your reader to take action *262* The 6 basic rules for writing powerful and masterful letters *263* How to use the hook technique in your letters *265* A 5-point format for a persuasive letter using the *hook 266*

Chapter 21:
The 7 Cardinal Sins of Conversation
and How to Avoid Them *269*

The enormous benefits that you can gain *270* The techniques you can use to gain these fantastic benefits *270* The first cardinal sin of conversation is not to listen attentively to the other person *271* How to correct the first cardinal sin of conversation *271* The second cardinal sin of conversation is interrupting others *272* How to correct the second cardinal sin of interrupting others *272* The third cardinal sin of conversation is criticizing the other person in public *273* How to correct a person's mistakes without criticism *274* The fourth cardinal sin of conversation is to use sarcasm and ridicule *274* How to correct the fourth cardinal sin of conversation *275* The fifth cardinal sin of conversation is talking down to people *276* How to correct or avoid the fifth cardinal sin of conversation *276* The sixth cardinal sin of conversation is participating in idle and malicious gossip *276* How to keep from committing this sixth cardinal sin of conversation *277* The seventh cardinal sin of conversation is using the big "I" and the little "you" *277* How to correct the seventh cardinal sin of conversation *278*

Chapter 22:
A Magic List of Successful Openers and Closers
for a Conversation, a Talk, or a Speech *281*

The magic method you can use to strike up a conversation with a complete stranger *282* How to talk with a woman if you're a man *283* How to talk with men if you're a woman *284* How to use topic teasers to stimulate immediate interest *284* A magic way to open and close a telephone conversation *285* Seven ways to open a talk or a speech *286* How to use leading questions to start off a business conversation or talk *287* How to know when to quit talking *288* Why I try not to talk too much *289* How to get the most out of your *Lifetime Conversation Guide 290*

Index *291*

PART I

Letting Your
Conversation
Take Charge
of
Your Social Life

Part One, which includes Chapters One through Five, covers social conversations. In Chapter One you will learn the 14 secret motivators that cause people to do and say the things they do, as well as how to use them to your own advantage. You'll also discover what subjects men and women best like to talk about.

In Chapter Two you'll be shown how to talk with strangers and feel completely comfortable about it. In Chapter Three you'll discover how you can use the psychology of conversation to build strong and enduring friendships. Chapter Four will give you the methods and techniques you can use to be well-liked and highly popular wherever you go. Chapter Five offers you 6 magic methods that will make your marriage and your home life much happier.

I have concentrated more on how you say something than on specific words to use. By that I mean that with few exceptions there are no magic words, but there is word magic in how you say it. You see, how you say something, the way you look, your eyes, the set of your mouth, your manners, and bearing will all tell whether you mean what you say, and if you are really saying what you mean.

As far as individual words go, certain specific courteous words and phrases that are used to praise a person or express love, for example, will never go out of style. Truly, they are magic words for they will literally work magic for you.

Otherwise, except for these few, I will not ask you to memorize set words and phrases to be used as responses to another person's remarks. If I were to do that, you would become nothing more than a parrot, a robot, or a computer programmed to give a specific response to a certain stimulus. And that would not help you establish the proper social relationships that you want with others.

Although Part I deals primarily with social situations, the principles, techniques, and methods you will learn here can also be used successfully in your daily business relationships.

It matters not whether you work for a large company, run your own business, or are engaged in sales work. Part I will be useful to you no matter what you do for a living.

chapter 1

Using a Person's
14 Secret Motivators
to Your Own Advantage
in Your Conversations

One of the first problems you must solve if you want to become a skilled conversationalist is selecting the proper subject to talk about. You cannot hold a person's attention for very long if you discuss something in which he has no interest whatever.

Most conversations start with "Hello . . . how are you today?" The expected answer is "Fine." The person asking the question isn't at all interested in hearing the minute details of how really sick the other individual is.

The next point to come up is usually a comment about the weather. "It's a beautiful day . . . warmer than usual . . . cooler than normal . . . I think it's going to rain." After that, there's no place to go and the conversation founders and dies in absolute silence.

If you want to avoid situations like these and become an excellent conversationalist, then you must give your listener an interesting verbal handle to grab onto. How can you do that? *Find out exactly what the other person wants or what he likes to talk about.* Let me give you a quick example of exactly what I mean.

How George Rogers Does It

"I've found that the quickest way to grab a person's attention and hold it is to pay him a compliment," George says. "Every person I've ever met wants to feel important in some way. When you pay a person a compliment, you feed his ego; you make him feel important, and he likes you immediately. He admires your good judgment.

"I'm susceptible like everyone else. After all, I'm human, too, you know. For instance, I have a new brown leather sport jacket that I like very much. The other night I wore it when my wife and I went out for dinner. The waitress said to me, 'Gee, that's sure a terrific-looking jacket, sir. That's the most beautiful leather I've ever seen!'

"That young lady made my day. Not only did she compliment me on my jacket, but in doing so she also praised my good judgment in making such a wise selection. She fed my ego; she made me feel important by just a few words. And she also benefited from that compliment, for her tip was much larger than usual."

4

So, instead of talking about the state of one's health or the weather, start the conversation off by paying the other person a compliment just as George does. When you do that, you'll feed that person's ego; you'll make him feel important, and that is one of the 14 secret motivators every person has that I'll tell you about later.

Three Major Points to Remember from This One Example

Although the friendly handshake, the big smile, and the cheerful greeting are all mighty important in making friends, they won't get you anywhere at all unless you *know exactly what the other person wants.*

You'll never gain your objectives or achieve your goals unless you stop thinking of what it is that you want from that person and *concentrate entirely on what you can do for him.*

To be able to do that, you must get inside a person's mind so you can find out what he really wants. You need to know exactly what actually makes that person tick. You'll want to *discover those secret motivators of his that really turn him on.*

Only then will you be able to understand why he says what he says; why he does what he does. And only then will you be able to guide and control the conversation for your own benefit.

You need not be a psychiatrist or a psychologist, nor do you need any sort of advanced degree to be able to understand human nature so you can discover the innermost secret needs and desires of others. The techniques you'll learn, not only in this chapter, but also in the rest of this book, are easy to understand, simple to use, and most important of all, you'll find that they really will work for you.

I can assure you of that, for I have spent my entire life studying applied psychology: why people say the things they say and why they do the things they do. Give me just a few minutes to listen to another person talk, and I can tell you what he wants out of life for himself even better than he can. With a bit of practice and experience, you can soon do the same. And when you do,

YOU'LL GAIN THESE MAJOR BENEFITS FOR YOURSELF

You'll Gain Power over Others

When you can guide and control the conversation, you will gain power over others. That great British statesman, Disraeli, once said, "Men govern with words." His statement is as true today as it was when he made it.

When you know and understand these 14 secret motivators that cause people to do and say the things they do, when you learn their innermost needs and desires, and when you make every effort to help them get what they want most of all, you will gain power over others that will work like magic for you. People will always do what you ask them to do.

You'll Be Able to Guide, Direct, and Control the Conversation for Your Own Benefit

As you study human behavior to perfect your understanding and knowledge of people—as you discover why people say the things they say; why they act the way they do—and as you learn to analyze their words and actions to find out what their hidden secret motivators are, you'll find that your ability to influence, control, and guide the conversation continues to improve. You will become a superb conversationalist. You'll truly be able to control people by what you say.

You'll Become a Brand-New Person with an Exciting and Powerful Personality

As you learn to use conversation to get what you want, you'll become a completely changed person. Your new personality will begin to pay off for you at once. For example, you'll see how you will soon be able to speak your mind in a way that everyone wants to, but that few people have the courage to do. You'll accomplish many things that others dare not even try.

As you develop in your ability to guide and control the conversation, you'll also gain new self-confidence. You'll become more poised. Your bearing and your manner will reflect your powerful and exciting new personality.

TECHNIQUES YOU CAN USE TO GAIN THESE MARVELOUS BENEFITS

First, I want to tell you about those 14 secret motivators that cause people to do and say the things they do. Then I'll show you how you can use these secret motivators to guide, direct, and control the conversation to your own advantage.

The 14 Secret Motivators That Turn People On

It will be extremely easy for you to understand all human behavior when you realize that *people do and say the things they do because they have certain deep needs and desires that must be fulfilled.*

Everything a person says and does is aimed at achieving those basic needs and desires. Some of these motivators are purely physical. Others are acquired through the learning process as one goes through life.

Physical Needs

The satisfaction of a physical need can become a specific goal that causes a person to behave in a certain way. Those basic needs are the ones that have to do with a person's physical existence and survival: food, drink, sleep, clothing, shelter, and normal body functions.

In the average social situation, you will seldom have the opportunity to exploit a person's physical need to your own advantage unless that basic need of his has become an obsessive want because of greed. Let me explain that to you more fully.

Greed at times motivates all of us. Greed will make a person want a larger house than he needs, a more expensive car than he requires, better clothes, finer food, and so on.

When a person's need becomes a want, it is also because he is driven by a deep learned desire—*ego-gratification*—a need for a feeling of importance and pride—plus a desire for more money and all the things that money will buy.

Don't misunderstand me now. I'm not putting down money or the good material things in life. After all, I'm susceptible, too. Give me the choice between a Chevrolet and a Cadillac and I'll take the Cadillac every time. I'm only saying that when a person's requirement for these basic fundamental needs becomes a burning, driving, overpowering obsession to get more of them than he can ever use, it is always because of greed.

And you can always use a person's greed to your own advantage. You can use it to influence and control the conversation, and ultimately, to influence and control the person's actions. All you need remember is this:

When all other human motives fail, you can always appeal to a person's greed to get your own way.

Desires or Learned Needs

Desires or learned needs are acquired by a person throughout his life as he discovers the values held by other people and the importance of certain social attitudes and ideas. Psychological needs such as the desire for power, approval, recognition, ego-gratification, liberty and freedom can be even stronger than the basic physical ones. People will do whatever is necessary to achieve them, be those methods legal or illegal; moral or immoral.

The basic desires or learned needs that every normal person has are these:

1. A sense of personal power, mastery over others
2. Ego-gratification, a feeling of pride and importance
3. Financial success: money and all the things that money will buy
4. Recognition of efforts, reassurance of worth
5. Social or group approval, acceptance by one's peers
6. The desire to win; the need to be first, to excel, to be the best
7. A sense of roots, belonging somewhere, either to a place or a group
8. The opportunity for creative expression
9. The accomplishment or achievement of something worthwhile
10. New experiences
11. Liberty and freedom, privacy from intrusion
12. A sense of self-esteem, dignity, and self-respect
13. Love in all its forms
14. Emotional security

Except for the first two—the desire for power and the need for a feeling of importance—which psychologists feel are the two greatest motivators of all, I have not listed the rest of these basic desires or learned needs in any particular order of importance. The point is, however, that a person will not be completely happy and contented if any one of them is not being satisfactorily fulfilled. Everything an individual does is directed toward their fulfillment. Every waking moment—every thought, word, and act—is aimed at achieving these goals.

Using These 14 Secret Motivators of People to Your Advantage

It should be immediately apparent to you that if you can help your listener gain his desires by what you say, you'll have him under your complete control. He'll gladly do what you ask if he can see how he can benefit by doing so.

It will be up to you to find out which one or more of these desires is dominant in your subject. You'll need to discover which ones you can use to influence and control his actions. Find out what he wants above all else in life. Do that and you will be in complete command of the situation at all times.

Although a person needs fulfillment of all 14 of these basic desires, you'll soon discover that *whatever a person is lacking at the moment, he has the greatest need and desire for.*

By the same token, *a surfeit of any one of these basic needs or desires will prevent you from using it at this particular time to gain control of the situation.*

These two points may seem self-evident to you, and you might wonder why I mention them, yet I have often seen people try to gain power with an individual or take control of a situation by trying to fulfill a desire that has already been satisfied.

Nothing is a bargain if it is not needed right then. So it will be up to you to find out which specific need or desire is most important to a person at that particular time.

Remember also that a person's needs and desires are never static. They change constantly. What a person wanted most of all a month or a week ago he may not want at all today. That's why you'll want to keep up-to-date and completely informed about a person's current needs and desires. To do that, listen for clues in his conversation. If he's reluctant to talk, you must draw him out so that he will.

Five Sure-Fire Guaranteed Methods You Can Use to Draw a Person Out

The most dependable way to draw a person out so you can discover what he wants most of all is to ask him questions. Of course, you can't be blunt about it. You must be subtle in your questioning techniques. You can use the following five guidelines to get a person to talk about himself and what he wants most of all.

1. Be genuinely interested in people—in each person and his individual problems.

2. Be a good listener. Watch for what he does *not* say as well as for what he does. Infinite patience is absolutely necessary to become a good listener.

3. Encourage the person to talk about himself. Ask him *leading questions* to help him get started.

4. Always talk in terms of *his* interests so you can find out what *he* wants. Never tell a person what you want out of the transaction; he couldn't care less about that.

5. Make the other person feel important. Feed his ego and do it sincerely.

To get specific answers to your questions, it's always best to use the Five Ws: *Who? What? When? Where? Why?* You can also use *How?* to get additional information about the person.

How to Ask Questions That Get Honest Answers

An insurance salesman, Byron Kent, kept a record of hundreds of interviews to find out why people bought or failed to buy. He found that in more than 60 percent of cases, the original objection raised by the prospect against buying insurance was not the real reason at all.

Byron found from his research that a person usually has two distinct reasons for doing anything: *a reason that sounds good to his listener, and the real one that he keeps hidden all to himself.*

Byron says that to find the real reason behind a person's words and actions, you should simply keep asking, "Is there any other reason?" or "And in addition to that?"

Specific Subjects People Like to Talk About

No matter who the person is, how important he is, how much money he has, or how successful he is, the most important subject in all the world to him is himself. He loves to tell you all about himself, how he started from nothing and became something, how much money he's made, how important a figure he is in the community, and on and on. Let me give you a classic example of this so you can see for yourself how you can use this human weakness to your own advantage, just as Paul J. Meyer did.

Paul J. Meyer is the founder and president of SMI International of Waco, Texas. SMI is the world's largest producer and distributor of recorded personal motivation, leadership development, and sales training courses.

But before Mr. Meyer founded SMI, he was selling insurance in Florida. While at a yacht basin in Jacksonville, a flash of inspiration came to him. Mr. Meyer reasoned that anyone who had a yacht must also have some good ideas on how to become successful. Jotting down the license numbers of those yacht club Lincolns and Cadillacs, he traced the owners, and then asked each one of them, honestly and sincerely, to what they attributed their success.

These people were so impressed by Mr. Meyer's sincere approach that they answered his questions readily without hesitation. You see, in spite of all their money, these rich people craved attention. They still needed ego-gratification; they wanted to be important.

By recognizing this basic desire of theirs, Mr. Meyer got the information he wanted. He took their answers, sifted them, expanded them, and reassembled them along with some original concepts of his own. The net result of all these ideas became his own personal "Blueprint for Success," and the foundation for Success Motivation Institute's first course.

This brief example shows that a person's favorite topic for discussion is always himself. Closely following that is an extension of himself: his wife, his children, his grandchildren. Other closely related subjects are his business or occupation, his hobbies, politics, religion.

As you can see from this, there are a lot more profitable subjects to talk about than one's health or the weather.

Why Accurate Information About What People Want Is So Important

To gain power for yourself so you can control any given conversational situation, you must know without a doubt what a person wants so you can help him get it. That's why accurate information about what a person desires is so important to you.

I can best illustrate this point by giving you a specific example with which I am personally and closely acquainted. A certain electronics manufacturer was having all sorts of personnel problems. Individual morale and organizational esprit were both at rock-bottom. Quality control was turning back about 30 percent of production. Absenteeism was running 25 percent above normal. The company's profit margin had been squeezed down to nearly nothing.

The company called in a management consulting firm to see if it could find out exactly what was wrong. The consulting firm, after talking to a number of employees, made up a questionnaire listing 8 specific human desires. Then all employees were asked to list those 8 basic requirements in their order of importance.

The consulting firm also asked company executives and management personnel to rate those same 8 items in the order they thought their employees would list them.

Shown below are the results of that survey. Management's rating of those 8 basic desires is shown on the right in parentheses for comparison purposes.

Employee's Rating	Eight Basic Wants or Desires	Management's Rating
1.	Credit and recognition for work done	(7)
2.	Interesting and worthwhile work	(3)
3.	Fair pay with salary increases	(1)
4.	Attention and appreciation. . . .	(5)
5.	Promotion by merit, not seniority	(4)
6.	Counsel on personal problems	(8)
7.	Good physical working conditions	(6)
8.	Job security	(2)

As you can see, the emphasis that employees and employers placed on these 8 items is not the same at all. When management placed its emphasis on what employees wanted—rather than guessing what they wanted—the company's troubles stopped, almost overnight. That was nearly 10 years ago. Today, that company is one of the top manufacturers of electronic products in the United States, with markets all over the world.

The survey shown here was the original one. The company has continued to take this survey on an annual basis. During the recession in the early '80s, when work was much harder to find and unemployment was at its height, job security moved from the number eight position to the number three spot. This in itself emphasizes the need for a constant reevaluation of an individual's needs and desires.

My reason for giving you this example here is to show you that you cannot control a situation by guessing what the other person wants. You must know what he wants so you can help him get it. Only then will you have the power to control both him and the situation to your own advantage. The only way to gain that information is through conversation, specifically by asking questions.

Two Examples of How to Use a Person's Secret Needs and Desires for Your Own Benefit

1. My insurance agent, Ted J., was making an average living by using the old-fashioned standard approach of plugging financial security for the family if the man of the house died.

His secretary, Patricia, attended several of my lectures on speech improvement and word usage. She suggested to Ted that he might profit by changing his sales approach to offer the prospect the opportunity to control and dominate his family, even after his death, with the proper life insurance program.

Ted called me the other day to tell me how much his business had improved with these new tactics. "When I offered a man only security for his family, I was offering him a benefit he could never use himself," Ted said. "In fact, I was making him think only of his death with that kind of sales pitch and he just couldn't accept that idea.

"But by offering him the chance to control and dominate, guide and direct his family's activities even after he was gone, he saw that he was in a sense still alive. He was not completely wiped out of the picture. My life insurance sales have quadrupled with this new approach, thanks to you and my alert secretary."

This point of people wanting to dominate others is a good one to keep in mind. Even though few individuals will admit the fact openly, it's a deep-hidden desire of almost everyone. Why is this so? Because if you can dominate another person and control his actions, that makes you more important than he is. And being important is one of the 14 basic desires we all have.

2. My neighbor, Jerry West, has a heating and air conditioning business. He found sales lagging after the energy crunch and higher utility rates that began back in the early seventies. People were willing to give up the physical comfort of air conditioning because of the high cost of electricity.

Jerry tried to come up with new customer benefits that he could use to stimulate sagging sales, but he was at a loss as to how to do so.

When he complained to me about his problem, I pointed out to him that with open windows instead of air conditioning, homes were much more susceptible to burglary. I suggested to him that he offer his prospects physical safety and emotional security as well as comfort and better health.

Jerry decided to try this new approach. To prove the point, he clipped police reports from the local newspaper and pasted them in a sales notebook to show prospective customers the rising crime rate in their community.

Then he would point out to his prospects that with air conditioning the windows would be closed, the house would be snug and tight and properly protected, and the person could sleep peacefully all night long, knowing that his family, his home, and his valuable possessions were safe and secure.

"I've sold more air conditioning using your idea than I ever did before," Jerry told me. "Older people are more concerned with their safety than with anything else, and we do have a lot of senior citizens here in Florida."

You can see from these two brief examples how easy it is to seize control of any situation when you use the correct motivator that will stimulate the person to take the action that you desire.

Now before we move on to the next chapter where you'll see how to use exact words and phrases to start a conversation with a total stranger, let me wrap up this first chapter this way.

It may seem to you that very little time has been devoted to the study of actual conversation in this chapter. And as far as specific words and phrases are concerned, that is true. But this chapter serves as the foundation for all conversation, both business and social.

When you know what a person's secret motivators are—when you know his deep needs and desires—you have power unlimited in your hands. You can control any conversation, business or social, that you have with that individual. And when you can control the conversation, then you can control the person as well. No doubt about it. As Disraeli said, "Men do govern with words."

If you will think more about what your listener wants to hear than about what you want to say, then the response you get will always be the one you're aiming for. And that puts you in complete control.

To quickly summarize this chapter, let me again list for you the 14 basic desires or learned needs that every normal person has:

1. A sense of personal power, mastery over others
2. Ego-gratification, a feeling of pride and importance
3. Financial success: money and all the things that money will buy
4. Recognition of efforts, reassurance of worth
5. Social or group approval, acceptance by one's peers
6. The desire to win; the need to be first, to excel, to be the best
7. A sense of roots, belonging somewhere, either to a place or a group
8. The opportunity for creative expression
9. The accomplishment or achievement of something worthwhile
10. New experiences
11. Liberty and freedom, privacy from intrusion
12. A sense of self-esteem, dignity, and self-respect
13. Love in all its forms
14. Emotional security

If you will do whatever is necessary to help a person fulfill these basic needs, you'll . . .

1. Gain much power over others
2. Be able to guide, direct, and control the conversation for your own benefit
3. Become a brand-new person with an exciting and powerful personality

If you feel at a loss as to how to start to find out what a person's deep needs are, you can always begin by feeding his ego—by making him important. The person does not live who does not want to feel important. So, make him feel important, and as he talks about himself, you'll quickly learn what his other needs and desires are. He can't help but reveal them to you as he talks about himself, his dreams, his hopes, his desires.

If you're at all doubtful about this. I suggest you try this experiment. Use this procedure for a week. See for yourself. You'll be amazed at the fantastic results that you'll get. And you'll quickly find out how much better things will go for you in talking with others. You'll get the results you want; I guarantee it.

chapter 2

Six Guaranteed Ways
to Strike Up
a Conversation
and Feel
Completely at Ease
with a Total Stranger

Do you feel at a loss about what to say or how to act when you meet a stranger? Do you want to hold the upper hand in the conversation so you can get your own way, but you don't really know how or where to begin? Perhaps you need to gain power over others so you can control a person's attitudes and actions the first time you meet, but you don't know how to do so. Maybe you'd just like to get better service from a waitress in a restaurant or a clerk in a store.

In this chapter, I'm going to give you some techniques that will let you do all these things, and much, much more. I'll show you how to get off on the right foot with strangers so you can master and control their attitudes and actions from the very beginning. To do that, you must always be able to . . .

Make a Good First Impression

Making a good first impression is more than half the job of getting what you want from a total stranger. The way you strike people at your first meeting will often decide how they're going to react to you for a long time to come.

If you rub a person the wrong way the first time you meet him, it could take months or even years to correct that initial bad impression he has of you. Your first few words are more important than the next several thousand.

For instance, suppose you've got a mean "I-hate-the-whole-world" look on your face the first time you meet a person. No matter how many times you see him after that, he will always remember that first bad impression he had of you. He will continually think of you as an old sourpuss with a miserable outlook on life.

For example, I was talking with Scott Kennedy the other morning at a Chamber of Commerce breakfast. Another person, a local businessman—let's just call him John—joined us in small talk for a moment.

After he left, Scott said, "I can't stand that man. He's got a rotten temper. Treats his help horribly."

I was astonished at Scott's remark and I said, "I don't understand that at all, Scott. I've known John for a long time now. He's one of the most pleasant, best-natured fellows in the whole town. I've never seen him lose his temper or raise his voice in anger in all the years that I've known him."

"Well, all I know is I went into his store one time," Scott said, "and he was chewing out one of his clerks up by the cash register in front of all the customers. He was really raising Cain. He was all redfaced and yelling like crazy. Didn't even have the courtesy to reprimand his employee in private."

"I'm really surprised to hear that, Scott," I said. "It sure isn't like John at all. Something really bad must have happened to cause him to act that way that one time. I know it had to be the exception because he's one of the most even-tempered men I've ever known."

"Maybe so," Scott said, "but I've never gone back in his store since then and I'm not going to. Once was enough for me. I have absolutely no use for employers who use their positions to mistreat and degrade people that way."

Actually, I do happen to know that John is one of the most patient, kind, and thoughtful employers I've ever met. He goes out of his way to be decent to his help. I also know that he has made several interest-free loans to some of his employees to help them get their children through college. But unfortunately, he had lost his temper the one time that Scott saw him; and Scott's first impression of John was a lasting one.

So it's highly important for you to know how to make the right impression on people the first time. Therefore, I want to use the rest of this chapter to show you how to get off on the right foot with strangers so you can influence their attitudes and actions and control the conversation from the very beginning. When you know how to do that,

YOU'LL GAIN THESE 6 HIGHLY SIGNIFICANT BENEFITS

1. When you use the first technique I'll give you, you'll gain the benefit of knowing how to strike up a conversation with a total stranger with tact and diplomacy.

2. Use the second technique and you'll be able to master the

other person immediately. You will automatically take control of the conversation.

3. The third technique will show you how to get quick and deferential service from a waitress, a clerk, even a snobbish government bureaucrat.

4. When you use the fourth technique, you'll see how to get a complete stranger to go out of his way to help you.

5. The fifth technique will demonstrate how you can make a lasting friendship with a total stranger.

6. Use the sixth technique and you can control the attitudes and emotions of complete strangers. And when you can control their attitudes and emotions, you'll also be able to control their actions.

THE 6 TECHNIQUES YOU CAN USE
TO GAIN THESE BENEFITS

The Tactful Way to Strike Up a Conversation
with a Complete Stranger

A friend of mine, Ron, can strike up a conversation with a complete stranger as easily as you or I might talk with a long-time friend. I've studied his methods for a long time for I've often felt I could use his gifted techniques myself. What is Ron's secret? *He appeals to the person's ego . . . he makes that person feel as if he were the most important person in the whole world.*

Some of the many conversation openers Ron uses are these:

1. I've always been interested in computers, but I simply don't understand them at all. Could you tell me more about them? (This opening can be used for any occupation or profession.)

2. I've often wished I knew more about business management. Would you tell me something about your position as a manager and the kind of work you do? (This opening can also be used for any sort of work.)

3. I've never seen such attractive earrings before. Could you tell me where I might get a pair like them for my wife?

4. How do you manage to keep such a calm and serene attitude toward life with the hectic business pressures you have to put up with every day?

5. I've never met a minister I didn't enjoy talking with. Could you tell me more about your particular faith?

6. Your name fascinates me. Could you tell me more about its origin and meaning? (I'll discuss this point in more detail later on in this chapter.)

There is no limit to the list of conversation openers you can use. You can make up your own. The only guidance you need follow is to *use a leading question to get the person to talk about his own self-interests.* This is a guaranteed way to get an individual to open up and talk with you.

Simply concentrate your attention on what he's interested in, not on what you're interested in. Always feed the other person's ego. Make him feel important and you'll never go **wrong.** It's one of the best ways in the world to strike up a conversation with a total stranger.

How to Take Control of the Conversation Immediately

When two people meet for the first time, one will automatically become the leader and assume control of the conversation. The other person will then become the follower. You can always take control if you will simply remember that *everyone in the world is waiting for someone else to tell him what to do.* Let that someone else be you. You'll find that this amazing strategy will put a total stranger under your thumb immediately.

All you need do is take the initiative and you will instantly have the momentum on your side. If you adopt a positive attitude and assume that the other person is going to do what you want him to, you'll find that 95 percent of the time he will carry out your request or your command without hesitation or question. In 5 percent of cases, all he needs is a little extra push.

Other people will always accept you at your own appraisal of yourself. You are more responsible for how people accept you than anyone else. A lot of people worry about what other persons think of them. You can rid yourself of that unwarranted fear if you will just remember that *you are not responsible for what other people think of you. You are responsible only for what you think of yourself.* Others form their opinions of you based upon the opinion you have of yourself.

If you act like a nobody and put yourself down, people will treat you like a nobody and put you down, too. But if you act like a somebody with authority, people will treat you that way. It is a truism that a person can have whatever allowances or liberties he takes without opposition. Take the role of leader, seize control of the conversation, and others will immediately acquiesce to you.

How to Get Superior Service from a Waitress or a Clerk

One of the deepest desires every person has is the need to be important—the craving to be appreciated. Every time you deal with a stranger, you can fulfill that deep craving with a few words that won't cost you a single penny. Just pay the other person an unexpected compliment of some sort.

For example, whenever I go into a restaurant I make it a point to compliment my waitress in some way. Just the other morning the one who brought my water and menu seemed grouchy and out of sorts. I was determined to change her attitude at once.

"What a lovely fragrance you're wearing," I said. "You certainly make an old man feel young and lively again."

Her face brightened immediately and a smile appeared in place of her frown. "Thank you," she said. "That's the kindest thing I've heard this morning."

You can be sure my eggs were done just the way I wanted them, over medium well, not too soft, not too hard, just right. There was extra jelly for my toast and my coffee cup was kept filled without my asking, all because I'd paid her a simple compliment.

Have you ever wanted to get up close so you could see the show better in a nightclub? This same technique will get you the same results as a $20 bill, but will cost you absolutely nothing.

My wife and I were standing in a long line waiting for the dinner show at the Flamingo, one of those fabulous Las Vegas clubs. The maître d' was strolling up and down the long line looking at the guests. He was handsomely dressed in dinner clothes and had a magnificent beard, the kind that only a few people like Hemingway, Kenny Rogers, or Kris Kristofferson can wear well.

"I wish I could grow a beard that looks as handsome as yours does," I said to him. "I've always wanted to grow one, but I've never had the courage. I've had to content myself with my salt and pepper mustache."

"Why are you standing back here in line when you have a reservation for a front table?" he asked with a sly wink. "Come up here where you should be and I'll seat you and your lady immediately."

If you want to see the service improve next time you're in a restaurant or a busy store, pay the waitress or the clerk an unexpected compliment, and see for yourself how good things will start to happen for you right then and there. This procedure will even work to melt the icy and haughty manner of an imperious government bureaucrat, and that's the closest thing to a miracle I've ever seen!

How You Can Get a Complete Stranger to Go Out of His Way to Help You

If you want to get a total stranger to go out of his way to help you, if you want to get a person you've never met before to do whatever you ask him to do for you, then say something that will *let him know at once that he is superior to you in some way.*

The plain truth is that every person you meet feels he is better than you in one way or another. A sure way to his heart is letting him know that you recognize that superiority. All you need do is ask a person for his advice, his opinion, or his help, and he'll go out of his way to assist you.

I can well recall the time I went to a bait and tackle shop here in Florida to buy my first saltwater fishing gear. I simply didn't know how or where to start. The clerk was busy with several other customers so he couldn't help me immediately.

I lifted one rod after another out of the rack only to put it back. Then I looked at lines and hooks and weights, but I didn't know what to pick up or put down. I noticed a man on my left watching me sympathetically.

"Can you help me out and give me some advice?" I asked. "I've never done any surf fishing before and I simply don't know where or how to start."

"Sure, let me give you a hand," he said. "I've got an hour before I go back to work. I'll be glad to show you what to buy and, just as important, what *not* to buy."

"I don't like to bother you," I said. "I don't want to burn up your lunch hour for you. But I sure could use some good advice from an expert."

"Don't worry about my lunch hour," he said. "I need to lose a few pounds anyway. The important thing is to get you fixed up with the right kind of fishing tackle."

So he proceeded to tell me all about the differences in the various kinds of fishing rods. Then he showed me the type he used and recommended the same kind for me. After that he selected the reel and showed me how to put it on the rod. Then came the correct hooks, the right weights, line, leader, a pair of fishing pliers, a scaler, a fish filleting knife.

He spent nearly an hour with me. We'd completed my shopping and he was showing me how to assemble it all when he glanced at his watch. "I think you're all set now," he said. "I'm sorry to leave, but I must get back to work."

"I really appreciate your help," I said. "I don't know what I'd have done without you. But I'm afraid I've used up your entire lunch hour. I'm sorry."

"Forget it," he said. "I'm just glad I was here and could help you out."

If you'll just be willing to admit that people can be superior to you in some way and then ask them for their help, you'll soon find that a tremendous number of benefits will come your way. Specific phrases you can use to get the results you want are these:

1. Can you help me out with this, please?
2. Could I ask for your valuable advice?
3. What is your opinion on this?
4. I value your judgment on this matter.
5. Could you please show me how to do this?
6. I would much appreciate your telling me how to do this.
7. I know you're an expert in this field. Could you give me a few tips?

These phrases and others like them will help you strike up a conversation with a total stranger and feel completely at ease about it.

I know this. *Every man I meet is my superior in one way or another—in that I learn from him.* If you will just remember this idea, you'll have no trouble in putting this technique to work so you can gain the benefits for yourself. Try it; you'll like it. I guarantee it.

Three Sure-Fire Ways to Make Friends with a Total Stranger

It's ever so easy to strike up a conversation with a total stranger and make friends with him if you will just get your mind off yourself and what you want and concentrate on what the other person is interested in.

There are any number of conversation openers you can use to

control the situation and get the other person to talk, but the three I've found to be most effective are, in the order of their importance, a person's name, his vocation, and his hobby. Let me show you what I mean:

1. A man's name is the most important word in all the world to him, so all you need say is something like this:

"Your name is fascinating. I don't think I've ever heard it before. Would you tell me more about its origin and meaning?" Let me give you an example of this technique.

A friend of mine, Harry Bellows, is district sales manager for a large wholesale nursery house. His company had been trying for years to win a certain large retail account from a man named Peter Menosky. More than a half-dozen salesmen had called on this gentleman, but without results. Finally, the president called Harry in and asked him to have a go at it.

"The first thing I did was to check with each salesman," Harry said. "Each one told me the same thing. Mr. Menosky was really touchy about how his name was pronounced and how it was spelled.

"So I went down to the library to find out the exact ethnic derivation of the name, *Menosky*. Then I went calling on him.

"As soon as I was ushered into his office, I said, 'I've been anxious to meet you for a long time, Mr. Menosky. You see, I've always been interested in the ethnic derivation of names. It's a sort of hobby of mine.

"'I know your name is Slovakian in origin, but I haven't been able to find out what it means. I know your first name, Peter, means reliable and dependable, but the library is not able to give me the meaning of your last name. Can you tell me?'

"Mr. Menosky glared at me and said, 'How do you know I'm Slovak? How do you know I'm not Polish? All your salesmen seem to think so!'

"'Because your name is spelled with the suffix *sky*,' I said. 'If your name were Polish, it would be spelled with *ski*.'

"'By golly, you're a pretty smart fellow,' Mr. Menosky said. 'I think I'd like to do business with you!'

"He then told me about his father coming to the United States penniless and knowing no one. He talked for more than an hour about his family's origins, his father's native country, his children and grand-children, his hobbies and interests. I listened patiently and benefited by so doing, for I left with the biggest order we'd ever got from a retail nursery. He's been our steady customer ever since that day."

I'm just as touchy about my own name as Mr. Menosky is about his. Mine is of Dutch origin. My grandfather came to this country from Rotterdam, Holland, in 1870. All my ancestors are Holland Dutch, not German, and I dislike being thought of as German just as much as Mr. Menosky disliked being called Polish. We may all be United States citizens, but we still have a feeling of original ethnic pride about our names.

2. Every person likes to tell you what he does for a living. All you need say is, "I've always been interested in your profession. Would you tell me something about your position and the work you do?"

This is usually enough to keep the other person going for half an hour or more. In fact, you might end up feeling swamped with information as I did when I asked a young computer programmer to explain his work to me. He told me so much about computers, I thought I was going to drown in technical terms. I felt about like my father did when he used to say that the preacher told him more than he wanted to know. If this happens to you, be patient. Remember, your purpose is to control the situation and guide the conversation for your own *eventual* benefit.

3. Ask a person to tell you about his hobby. Most people have an avocation of some sort, be it hunting, fishing, bowling, golf, gardening, music, whatever. In a great many cases, people are as expert, if not more so, in their avocations as they are in their professions; and they always like to talk about their hobbies.

I have a neighbor, a pharmacist by profession; a botanist by avocation. Bill is a walking botanical encyclopedia. He can give a person valuable free advice about plants, shrubs, trees, vines, and everything else that grows. Bill can look at a plant or a shrub and tell me if it needs iron, magnesium, has too much water, not enough water, whatever. All you need do to become his A-number-one friend is to ask him something about his hobby.

How You Can Control the Attitudes and Emotions of Complete Strangers

When you study physics or chemistry, you find that positive attracts negative, like goes with unlike, acid neutralizes alkali. But this doesn't hold true when you're learning how to get along with people. When you're dealing with human beings, just the opposite is true. Like always attracts like. Let me show you exactly what I mean:

- Be kind to others, they will be kind to you.

- Be mean to others, they will be mean to you.
- Be courteous to others, they will be courteous to you.
- Be rude to others, they will be rude to you.
- Be friendly with others, they will be friendly with you.
- Be hostile toward others, they will be hostile toward you.
- Smile at others, they will smile back at you.
- Frown at others, they will frown at you.

As I told you earlier in this chapter, whenever two people are involved in a relationship, one will become the leader, the other will become the follower. If you assume the position of leadership as you should, the attitudes and emotions of others will depend entirely upon your attitude and emotions. The power you have over others and the ability to master and control their emotions and actions by your own emotions and actions is enormous.

In dealing with others, then, you will always see your own attitude reflected back in the other person's behavior. It is almost as if you were looking at yourself in a mirror. When you smile, the person in the mirror smiles. When you frown, the person in the mirror frowns back at you. Let me give you a simple example of this technique.

Take my own granddaughter, Dara Nicole, for instance. When I smile at her, she's happy and she smiles, too. But, if I frown the least little bit, or if I act irritated and impatient about something, she gets a worried look on her face and says, "Are you mad, Grandpa?"

Then I'll smile back at her and reply, "No, of course I'm not mad. Are you?"

A look of relief and joy comes over her face and she says, "Nope—I'm not mad either. I'm happy!"

You don't have to say a single word to influence another person. Smiles and frowns are both contagious. It's all up to you how you want to infect the other person. His attitude and actions will depend entirely on your attitude and your actions.

So, if you've been afraid to strike up a conversation with a complete stranger, practice the techniques I've given you in this chapter for a few weeks. To refresh your memory, let me list them for you again here.

1. To tactfully strike up a conversation with a complete stranger, *ask him a leading question so he will talk about his own self-interests.*

2. Take control of the conversation immediately by assuming

the leadership role. *Remember that everyone in the world is waiting for someone else to tell them what to do.*

3. To get superior service from a waitress, a clerk, even a haughty government bureaucrat, pay that person an unexpected and *sincere* compliment.

4. To get a complete stranger to go out of his way to help you, *let him know at once that he is superior to you in some way.*

5. Three sure-fire ways to make friends with a total stranger are these:

a. Remember that a man's name is the most important word in all the world to him. Be sure to spell it correctly and pronounce it properly.

b. Let the person tell you what he does for a living. Let him go into all the details.

c. Have a person tell you all about his hobby. Ask him questions to draw him out.

6. You can control the attitudes, emotions, and actions of complete strangers by your own attitudes, emotions, and actions. Remember that a smile always wins a smile, but a frown gets only a frown.

If you will use these 6 techniques, you'll soon find that your fears of talking with strangers will vanish. You'll develop the confidence you need to feel completely at ease and comfortable when talking to a total stranger.

And now, on to another important chapter, "How to Use the Psychology of Conversation to Build Strong and Enduring Friendships." When you use the techniques that you'll learn in Chapter Three, you'll find that you can convert strangers and mere acquaintances into lifelong friends. That's important; friends who'll help you out of a tough spot are invaluable. You can never have too many of them.

chapter 3

How to Use
the Psychology
of Conversation
to Build Strong
and Enduring Friendships

Most of us feel lucky if we can count our *true* friends on the fingers of one hand. Exactly what is a "true friend"? Well, my own definition of a true friend is one who will accept me just as I am with all my faults and frailties, and still love me in spite of those character defects. A real friend's attitude toward me, then, could best be expressed by this statement:

I like you *because* ... but I love you *in spite of* ...

That's the kind of true friend I'm talking about. Since friends are won or lost primarily by what you say, then your language—not only what you say but also how you say it—becomes extremely significant. I want to use this chapter to show you how to say the right thing so you will be able to make more friends and keep them through the psychology of conversation. When you do that,

YOU'LL GAIN THESE 6 TERRIFIC BENEFITS

1. A true friend is one who'll stick by you when the going gets rough. He'll not desert you at the first sign of trouble. He'll give you his wholehearted support and see you through your tough times.

2. A true friend will trust you and have full confidence in you, no matter what. As the old saying goes, "Never explain what you do to anyone. Your friends don't need it and your enemies won't believe it." You don't have to prove yourself to a person to hold his loyal friendship.

3. No matter what you say or do, a true friend will accept you just as you are. He won't criticize you for your faults and character defects. He may not like them, of course, but he'll tolerate them with kindness while praising your good points and fine qualities to others.

4. When you gain a person's friendship, you'll also gain his respect. True friends will respect you, your decisions, and your actions. They'll willingly and gladly do whatever they can to help you.

5. A true friend will never speak disparagingly about you. Not

only that, he'll do everything he can to squelch rumors or gossip that degrades you or blackens your reputation. He'll never say anything behind your back that he would not say to you in person.

6. As you learn the how-to of making close friends, you'll become an expert in the art of human relations, for making and keeping friends requires tact, diplomacy, and skill.

EIGHT POTENT GUIDELINES YOU CAN USE TO GAIN THESE MAGNIFICENT BENEFITS

How to Put the First Guideline to Work

If you will recall, in the last chapter I said that how you act toward others will bring the same sort of reaction to you. If you are kind to others, they will be kind to you. If you are courteous to others, they will be courteous to you. If you are friendly to others, then they will be friendly to you.

So the first point to remember about making friends is simply this: *If you want to get, then you must first give.* It is absolutely impossible to give of yourself to someone else and get nothing in return.

Now a petty, nearsighted person often refuses to give of himself because he cannot see how or where he's going to profit by so doing. Therefore, he gets nothing back because he gives nothing away. The maxim still holds true even in his case. He got back exactly what he gave away: nothing.

But the farsighted person gives of himself without any thought of return and gains friends because of that. Let me give you an example so you can see for yourself how well this technique can work.

Pete Randall is a cookie salesman from Des Moines who calls upon retail grocery stores in north central Iowa. Pete's cookies are good, but they're really no better than half a dozen other brands. Yet Pete outsells his competitors all the time. How does he do that? He gives of himself and takes the time to help the grocer sell his products.

"A small town grocer doesn't have the backing that big chain stores do for floor displays and advertising," Pete says. "Nor does he have the manpower to help him. If he's going to get it done, he has to do it himself or get his wife to help him.

"Now you don't walk into a man's place of business and tell him how to run things. That rubs him the wrong way and you could easily lose a customer. So I wait until the time is just right, when he either asks for help, or when I find him in the middle of putting up a cookie advertising display. Then I pitch right in and help him.

"I remember a store in Clarion, the So-Lo Market, where I helped the owner put up a display for one of my cookie competitors. The next time around, he wanted me to help him again, for he'd done a booming business with that display but this time he wanted to do it with my cookies.

"Now he pushes my brand all the time, and, in return, I bring him all sorts of suggestions for displays on everything from brushes and brooms to yams and yogurt.

"In 90 percent of the stores I service, my cookies outsell every competing brand. And just because the owners push my line instead of the others. I help them whenever I can and, in return, they go all out for me."

So the first guideline (actually a law of human relations) for making valuable friends is to first give of yourself to the other person. Do everything in your power to increase the happiness and success of the other person. That's exactly what Pete does. You've seen how he profits by so doing. You'll profit, too, by having more true friends than you ever thought possible when you use the same technique.

You'll also profit in other ways as well. When you build your friendships on the basis of benefit, profit, and success for others, you'll find that they'll be glad to help you by doing whatever they can to advance your interests, too.

How to Build Your Friendships on a Solid Foundation

Now that you know and understand the first law for making valuable friends, I want to show you a simple way of putting this principle of giving of yourself to others to work. I know you might feel you are not in a position to help others as Pete Randall did, but you don't have to be.

You can use this technique to win friends, no matter who they are—your boss, your employees, your associates at work or in church, your husband or wife, even your own children. All you need do is *praise the other person for what he has done.* Let me tell you first of all why praising another person is such a valuable technique to use.

To be praised by others is a basic human desire. We all want to be told how great we are and what a good job we've done. Even the United States Army found that praise worked far better than criticism in getting soldiers to do a better job. When soldiers were praised for their efforts, 9 out of 10 did a better job the next time around. However, when they were criticized, only 3 out of 10 did a better job the next time.

Praise a person and you'll win his loyal friendship. He'll love you for it. Tell him what a magnificent job he's doing—how you couldn't get along without him—how happy you are that he's your friend.

Be generous with your praise. Pass it around freely; the supply is limited only by you. Don't be stingy about passing out bouquets; they cost you nothing. Above all, don't act as if you expected something in return for your praise. Don't pay a person a compliment as if you wanted a receipt for it.

Not only does praise feed a person's ego and fulfill his desire to be more important, but it also satisfies nine more of his basic needs. Let me list them for you here so you can see for yourself what a valuable tool praise can be.

1. Recognition of efforts, reassurance of worth
2. Approval and acceptance by others
3. The accomplishment or achievement of something worthwhile
4. A sense of roots, belonging somewhere
5. A sense of self-esteem, dignity, and self-respect
6. The desire to win, to be first, to excel
7. Love
8. Emotional security
9. A sense of personal power

When you can fulfill all of these basic desires a person has just by praising him, then it makes good sense to do so. You can be sure he'll want to be your friend when he gets treatment like this from you.

Specific Ways You Can Praise a Person to Gain His Friendship

In the happiest marriages, husbands and wives are friends as well as lovers. If you're the husband, you can praise your wife in any number of ways to win her friendship. Just for instance, if your morning coffee is good, then tell her so. (If it isn't, tell her so anyway!) Be generous with your praise. Don't wait until she does something big or unusual to praise her. Praise her for her excellent cooking, her magnificent housekeeping, her beautiful appearance, her gorgeous new hairdo. And don't forget to thank her for what she does for you. That's also praise. The two simple words, "Thank you," can be a real morale-booster to a tired and worn-out housewife.

If you're the wife and you want your husband to be successful in his work, then you can help him by the simple act of praising him for what he does. Praise builds his self-confidence and helps him do a better job. Your praise can send him off each morning filled with the confidence that he can solve any problem that comes his way.

Always be sure to use praise, not flattery, to build strong and enduring friendships. To flatter a person means to praise him far beyond what is true, or to praise him insincerely. The dictionary says that flattery is praise that is usually untrue or overstated. In other words, to flatter is simply to lie. To be sincere means to be genuine and honest, free from all pretense and deceit.

Flattery is as phony as a three-dollar bill. People can always spot your phoniness and see through you immediately.

There's an easy way for you to determine whether you're praising a person sincerely or whether you're just flattering him. Flattery praises a person for what he *is*, not for what he *does*. Praise congratulates a person for what he *does*, not for what he *is*. Let me show you the difference between the two by these four brief examples:

FLATTERY: Reverend, you're the nicest preacher we've ever had.

PRAISE: That was an inspiring sermon you gave this morning. We can always use more like that.

FLATTERY: Tom, you're the best salesman in the entire company.

PRAISE: Congratulations, Tom. You had the most sales in the entire district last month. That's an outstanding record. Thanks a lot for your excellent work. I really do appreciate it.

FLATTERY: Miss Jones, you're really the most beautiful typist in the company.

PRAISE: Miss Jones, your typing is absolutely superb. I have no hesitancy about signing my correspondence now. I really do appreciate your excellent work. Thanks a lot.

FLATTERY: George, you're the smartest worker in the entire plant.

PRAISE: George, that suggestion of yours was an outstanding idea. It's going to save us a lot of time and unnecessary steps. Thanks a million for your help.

See the difference here? Flattery is vague, ill-defined, and usually confusing. It leaves the flattered person wondering *Why? How? When? In what way?* He doesn't know what he has actually done to deserve the praise, so he is in no position to repeat his performance. Flattery does nothing to help the person improve his work methods.

And in the case of Miss Jones, telling her she's the most beautiful typist in the company is really confusing. She's left wondering if the boss is talking about her typing or if he's getting ready to make a pass at her.

Genuine praise does not create this confusion. Not only that, when you praise a person for what he *does*, not for what he *is*, you are forced to find something to praise him for. That makes you look for his good points rather than his weak ones. Genuine praise requires thought, energy, and effort on your part, but it is well worth it in the long run. Praise others and you'll be able to build many strong and enduring friendships.

Finding a Common Denominator for Your Friendship

Turning casual acquaintances into lasting friendships usually depends upon having the opportunity to talk with people regularly on a friendly basis, with a regard for their needs, their desires, and their interests. Many social relationships are established, not only at work, but also by membership in some organization or group. The relationship might be political, religious, or athletic. It could result from lodge or club membership. Whatever it is, there has to be a common interest of some kind.

The best way to find a common denominator for your friendship is to take an active interest in what the other person likes to do. If he's interested in chess, for example, and you want to become his close personal friend, learn to play chess. Then you can both speak the same language and feel completely comfortable with each other.

However you do it, don't make the mistake I made when I was much younger and not as wise as I hope I am now. My boss was an avid golfer. He loved the game and played whenever he had the opportunity. He invited me to play with him, but I told him that I didn't know how.

"Wonderful," he said. "That's all the better. I can teach you to play the right way and make a top-notch golfer out of you."

When I still declined his invitation, he wanted to know exactly why I wasn't interested. "Because I like to bowl," I said. "No matter what the weather is, it doesn't matter. I can always go to the bowling alley. Besides, I don't have to hunt for my ball as you do. It always comes back to me. Frankly, I think it's silly to go chasing after a little white ball and spend half your time looking for it."

As you can no doubt guess, it took me a long time to repair the damage of that stupid remark. After several less capable individuals were promoted ahead of me, I finally began to realize that my success depended not only on my own business capabilities, but also on my ability to get along with other people, especially my boss. That one incident started me on my lifelong study of human nature, of people and their basic needs, desires, and motivations. I hope that I'm much wiser now than I was then.

Finding a common denominator for your friendship is especially important for people who retire and move to a new area. All their lifelong friends are now gone and there's no longer the opportunity to meet people at work as there was before. Of course, church and lodge memberships help, but if you want your next-door neighbors to become close friends instead of mere acquaintances, then find out what they're interested in and what they like to do so you can talk their language and do it with them.

Why You Should Accept a Person Exactly as He or She Is

To accept a person exactly as he or she is provides not only the sound basis for a solid friendship, but it is also one of the secrets of a happy and successful marriage as you'll learn later on in Chapter Five.

If you want to be able to accept a person exactly as he (or she) is, then concentrate on his good points, and overlook his defects. We all have defects of some sort. The person doesn't live who has achieved perfection. To the best of my knowledge, only one person ever lived who was perfect and He was crucified for it.

Never criticize a person if you want to be able to accept him exactly as he or she is. Criticism is a quick way to destroy a friendship. When you tell a person that he's wrong or he shouldn't do this or that, his feathers are immediately ruffled, he becomes defensive, and he resents your comment, no matter how well-intentioned it might be. Let me give you an example of how to avoid criticizing someone even when you know he's wrong.

Last year I was on the Chamber of Commerce committee that

was responsible for soliciting money from business people to buy toys for poor children at Christmas time.

Gene Baxter and I went together on most occasions, feeling it was easier to collect with two people rather than only one. One old grumpy fellow complained loudly about giving. "I don't believe in charity," he said. "No one ever gave me anything. The Bible says 'God helps those who help themselves.' "

"I agree with you," I said, "but we're not asking for much. Besides, it's the children we want to help. After all, they're not old enough to help themselves yet as you so wisely suggest."

He relented then, and after we left with his check in hand, Gene said, "Jim, I've never heard that Bible quotation before, have you?"

"No, Gene, I haven't," I said, "because it doesn't come from the Bible. But if we had told him he was wrong, we wouldn't have his check, now would we?"

There's no point in telling a person that he's wrong. When you do, you're criticizing him and criticism destroys friendships. Not only that, it creates enemies. And life is too short to have enemies. Even one is one too many.

Don't show up another person for this is merely an oblique way of criticizing him. For instance, it's terribly embarrassing to an employee to have his boss show off at his expense by doing a job faster or better than he can.

Of course, it's only to be expected that the boss can do a better job. If he couldn't, chances are he wouldn't be the boss. But if you do happen to be the boss, you don't need to prove your point that way. Showing a person how to do something is one thing, but showing him up is quite another.

It's important to a person's dignity to be able to do something well on his own. When you do that job faster and better than he can, you destroy his self-respect and self-esteem. Instead of helping him fulfill one of his basic desires, you're taking it away from him.

Let me wrap up this idea this way: If you want to treat a person with dignity and respect, then *treat every man like a gentleman and every woman like a lady.* Do that and you'll end up with more friends than you care to count.

Avoiding Arguments and Disagreements at All Costs

As I've just said, one of the best ways to keep out of arguments and avoid disagreements is never to criticize the other person. But there'll be times when a person becomes angry with you for one reason or another. Here's the best way to handle that kind of situation.

When a person becomes angry with you, you have your choice of doing one of two things. You can retaliate, get mad and fight back, or you can do exactly the opposite—appease his anger.

If you fight back—which is exactly what the other person expects you to do—you will lose complete control of the situation and only make things worse. You will accomplish absolutely nothing by losing your temper, too.

What happens, then, if you don't fight back? Does this mean the other person automatically wins? Of course not. The only time you can be sure of winning is when you don't lose your temper and retaliate. It always takes two to make a fight. When you refuse to become angry, then the other person's anger simply has to burn itself out.

Gary Nichols, a friend of mine, tells me he handles arguments and disagreements this way:

"I have a neighbor with a short fuse who flies off the handle at the slightest provocation," Gary says. "When he used to come over raising the dickens about something, I'd get mad, yell back, and we'd get nowhere. We fought like crazy until I learned how to handle his temper tantrums. Now when he gets upset or mad about something, I stay calm instead of flying into a rage. When I refuse to fight, he realizes that he might just as well cuss out a tree or a bush, so he throws in the towel and gives up."

The best way to turn off a person's anger immediately and keep out of a disagreement with him is to respond in a kind and friendly manner. Remain calm and say nothing for a few moments until he's drained himself emotionally.

Then answer him quietly and softly for as the Bible says, "A soft answer turneth away wrath," and that's ever so true. If you use a soft, quiet tone of voice, it will not only calm down the other person, but it will also keep you from getting angry as well.

When you refuse to fight back, when you speak softly, the angry person suddenly realizes he's the only one shouting. This embarrasses him and makes him feel awkward. He suddenly becomes extremely self-conscious and anxious to get the situation back to normal as quickly as possible.

You can use these facts of applied psychology to control and quiet down the other person's angry emotions. When you find yourself in a tense situation that threatens to get completely out of hand, deliberately lower your voice and keep it down. This in turn motivates the other person to lower his voice. As long as he speaks softly, he cannot remain angry and high-strung for very long.

Hŏw You Can Mix Friendship and Business Successfully

Although Part I deals primarily with social conversations and social relationships, I do want to touch upon this point here. Any person who says you cannot mix friendship and business doesn't know much about business. Let me ask you this: Would you do business with a person you didn't like? Of course not. Neither would I.

Friendship is the best sales technique of all, no matter what your business is or what your job happens to be. Friendship is responsible for more good human relations in business, for meeting more sales quotas and building more bank accounts than anything else. Remember Pete Randall, the cookie salesman? He mixed friendship and business very successfully and so can you.

A top executive I know has an open-door policy and is on friendly terms with every person in his entire company and it's a big one. He has never become snobbish or high hat about his position or his success. He still approaches his people with comments like these:

1. Do you think this procedure would be a better one?
2. Thanks for doing such a terrific job for me.
3. I'm sure you understand this, but I can't figure it out. Would you explain it to me?
4. I've always admired your good judgment in matters like this.
5. I'm sure you could solve this problem in no time at all for me.
6. What is your own opinion on this? I'd like to know what you think about it before we decide.
7. What's your solution to this problem? I know you're an expert in this field.
8. Could you help me out of this mess?

As you can see, all these comments appeal to a person's ego and make him feel important. As you could readily guess, every employee in the plant goes all out and does his level best for this man.

Fifteen Ways to Keep Your Friendships Warm and Cordial

It takes a lot of effort to keep your friendships warm and cordial. Neglect them and they'll die from lack of care. Use this fifteen-point checklist to keep your friendships alive.

1. Always maintain a warm and friendly attitude toward others.

2. Go out of your way to perform some unexpected service for your friends.

3. Compliment another person and praise him for something he's done.

4. Always keep your word. Never make a promise you cannot keep or a decision you cannot support.

5. Treat your associates at work as close friends of long standing, not just casual acquaintances.

6. Establish a reputation as a reliable person who can be depended on so your friend will trust you.

7. Go to work with a smile on your face, leaving your personal problems and troubles at home.

8. Never use your position for personal gain at someone else's expense.

9. Don't play favorites; treat every one equally.

10. Have respect for every person's dignity. Treat every woman like a lady and every man like a gentleman.

11. Be sincere in your relationships with others. Don't be a phony. Really mean what you say and say what you mean.

12. Practice the Golden Rule with everyone, especially the daily associates with whom you work.

13. Maintain a strong belief in the rights of others.

14. Have an abiding interest in the other person's welfare.

15. Be willing to deal with every person as courteously and considerately as if he were your blood relative.

Let me summarize for you the 8 techniques you can use to build strong and enduring friendships:

1. Give of yourself to the other person first. Do everything in your power to increase the happiness and success of the other person.

2. Build your friendships on a solid foundation. One of the best ways to do that is to praise the other person for what he has done.

3. Use praise, not flattery, to gain a person's friendship. Praise compliments a person for what he *does*; flattery for what he *is*.

4. Find a common denominator to build a solid friendship.

5. Accept a person exactly as he or she is; never criticize him if you want to retain his friendship.

6. Avoid arguments and disagreements at all costs. They gain you no benefit whatever, but they can generate a great amount of ill will.

7. Learn how to mix business and friendship successfully.

8. Practice daily the fifteen methods I gave you to keep your friendships warm and cordial. Please see the checklist beginning on page 39.

When you practice these eight techniques, you'll gain the following 6 magnificent benefits:

1. You'll have friends who'll stick by you when the going gets rough.

2. Your friends will trust you and have full confidence in you.

3. Your friends will accept you just as you are. They will not criticize you or find fault with you.

4. Your friends will respect you, your decisions, and your actions.

5. Your friends will never speak disparagingly about you. They'll do everything possible to squelch rumors that degrade you or blacken your reputation.

6. As you learn the how-to of making close friends, you'll become an expert in the art of human relations, for making and keeping friends requires tact, diplomacy, and skill.

chapter 4

How to Be Well-Liked and Highly Popular Wherever You Go

What does it really mean to be popular? Well, the basics of being popular and well-liked boil down to being the kind of person others want to have around. Ask yourself now, do you enjoy being with people who are egotistical know-it-alls . . . who have the answer to every question, the solution to every problem . . . who are never wrong . . . who usurp all the conversation . . . who never listen to what you say, but constantly interrupt you to change the subject . . . who try to show off and put on airs? I'm sure you don't and neither do I.

Well then, what kind of people do you like to associate with? If you're at all like I am, then I'm sure you enjoy being with those people who are the complete opposite of the kind I've just mentioned. And if that's the kind of person you like to be with, then that's the sort of person you ought to try and be.

To be that kind of person takes practice, perseverance, and self-discipline, but it can be done. In fact, if you will just practice the techniques you'll find in this chapter, you'll be well-liked and highly popular wherever you go. I guarantee that.

SEVEN FABULOUS BENEFITS THAT WILL BE YOURS

1. People will really enjoy being with you.

2. You'll gain many, many true friends.

3. You'll even convert your enemies into friends.

4. People will admire and respect you.

5. You'll be invited to more places than you can go.

6. People will be anxious to please you, to do what you ask.

7 You can get whatever you want from people, for these techniques will work like magic for you.

44

FIVE BIG SECRETS OF BEING WELL-LIKED AND HIGHLY POPULAR

How to Practice the First Big Secret of Popularity

If you want to be well-liked and highly popular wherever you go, then learn to *give your wholehearted attention to the other person.* Every individual in this world from the smallest baby to the oldest man or woman wants the attention of others. He wants to be listened to; he wants to be heard. He wants others to listen to his ideas, his opinions, his suggestions, and his recommendations. He has a deep and burning desire—yes, even an insatiable craving—to be important, to be great, to be famous. And one of the best methods you can use to make a person feel important is to pay attention to him and to what he says.

Just, for instance, take the fellow who's never had his picture in the paper since his high school graduation. Why, he'll jump at the chance when it's offered to him. That's why people always wave when the TV camera swings their way. It's an automatic reaction to gain attention and feel important.

Let me explain that last statement more fully. You see, our actions to attract another person's attention are simply the outward manifestations of our inner desires for importance. We yearn for attention. We want our ideas and opinions to be heard. The desire for attention is present in every single one of us. If you think not, let me ask you this: Have you ever been snubbed by a haughty waiter, left standing on a corner by an independent bus driver, or been completely ignored by a government bureaucrat or store clerk? How did you feel? Now you know what I'm driving at, don't you?

Psychologists, psychiatrists, ministers, criminologists, management consultants, marriage counselors, all these experts have come to one simple conclusion in this art of human relations, and that is, if you want to be well-liked by others, then you must learn to give your wholehearted attention to the other person. It's the only sure way of establishing solid friendly relationships with other people.

This first big secret of how to be well-liked and gain popularity will work miracles for you, not only with people outside your family, but also with your spouse and children. Let me give you a couple of brief examples of this:

How to Go Out of Your Way to Pay Attention to Your Wife

You don't have to send your wife flowers or candy every day or buy her expensive gifts all the time to show her how much you love and appreciate her. My technique will cost you absolutely nothing and it's even more effective. I know a couple who's been happily married for more than 40 years now, and I know this man doesn't give his wife any presents except on her birthday, their anniversary, and Christmas.

"What's your secret, Sam?" I asked him one day.

"Very simple, Jim," he said. "I always pay attention to my wife. I let her know by my actions that I know she's around. I still say *please* and *thank you* even after all these years. So does she; it sort of builds a mutual respect between us. And I never get up from the table without saying, 'Thanks, honey; that was a terrific meal,' or 'Thanks a lot, dear; you're sure a wonderful cook.'

"Or when we pass each other in the house, I reach out and touch her gently. Or I bring her a glass of water when she's watching TV in the evening. Or a cup of tea in the afternoon while she's sewing or knitting. What if she doesn't want it? you say. What if she's not thirsty? Don't worry about that. She'll drink it anyway just to show her appreciation for my giving her my wholehearted attention. If you don't believe that, try it on your own wife. You'll soon see for yourself."

I know these might sound like tiny, inconsequential things to you at first. But just as Sam says, they serve as proof positive to your wife that you still love her and that you still appreciate her. So if you want to maintain a harmonious relationship and a pleasant atmosphere in your home, all you need do is give your wholehearted attention to your wife, too. You'll be mighty happy when you do. When you do these little things for her, your own benefits will multiply. You'll never want for a clean shirt, you'll never put on a pair of unpressed pants, or you'll never sit down to a cold supper. Your wife will love all those *little inconsequential, unimportant extras* and she'll want to make sure they keep coming. And if you're the wife, this technique will work both ways. You can use it on your husband, too.

As I told you in the beginning of Part I, there are very few magic words or phrases as such, but as you can see from this last example, *please* and *thank you* are two of them. Use them constantly, for they'll work magic in your own relationships with others.

I know that to be a fact, for there's a grocery store less than three blocks from my house, but I never go there. The checkout clerks are always sour-faced and don't know how to say "Thank you." So I drive nearly three miles to a different supermarket simply because the people there are friendly and courteous and never fail to say "Thanks." Who says you can't mix friendship and business?

This technique will work on your children, too

If you've been having disciplinary problems with your children, this technique of paying attention to others will go a long way toward solving them. I know, for I raised three children of my own.

Many parents make the mistake of not paying attention to their children. They don't want to be bothered with them or their problems. But children need and want attention just as much as grownups do.

Now it doesn't take a lot of extra effort to give your children that special attention they need so much. Ask them to play with you; perhaps a game of pool, ping-pong, cards, chess, checkers, Monopoly—whatever you have in your home.

Larry, my youngest son, and I used to battle it out with a cribbage board in front of the fireplace on many a stormy winter night. In the summer time, you had to get in line to play ping-pong in our garage.

So learn to play with your children; pay attention to them. It'll improve all of your family relationships. Your kids will learn to like you as well as love you. You'll not only be their parents, but you'll also become their friends, and that's ever so important. A good healthy game of ping-pong in the garage with your teen-age son or daughter will do more to reduce that generation gap than all the lectures you can give them in the back bedroom.

How to Put the Second Big Secret of Popularity to Work

I know of no faster way to drive people away from you and become extremely unpopular with everyone than to continually talk about yourself and your own accomplishments. Not even your best friends can put up with your never-ending stories of how important you are. Even they will reach the limits of their endurance. So the second big secret of how to be well-liked and popular with everyone is to *forget yourself completely and become genuinely interested in other people.*

If you believe you can be well-liked, popular, and win friends by getting them interested in you and your affairs, then I must tell you quite bluntly: you are dead wrong. The only way you can ever win lasting friends is to become truly interested in people and their problems.

The selfish person who has no interest in his fellow man and his problems always has the greatest difficulties in life and ends up causing the most harm, not only to others, but also to himself. That individual is bound to fail unless he changes his basic selfish attitude toward people. If you do by some rare chance happen to find yourself in that rut, here are two giant steps you can take to get out of it so you can become genuinely interested in others:

1. Forget yourself completely.
2. Think that other people are important.

How to Forget Yourself Completely

All of us are self-centered almost all the time. To me, the world revolves around me. But as far as you are concerned, it revolves around you. Most of us are busily trying to impress someone. We are constantly seeking the spotlight. We continually want to be in the center of the stage. Most of our waking moments are spent in trying to achieve status of some sort.

But if you want to be well-liked and popular with others, you must learn to forget yourself completely. You can do that easily when you give service of some sort to others. If you want to win the hearts and support of people, then you must be willing to help them in any way that you can.

To be able to do this with sincerity means you'll have to place more emphasis on what they want instead of on what you want. And you'll need an attitude of complete unselfishness to do that.

I know this much for sure. If you are sincere, if you will become genuinely interested in helping others, you'll never run out of work. I guarantee that the willingness of people to accept your help will always far outrun your ability to do so. But when you do, you'll have more friends than you can count. Everybody will be able to say a good word for you. You'll be well-liked and popular wherever you go.

How to Think That Other People Are Important

This is the second step I mentioned that you can use to become genuinely interested in others. Jesus once said, "Believe that you have got it and you shall have it." The same principle applies here. In other words, all you need do to think that other people are important is just to *pretend that they are and they will be.*

Simply tell yourself once and for all that other people and their interests are more important to them than you and your interests. When you adopt this attitude and practice it sincerely, it'll come through as clear as a bell to the other person. You won't have to put on a phony face and butter him up to win his friendship.

With this new approach, you can stop looking for gimmicks to become well-liked and popular. You won't need any for you'll have put your dealings with other people on a firm, sound, sincere, and honest basis. Sincerity and honesty are better than a gimmick any day of the week, for you can't make a person feel important if deep down inside you really feel he's a worthless nobody.

The beauty of this method is that you no longer need participate in the games people play to impress each other. All you need do to make this technique work is just to think that the other person is important and then treat him that way. Pretend that it is so, and it will be.

How to Use the Third Big Secret of Popularity

The third big secret of popularity is to *learn to listen with everything you've got.* Listening is hard work. It requires your complete concentration. You need to use not only your ears, but also your eyes to listen. Watch for facial expressions, the frown or the smile that can often tell more than the words the person is using.

If you don't listen intently to the other person, you will insult him and turn him off completely. And you'll lose a friend in the process. To tell the truth, I know of no quicker way to insult a person or hurt his feelings than to brush him off or to turn away when he's trying to tell you something.

How many times have you been right in the middle of a story only to have one of your listeners turn away or interrupt you and start talking on a brand-new subject? You'd have liked to strangle that individual with your bare hands, right?

Children feel the same way when their parents brush them aside, ignore them, and pay no attention whatever to their problems. And if youngsters feel that way, what reason do you have to believe that grownups don't react in the same exact manner?

"You must give your child more than board and room," says Doctor Daniel Post, director of a family guidance and counseling center for wayward

children and their parents in Phoenix, Arizona. "I hear the same complaint over and over from upset parents. Time and again they say to me, 'But Doctor, I just don't understand what's wrong with our son. Why should he want to steal or run away from home? We give him everything he needs!'

"They do give him everything he needs physically, perhaps, but not the two most important things he needs psychologically: *love and attention.* When I listen to the youngster who's broken the law, he tells me a completely different story: 'My parents never pay attention to me. My dad never listens to what I have to say. He never even looks at me when I talk to him. He's either reading the evening paper or watching TV so he doesn't want to be bothered. My mother's always yelling about my long hair or dirty jeans or why I don't wear socks, but she never listens to me either. That's all I ask 'em to do. Just listen tc what I have to say once in a while. I'm important, too, aren't I?'"

Learning to listen to the other person with everything you've got means putting aside your own interests, your own pleasures, and your own preoccupations, at least temporarily. For those few moments of time you must concentrate 100 percent on what the other person is saying. You should focus all your attention on him. Listen to him with all the intensity and awareness that you can command.

How to Listen Between the Lines

A lot of times you can learn more by what the other person doesn't say than by what he does. So learn to listen between the lines. Just because he didn't say he doesn't want to do things your way is no sign that he does.

The speaker doesn't always put everything he's thinking into words for you. Watch for the changing tone and volume of his voice. Sometimes you'll find a meaning that is in direct contrast to his spoken words. And watch the facial expressions, his mannerisms, his gestures, the movements of his eyes and his body. To be a good listener and listen with everything you've got means you'll have to use more than your ears to listen.

How to Be Considered a Conversational Whiz Just by Listening

You can use the following five techniques to get people to open up and talk with you. When you do, you'll be considered to be a whiz at conversation.

1. *Look directly at the person while he's speaking*. Don't be disturbed by anything else. The person talking will notice your lack of attention immediately and be upset by it.

2. *Show interest in what he is saying*. You don't have to say a word. Just nod your head and smile when it's called for. That's usually all you need to do.

3. *Lean toward the person*. This demonstrates a deep interest on your part in what the person is saying.

4. *Use feedback to keep him going*. You can keep the person talking and show your interest by saying such things as "Oh yes . . . I see . . . that's right."

5. *Ask questions if necessary*. All you need do is say something like, "And then what did you say?" "And then what did you do?" That's enough to keep the person talking indefinitely.

Remember that people are more interested in what they have to say than in what you have to say. They like to talk about themselves, their successes, their families, their hobbies, their own interests. Use the 5 techniques I've just given you to encourage them to talk and they will feel that they've met, not only a good listener, but also an excellent conversationalist. This kind of behavior on your part makes a positive favorable impression on others. If you can be a good listener and get the other person to open up and talk, you'll be well-liked and popular wherever you go.

How to Put the Fourth Big Secret of Popularity into Action

I attended a small social gathering one afternoon at a friend's house. One of the people present was a talkative woman who constantly forced her opinions on everyone. Whatever subject was brought up, she'd either done it before or knew all about it. She was an expert on everything, at least according to her account of it.

"My God, is there anything that woman doesn't know?" Jack J. asked me.

"Evidently not, Jack," I replied. "But I doubt if she'll ever be invited here again."

So the fourth big secret of popularity is not to be a *know-it-all*. A know-it-all rubs people the wrong way. This kind of person embarrasses others, makes everyone uncomfortable, and is highly unpopular. Nobody likes the perfect person who has all the answers to everything. No one feels at home with perfection.

I don't mean you must always run yourself down or be considered ignorant to be popular and well-liked. But it is utterly refreshing to hear a person say, "I don't know."

I don't know are three more magic words you can use to great advantage. If you don't know and the other person does know, he'll be sure to tell you. And even if you already know, so what? Your aim is to be well-liked and popular, not to show off your knowledge. You'll never achieve your goal if you're going to be a know-it-all.

So even if you do know all the answers when someone is trying to introduce an interesting subject, just be tactful and diplomatic enough to say "I don't know" and give the other person a chance to shine.

Practicing the Fifth Big Secret of How to Be Popular and Well-Liked

The fifth technique you can use to be popular and well-liked is to *admit your mistakes,* especially when you've hurt the other person's feelings by what you've said or done. It takes courage to say, "I'm sorry . . . I was wrong . . . I made a mistake and I apologize." But these are magic words, too, for they will work miracles in human relationships for you.

Now this sort of humbleness does not degrade or humiliate you. In fact, just the opposite is true. People admire you for your decency and courtesy and it will pay you dividends to admit you were wrong and apologize to the other person. Let me give you a personal example of that.

I once had occasion to write to a lawyer with whom I was extremely displeased. I felt the fee he'd charged me for a certain legal service was far too high and I told him so. I guess I got carried away, for my letter became much more caustic than I'd meant it to be.

At any rate, he called me to tell me in no uncertain terms exactly what he thought of both me and my remarks. He was really angry with me and he laid it on hot and heavy. When he finally paused for breath, I said, "Brad, I'm truly sorry I wrote that letter in such haste. I should never have done so. You have a perfect right to be angry with me. I apologize for what I said. Please forgive me."

He was quiet for a long time. Finally he said, "That's all right, Jim. I respect you for having the courtesy to say you're wrong and for apologizing. Could be my fee was a bit high, so I guess I owe you an apology, too. I should have enclosed an explanation with the bill. I'll send you a new one. Let's be friends and start all over, okay?"

So you see, to promptly admit your mistake when you are wrong and apologize to the person you've hurt can immediately turn his anger into a lasting friendship. But you can go even further than that for even better results.

All you need do is to *say you're sorry even when you're not at fault*. When you're not in the wrong, you can afford to be big about it. If just saying you're sorry will restore peace in your family, or mend the broken relationships between two people, then say it so you can get on with the more important business of enjoying each other's companionship, rather than stewing and fretting about who's right or who's wrong.

How Max W. Practices These Techniques to Be Popular

Max W. is one of the most popular and well-liked persons I've ever met. He is always being invited somewhere. Someone is constantly after him to go to a party, have lunch at the club, be the guest speaker at the Rotary or the Kiwanis, play golf or tennis.

One evening I was a guest at a small social affair. I spotted Max sitting in a corner with the prettiest girl there. Out of curiosity I watched for a while from a distance. I noticed the young lady was talking constantly, but Max never seemed to say a word. He would smile and nod his head every so often and that seemed to be it. After a while, they got up, thanked their host and hostess, and left.

The next day I saw Max in a restaurant eating lunch alone for a change. I asked if I could join him. "I saw you with the most gorgeous girl at the Swansons' last night," I said. "She seemed totally engrossed in you. How did you hold her attention so well?"

"Easy," Max said. "When Mrs. Swanson introduced Jo Ann to me, I simply said to her, 'You have a gorgeous tan. And right in the middle of winter, too. How did you do it? Where have you been? Acapulco? Hawaii?'

"'Acapulco,' she said. 'It was so wonderful. Have you ever been there?'

"'I never have,' I said to her. 'I'd love to know all about it. Would you tell me about your trip?'

"'Of course,' she replied. So we sat down in a quiet corner and for the next two hours she did exactly that.

"This morning Jo Ann called me to say she enjoyed my company very much. She said she was anxious to see me again, for I was a most interesting person to talk with. But honestly, I didn't say more than a dozen words all night long."

Have you figured out the secret of Max's popularity? He used four of the five major secrets of how to be well-liked and popular. First, he gave Jo Ann his undivided attention. Second, he forgot himself completely and showed genuine interest in what she had to say. Third, he listened intently to her with undivided attention. Fourth, he motivated her to talk when he said he knew nothing about Acapulco, but was anxious to hear about her trip.

So if you, too, want to be well-liked and popular with everyone, never, never talk about yourself. Instead, get the other person talking about *his* interests, *his* business, *his* golf scores, *his* successes, *her* hobbies, *her* trips, *her* children, and so on.

Get people to talk about themselves, listen with rapt and undivided attention and you'll be well-liked and popular too. You'll be welcomed wherever you go.

Six Ways to Become a Loner and Not Be Invited Anywhere

I normally do not like to offer negative suggestions, but in this case, I think they will be well worthwhile. If you want to be well-liked and popular, it would be wise for you to avoid making the following mistakes:

1. Monopolizing the conversation
2. Talking in a loud voice
3. Interrupting others constantly
4. Forcing your personal opinions on everyone
5. Letting people know how wrong they are
6. Being negative about everything

How to Win a Popularity Contest: A 12-Point Checklist

1. Be yourself. If you try to be someone you are not, you'll appear phony and artificial.
2. Listen carefully to other people's opinions.
3. Ask questions that encourage others to talk.
4. Offer opinions rather than irrefutable facts.

5. Maintain a sense of humor. Don't take yourself too seriously.

6. Accept criticism gracefully for your mistakes.

7. Be cheerful, friendly, and optimistic. Smile.

8. Never argue with anyone. Give ground on unimportant trifles.

9. Don't gossip or be a rumormonger.

10. Talk about subjects the other person is interested in.

11. Don't be a know-it-all or a perfectionist.

12. Don't set up your own standards of right and wrong.

Let me give you a summary checklist of how to be well-liked and popular wherever you go.

1. The first big secret of popularity is to give your wholehearted attention to the other person.

2. The second big secret of being well-liked is to forget yourself completely and become genuinely interested in other people.

3. The third big secret of being popular with others is to learn to listen with everything you've got.

4. The fourth big secret of popularity is not to be a know-it-all. *I don't know* are three magic words that can be used to great advantage.

5. The fifth big secret of how to be popular and well-liked is to admit your mistakes, especially when you've hurt the other person's feelings by what you've said or done. Learn to say you're sorry even when you're not at fault. This act alone will pay you far bigger dividends than you realize.

If you will use these techniques for the next 10 days or so, you'll be amazed at how rapidly people's attitudes toward you will change for the better. There will be a marked improvement in your relationships with others. You'll be able to be popular and well-liked wherever you go. It's like waving a magic wand and watching miracles happen.

chapter 5

Magic Methods
That Will Make
Your Marriage and
Your Home Life
Much Happier

In Chapter Three, I said that husbands and wives who were friends as well as lovers always had the happiest marriages. I also showed you how you could use praise to win your spouse's friendship. Then, in Chapter Four, I said that one of the best ways to have a harmonious family relationship is to pay attention to your husband or your wife and, also, to your children.

In this chapter, I'll not only amplify and expand these ideas but I will also give you nine additional magic methods that you can use to make your marriage and your home life much happier. When you use these valuable techniques,

YOU'LL GAIN THESE 6 HUGE BENEFITS

1. There will be a peaceful and pleasant, happy and joyful atmosphere in your home.
2. A spirit of cheerful cooperation and helpfulness will be evident in your entire family.
3. There'll be a willingness on everyone's part to work together to solve common family problems.
4. You'll be loved and respected by each member of your family.
5. Your spouse and your children will look to you for guidance and direction.
6. Arguments and disagreements will be virtually nonexistent in your home.

NINE MAGIC METHODS YOU CAN USE
TO GAIN THESE BENEFITS

How to Create a Happy Family Atmosphere by What You Say

Each and every one of us possesses a power we often fail to use properly. *That power is the freedom of choice.* Many people choose to be poor when they need only choose to be rich. Some choose failure instead of success because it is easier. Others choose to be afraid of life when all they need do is step out with courage and take what is rightfully theirs.

What you choose to do about your family life is exactly the same. You have the power to choose the kind of atmosphere that you want in your home. You can choose one that is fun: one that is filled with excitement, joy, and happiness. Or you can choose a home life that is constantly filled with anger and resentment, arguments and bickering. It's all up to you. Let me give you an example of how well this technique will work when it is properly used.

I had an uncle whom I admired greatly, Warren Roland. He and my aunt Mary were married for more than 50 years before he died. They were always extremely happy together. I never once heard a harsh word from either of them for the other, nor did I ever see even an angry glance exchanged between them.

Just before I was married, Uncle Warren asked me to drop by his place for a chat. "Will you accept a small bit of advice from your old uncle?" he asked. When I said I'd be more than glad to, here's what he told me.

"You can be happy in your marriage if you just choose to be," he said. "That's what your aunt and I did when we were first married. We chose to be happy. If you want your marriage to be successful, I recommend that you do the same: *choose to be happy.* It's really just that simple when you don't complicate it."

If you make that same choice, then you will automatically say kind and courteous, happy and cheerful things to the members of your family. You just can't choose to be happy and then growl and bark at your family or argue and disagree with them. The two emotions are incompatible.

Remember the rule that if you want to get, you must first give. If you use courtesy and tender loving care in family discussions, that's what you will receive in return. You cannot expect to give nothing to your family and get something back just because it's your family. It won't work. You must make the first move yourself.

All you have to do is choose to have a happy home life and the right words will come to you. You won't have to agonize over what to say or how to say it.

Even if you've been married a long time and things don't seem to be going too well, it's never too late to make the decision to be happy with your spouse. When you choose to be happy, kindness and courtesy will flow from you with every word you speak. No matter how bad things might seem to be at times, they'll always get better when you make that one simple decision: *Choose to be happy.*

How to Get Up on the Right Side of the Bed

Even though it might be a cliché and sound old-fashioned to you, getting up on the right side of the bed in the morning is still an extremely wise procedure. So get in the habit of starting the day off right. Again, it's simply a matter of choice. You can be happy or miserable, whatever you decide to be.

How to do it? Simple. There's another old saying you can use that will help you. Instead of saying to yourself, "Good God, it's morning," just say, "Good morning, God," and go on from there. Greet your wife or husband with a cheerful "Good morning, dear. You must have rested well. You look fine this morning."

I don't care whether the sun is shining or whether it's raining or snowing; it can be a terrific day if you choose to make it so. Life can be a lot more enjoyable for both you and your family if you start the day off pleasantly with a kind word and a smile instead of a growl and a frown.

Tell yourself that today is going to be the best day of your life and it will be. Yesterday is gone, tomorrow isn't here, so concentrate on making today an outstanding one. Use that attitude and you can infect your family, too.

A former business associate of mine always came to the office with a big smile and a cheerful "Good morning, Jim."

"What's your secret, Hank?" I once asked him. "How do you manage to be so happy at nine in the morning? Most people don't feel that good until quitting time at five."

"Oh, that's easy, Jim," he said. "My wife wakes me every morning by putting her hand gently on my forehead and saying, 'It's time to get up, dear. It's a beautiful morning. Your coffee's ready and the morning paper is on the dining room table. I love you.' How could I help but feel good with a greeting like that every morning?"

Something tells me that Hank's wife is one smart woman. She knows the secret of a happy marriage.

How to Get in the Habit of Saying
the Cheerful, Pleasant Thing

It is especially important to develop the habit of cheerful and pleasant conversation when the family is all together if you want to have friendly and harmonious relationships in your home. So always be pleasant to your family no matter how rotten you might feel inside. There's no point in making them miserable just because you're down in the dumps for one reason or another.

It is particularly important to develop the habit of pleasant and cheerful conversation when the family is together. This is especially true at meal times. Do not upset everyone's digestion—including your own—by making the family meal a recitation of troubles, anxieties, fears, warnings, and accusations. Discipline and dinner do not go together. Make every meal a joyful and happy festive occasion.

Our next-door neighbors have two small grandsons who visit them every summer for several weeks. One day the younger one, a six-year old, struck up a conversation with me.

"How do you like staying with your grandpa and grandma?" I asked him.

"I like it," he said. "Boy, my grandpa and grandma sure get along real good. They're always saying nice things to each other. They say nice things to me and my brother, too. They never fight or get mad like my dad and mom do."

Children are especially cognizant of the kind of family atmosphere they are raised in, no matter how young they are. It's a known fact that abused children grow up to be child abusers themselves. And children with mean and grouchy parents will grow up to be mean and grouchy themselves. So, if you want your children to grow up and be the kind of adults whose company other people will enjoy, raise them in a cheerful and pleasant family atmosphere.

A Technique That Will Work Magic in Your Marriage for You

If you will remember, I said that one of the vital factors in gaining good friends was to accept people exactly as they are. That principle applies just as much, if not more so, to your relationship with your spouse.

One of the real secrets to complete joy and happiness in your home is accepting your partner exactly as he or she is. Don't try to change your spouse and make him or her over into a second edition of yourself. Don't nag or criticize. You'll never change a person that way. You'll never get a person to do what you want him to do with criticism.

Take your own husband, for instance. Have you ever been able to change him very much through all your years of marriage by nagging and finding fault with him? I know that you probably thought you had good intentions. You felt that you could make him over into the kind of person you thought he ought to be, but did you ever really succeed? I doubt it. I know my wife never did.

Or if you're thinking of making your wife over to fit your own specifications by using criticism, forget it. I failed at that, too. I haven't been able to change her one little bit through all these 40 and more years. She's still the same woman I married. But thank God I failed in my attempts. I know now I couldn't have improved on her at all.

This is a most valuable point for you to remember if you will. *The only person you can ever really change in your life is you, yourself, and you alone—no one else.* So accept your partner just as he or she is. You'll never be able to achieve total joy and happiness in your marriage until you do.

How to Work This Technique If You Are Newly Married

When a couple is first married, they are completely blind to each other's faults. They're too much in love to notice the other person's bad habits. But after the honeymoon is over and they realize there are some adjustments that must be made, there can be a tendency to find fault and criticize each other. Then love goes out the window.

But this doesn't have to happen. Let me give you some methods you can use to get what you want in your marriage without destroying your happy and loving relationship:

SITUATION: Husband is always leaving the cap off the toothpaste tube.

WRONG: For God's sake, when will you learn to put the cap back on the toothpaste tube? I'm sick and tired of trying to get the toothpaste out when it's all dried up!

RIGHT Darling, would you mind putting the cap back on the toothpaste when you finish? I'd sure appreciate it. Thanks a lot for being so thoughtful.

SITUATION: Wife hangs her stockings over the shower rod to dry and leaves her cosmetics scattered all over the bathroom counter.

WRONG: Why the devil do you always hang your stockings on the shower rod? Can't you find somewhere else to dry them? I can't take a shower when they're in my way. And I need a broom to clean up your mess on the bathroom counter.

I've never seen so much junk. I can't even find a clean place to shave and wash up.

RIGHT: Honey, I'd appreciate it if you didn't hang your stockings over the shower rod until after I take my shower. I don't like to get them wet or cause you to wash them all over again. And I wonder if you could pick up the bathroom counter when you're through putting your make-up on. I don't want to spill any soap or water or shaving cream on your things while I'm cleaning up. Thanks so much. I love you for it.

SITUATION: Husband throws his dirty clothes in a corner, tosses his pants on a chair, and drops his shoes where he comes in the door.

WRONG: I'd swear your mother raised a pig instead of a son. If you think I'm going to follow you around picking up after you, you're crazy. I'm sick and tired of your filthy lazy habits.

RIGHT: Honey, I'd appreciate it if you'd put your dirty things in the clothes hamper and hang your trousers up so they won't get so wrinkled. And this morning I nearly fell over your shoes in the hallway when I was getting ready to go to work. Darling, I can't hold down a job and keep a clean house, too, unless you help me. Would you please do that? Thanks for your cooperation, dear. I surely do appreciate it.

I could go on and on with examples like these, but these three should be enough to show you how to solve those small irritating problems with courtesy and kindness instead of nagging and criticism. Do that, and you'll be able to keep the fires of love and romance burning all of your life.

How to Have a Family Love Feast

A technique you can use to help establish pleasant and cordial relationships in your home and make your marriage and your home life much happier is to hold a family love feast. Only two rules apply: one, no criticism is allowed; two, only compliments are to be handed out. Here's how to do it.

Gather your entire family in a comfortable setting such as the family room, the den, or the living room. Soft, pleasant background music is permissible if it's turned down low, but no television and no other interruptions are allowed. Each person takes turns being the subject while all the others tell him the good points they see and like about him. Let me give you some examples:

"I love your awareness of natural beauty. You call my attention sometimes to a beautiful sunset or a gorgeous full moon and I think that's terrific for we can watch it together."

"I want to thank you for picking a hibiscus flower and putting it on the table for me each morning. I do appreciate your loving thoughtfulness."

"I appreciate the way you always put the cap back on the toothpaste tube so it won't dry out."

"You're a warm, loving, and compassionate person, and I love you for that."

"Your smile and a cheerful 'Good morning' get me off to a good start each day. Thanks a lot.

"You really look fantastic in blue (or red or green)."

"I love to hear you sing. You have such a beautiful voice."

"You really have a way with words. You explain everything so clearly so I can understand it easily."

"You hit the ball better than anybody I know."

"You're an outstanding speller. I wish I had your talent for that."

"I really love the cutting board you made for me in your shop class. Thanks a million."

There's no end to the good things you can say to each other in a family love feast. And it helps the entire family to get along better, to understand each other, to appreciate each other more, to have fun with each other, and to look for the good qualities instead of the character defects in people.

You can use the same techniques with your friends and associates as well as with your family. Praise and kind words of love and appreciation for others can make irritable people become warm and outgoing. Sad and despondent persons can become confident and enthusiastic when they are treated to a love feast like this. So, before you dismiss this technique as so much syrupy mush, give it a whirl.

When you do, you'll quickly change your mind. You'll find it's a magic method that makes darned good sense.

How to Guide, Direct, and Control Your Children Without Effort

To guide, direct, and control your children without effort so they'll always do what you know is best for them to do, *make them happy*. When they're happy, they'll be only too glad to do as you desire.

How do you make a child happy? It takes a lot more than money and material possessions. You can start off by telling your child you love him and then proving that you do by giving him your full and undivided attention. This is something every child usually needs the most and yet gets the least of: *attention*. As a result, children often feel left out. Lack of attention makes them feel unwanted. You can give them a real sense of being wanted and fulfill their deep need for emotional security by giving them your wholehearted attention.

Praise is the best way to give a person your full attention. Children respond to praise just as much as adults do. If you want your son or daughter to get better grades in school, then praise them for their efforts. If you criticize them for their poor grades, those grades will go even lower. I guarantee it. I know that from personal experience. You see, mine has been a learning process, too.

I do know that sometimes you must discipline your children. After all, I raised three of my own. Discipline should be reasonable and firm, yet kind and friendly. Parents in unhappy families don't realize this, but in a happy family there is seldom any reason for discipline. People usually discipline themselves in happy families.

So give your children a happy, pleasant atmosphere, encourage their efforts with kind words of praise, work with them, play with them, make them feel they belong by letting them take part in family projects, and you'll find that the necessity for discipline seldom exists. Your children will do what you want them to do. When discipline is handled in this way, you can enjoy your children, just as Mike Turner does.

"One summer a few years ago when Bob was 16, he and I went on a month-long trip throughout the west in a camper, just the two of us," Mike told me. "We did everything together just as two buddies would. We took turns driving the pickup truck, cooking the meals, washing the dishes, making the bed. Not once during the trip did I tell him what to do. I treated him as an equal.

"After we were back home, Bob paid me a compliment I will always remember. 'Dad, this has been the best time of my life,' he said. 'I'll always remember this trip for I've learned that you're my friend as well as my father.'"

I know you must give guidance and counsel to your children, but if you really want to enjoy them and make your home life much happier, drop that parent role as often as you can so you can be a friend as well as a father or a mother. This approach will bring you a wonderful new relationship with them.

How a Wife Can Help Her Husband Become Highly Successful

A wife can help her husband become highly successful by the simple act of using words of praise for what he does. If you want your husband to get ahead and be successful in his work, then don't criticize him for not bringing home a bigger paycheck. Instead, praise him for his hard work and for all he does for you. Praise builds his self-confidence and helps him get ahead. Let me show you how important that can be.

Charles H., president of a large company employing several thousand people, told me that big businesses and corporations want to find out more about the wife before a man is promoted to a top-level of responsibility.

"I myself am more interested in whether a wife can give her husband a feeling of confidence in himself than I am in her good looks and social acceptability," Charles says.

"You see, if she gives her husband the feeling that she is pleased with him and with his work, and if she praises him in every way possible, it's about like getting a shot of adrenalin every time he comes home.

"His wife's praise sends him off each morning filled with the self-confidence that he can solve any problem that comes along. That's the kind of person we need in our top executive positions. That kind of wife can help put him there."

How to Make Your Spouse the Most Important Person in Your Life by What You Say

Of the 14 basic needs and desires we all have, the desire to be important is the most dominant one of all in nearly everyone. So, make your mate the most important person in your life, and you will never fail. Here are three specific ways you can do exactly that:

1. *Think that your mate is the most important person in the world.* The first rule is simply to convince yourself that your spouse is the most important person in your life. Do this, and you won't have to pretend. Your attitude will come across loud and clear without even trying.

Not only that, you won't have to use any phony gimmicks or artificial tricks to make this technique work. Your relations with your mate will be on an honest and sincere basis, as they should be. As you think, so shall you believe, and as you believe, so shall it be. Act as if it were true and it will be true.

2. *Pay close attention to everything he says and does.* The most common complaint of wives is this: "He never notices me . . . never pays any attention to me or what I say . . . takes me for granted . . . treats me like an old shoe . . ."

Does your wife have a new hairdo? Tell her how beautiful it makes her look. Is she wearing a new dress? Compliment her on her choice. Thank her for the wonderful dinner she prepared for you. The same sort of advice can work for the wife, too.

3. *Always praise . . . never criticize.* You've heard me talk about this several times before, but it is such a valuable technique I could never discuss it too often. Praise is the most powerful tool you can use to feed a person's ego and make him feel important.

By the same token, criticism destroys. Criticism detroys people. It creates enemies. It ruins friendships. It destroys love and marriages. In fact, I cannot think of a single thing criticism does that is of any value whatever to anyone.

So if you want a harmonious and friendly relationship with your spouse, never criticize. Praise instead. Praise creates energy. It makes a person work harder, more effectively, and with greater enthusiasm, because praise makes the person feel proud of himself and what he has done.

Simply say to your spouse, "I am so proud of you." These are magic words, for he'll do whatever you want him to do when he hears them. You just can't miss when you praise a person for what he has done

PS: Don't Do Too Much for Your Spouse

I never realized that you could do too much for your spouse until I listened to one of my wife's friends one day.

"Keith does everything for me," Nancy said. "I know he loves me, but he doesn't really need me. Why do I say that? Because he never lets me do anything on my own. No matter what I mention or start to do, he takes over and does it for me. He makes me feel so useless and unnecessary. I wish he would realize that just once in a while I'd rather do something for myself instead of having him do it for me."

Grownups are just like children in this respect. If they can't do something on their own, they have nothing to be proud of. Everyone wants to feel important and be proud of his own accomplishments, no matter what they are. Nancy's remarks brought the words of my own granddaughter, Christina, back to mind. When she was small and I tried to help her do something, she would say, "Don't help me, Grandpa. I want to do it myself."

Let me enumerate again for you the 9 magic methods you can use that will make your marriage and your home life much happier.

1. Learn to create a happy family atmosphere by what you say You can do that easily if you simply choose to be happy.

2. Always get up on the right side of the bed. I know it's a cliché, but the point is, it works, and that's important, cliché or no cliché. It's simply a matter of choice.

3. Get in the habit of saying the cheerful and pleasant thing. Remember that discipline and dinner do not go together.

4. A technique that will always work magic in your marriage for you is to accept your partner exactly as he or she is. Remember that the only person you can ever really change in your life is you, yourself, and you alone—no one else. When you realize that, you'll also realize that criticism of another person is completely useless.

5. If you're a newlywed, learn to solve small irritating marital problems with courtesy and kindness rather than with nagging and criticism. Do that, and you'll keep the fires of love and romance burning all of your life.

6. Have a family love feast where you hand out compliments to members of your family. No criticism is allowed.

7. You can guide, direct, and control your children without effort when you make them happy by giving them your full and whole-hearted attention. Praise is the best way to do this. In happy families, there is seldom any reason for discipline.

8. If you're a wife, you can help your husband become highly successful by praising him and sending him off to work each morning feeling confident that he can solve any problem that comes along.

9. Three ways to make your spouse the most important person in your life are these:

    a. Think that your mate is the most important person in the whole world.

    b. Pay close attention to everything he or she says or does.

    c. Always praise; never criticize.

When you use these 9 valuable techniques, you'll gain these 6 huge benefits:

1. There will be a peaceful and pleasant, happy and joyful atmosphere in your home.

2. A spirit of cheerful cooperation and helpfulness will be evident in your entire family.

3. There will be a willingness on everyone's part to work together to solve common family problems.

4. You will be loved and respected by each member of your family.

5. Your spouse and your children will look to you for guidance and direction.

6. Arguments and disagreements will be virtually nonexistent in your home.

This concludes Part I about social conversations. In Parts II, III, and IV, I will take up the three major kinds of business conversations.

However, please remember that the principles and techniques you've learned in Part I for social conversations can also be used in almost all business situations.

This is especially true of Chapter One, where I discussed the 14 secret motivators that every person has and how you could use them to your own advantage in your conversations. In fact, these points are so important for you to remember, it would be helpful for you to make a list of them and keep it handy for ready reference at all times.

PART II

Business
Conversations
That Order,
Command, or Direct

Business conversations have three primary purposes and can be divided into three main categories: those that order, command, *or* direct *and tell a person* what *to do; those that* inform *and tell a person* how *to do something; those that* persuade *and tell a person* why *something should be done.*

These three general purposes sometimes overlap, as when a conversation that directs a person what *to do also explains* why *the order must be carried out. Or if you were trying to get your superior to approve some new procedure, you would not only want to inform him* how *your new system would work, but you would also want to let him know* why *it was so important that the proposed change be made.*

However, for clarity and better understanding, I will discuss each of the primary purposes of a business conversation separately. In Part II, I will take up those that order, command, *or* direct *a person* what *to do.*

chapter 6

How to Give Orders and
Commands That Will
Always Be Obeyed
Without Fail

Telling others what to do is a subtle art that requires a great deal of skill and expertise. If you want to become highly successful in business or industry, you must know how to control and direct people's actions by your orders and commands. Since you cannot use force to control people, you must learn how to use techniques that will command both respect and obedience.

When you can command words to serve your thoughts and feelings, you are well on your way to commanding people to do your will and serve your purposes. You'll be able to give orders that will always be obeyed without fail.

THE 5 OUTSTANDING BENEFITS YOU'LL GAIN

1. *People will respond quickly to orders and directives that are concise, clear, and easy to understand.* If you overstate your order by adding too many details, you will only create confusion. The perfect example of the most concise and clear-cut order of all time can be found in Matthew 9:9 where Jesus simply said, "Follow me." And the Scripture says that "Matthew arose and followed Him."

2. *People work better when they know the results you want.* They will do a far better job for you when you tell them what their exact responsibilities are, precisely what you want done, and the specific results you expect.

3. *To decentralize the work effectively, issue orders that are easy to understand.* This is especially important in business and industry where a person always seems to need more time than is available. When people understand your order and know exactly what you want, you'll gain more time to do your own work and supervise the work of others.

4. *Use mission-type orders and you can emphasize results, not methods.* A mission-type order tells a person what you want done and when you want it, but it doesn't tell him how to do it. The *how-to* is left entirely up to him. A mission-type order opens the door wide so a person can use his imagination, initiative, and ingenuity to do the job

for you. No matter what your line is, this can lead to a better way of doing things. If you're in business, improved methods can mean increased profits for you.

5. *You can get rid of waste, confusion, and duplication of effort.* When you use clear, concise, and simple orders that are easy to understand, people will know what you want done and they'll do it right the first time. They'll not have to come back to you time and again for clarification of what you said. *Simplicity is an absolute must to insure complete compliance with your commands.* This is a hard and fast rule for you to follow.

NINE TECHNIQUES YOU CAN USE TO GAIN THESE BENEFITS

How to Give Orders That Will Always Be Followed Without Question: The First Requirement

The first requirement is to *make sure the need for an order actually exists.* Certain administrative details in your work become so routine that it's unnecessary to issue any sort of order about them. For instance, you don't need to give your people an order at the end of each day to come back to work the next morning.

Most of the time, the details of any business or office are handled by some sort of an established and accepted standing operating procedure, whether it's a written one or not. The only time an order would be needed then would be if a change in time or procedure takes place.

For example, if you've left standing instructions with your secretary to bring the morning mail to your desk as soon as it comes in, you shouldn't have to tell her every single day to do that. If you have to keep repeating that order, you need a new secretary! Or if you've left instructions for the night shift to leave a production report on your desk each morning, then a one-time order should be enough.

Some people make the mistake of thinking they have to issue an order just to prove that they're the boss. That is not necessary. If you're in charge, people already know that. You don't have to issue an order to prove it.

When a foreman or supervisor is new on the job, you'll often see this happen. Once in a while, an executive will go "power mad" and start punching buttons just to see people jump. In the army, young second lieutenants and newly promoted corporals are prone to make this mistake. But the services are not unique in this respect. I've seen this first basic rule violated time and again in business establishments and industrial plants.

Here's how you can determine whether an order is required or not. An order is needed in only four specific situations:

1. To start some action
2. To correct a mistake in the action or to solve a problem
3. To speed up or slow down the action
4. To stop the action

Now I'll bet you're sitting there right now trying to think up other times when you might need an order. You might be thinking, "What if I have to change direction?" Do me a favor, will you please? Just slip that question under number two—to correct a mistake in the action or to solve a problem.

If you don't need an order, don't issue one. You make yourself look like a fool when you do. But by the same token, if you do need to issue one to get the job done, do so at once. Don't be afraid of hurting someone's feelings by telling him what to do. If that's your job, do it.

How to Give Commands That Will Always Be Obeyed: The Second Requirement

The second requirement in issuing commands that will always be obeyed is to *know exactly what you want before you issue an order*. It's absolutely essential that you know precisely the results you're after before you tell anyone to do anything. Too many orders grow like a rambling rose, creeping ivy, or the crabgrass in my yard.

Incomplete, vague, and ambiguous orders will get you the same kind of results. If you are not sure of exactly what you want, then no one else will be either. You're not yet ready to issue an order.

To help you determine the results you're after, follow these seven simple guidelines so you can use the same thinking pattern each time you issue an order:

1. *What* exactly is it that I want to get done?
2. *Why* exactly is the job necessary?
3. *When* does the work have to be done?
4. *Where* is the place for the work to be done?
5. *Who* is the person best fitted to do this job?

6. *How* will the job be done? What tools, equipment, and facilities are needed?

7. *How much* will it cost to do the job?

By following these seven points, you'll box yourself into a corner and force yourself to answer the relevant questions of *who, what, when, where, why, how,* and *how much.* You're bound to improve your ability to issue orders when you do this; and your skills to make sure the job is understood, supervised, and accomplished will also improve.

Keep in mind that you should concentrate primarily on *results,* not methods, so you'll be able to know exactly what you want before you issue an order. Once you know the results you're after, just tell your subordinates what it is. Then getting the job done will be no problem at all.

How to Issue Orders That Will Always Be Carried Out: The Third Requirement

The third requirement in giving commands that will always be obeyed is to *let a person know exactly how he's going to benefit by carrying out your order.* So before you tell a person what to do, think the situation through thoroughly. Reverse your roles mentally so you can look at your order from his viewpoint. That way you'll be able to tell him exactly how he will be rewarded by doing as you ask. You must give him the proper incentive to obey your command. Let me give you a few examples of that:

1. If you finish this job by 3 o'clock, then you can go home a couple of hours early and still get paid for it.

2. If you'll do it this way, you can increase your hourly output and make more money for yourself.

3. Then there's the example of a well-known country and western recording artist and television star. For purposes of illustration, I'll just call him "Joe." A long time ago, Joe was playing guitar with a small group in a little California bar. One night the owner said, "Joe, I want you to sing, too. We need more voices." Immediately Joe said, "But you're paying me just to play the guitar. What do I get if I sing?" To which the boss promptly replied, "You get to keep your job!" This is one of the best incentives of all to use at times.

No matter what your order is, your listener always wants to know first off exactly what's in it for him. So tell him that. Let him know right away how he's going to benefit by doing as you say. This is especially true if you're going to tell a person how to correct his mistake.

Of course, if he's working for you, then, like Joe, he may have no other choice than to do as you say if he wants to keep his job. But even if you're the boss, unless you stress the advantages the person is going to gain by doing as you want, he'll carry out your order grudgingly. You'll get only the bare minimum results from him.

Even in the military where a person has no choice but to obey, explaining why an order must be carried out will make the difference between a superior unit and a mediocre one.

So let a person know how he can fulfill his basic needs and desires when he does as you say. It will be up to you to find out which secret motivator you can use to get him to follow your order to the letter.

How to Get Him in the Mood to Follow Your Orders

You can use these three simple techniques to set the stage so the person will be in the mood to obey your commands without question:

1. *Use praise, recognition of efforts, reassurance of worth.* If you want a person to go all out for you, if you want him to follow your commands implicitly, then praise him. Tell him what a terrific job he's doing . . . how much you need him . . . how you can't get along without him . . . how happy you are that he's in your company.

"Praise is the quickest and most reliable way to make a person feel important," says Carol Taylor, a highly successful local businesswoman. "It's also the least expensive for it costs you absolutely nothing to praise a person's work. It's one of my favorite motivational tools. I've used it for years now with fantastic results."

If you will remember, credit and recognition for their work was the number one desire of the electronic factory's employees that I told you about back in Chapter One. If praise worked for management there and for Carol Taylor, it'll work for you, too.

So give the person the praise he needs so much, the importance he craves, the credit and recognition he wants, and he'll always obey your commands without fail.

2. *Make his job interesting and worthwhile.* Let a person know why his job is important and how it contributes to the success of the entire group. This, too, feeds his ego and fulfills his basic desire to be somebody. *Everybody wants to be somebody.* When a person understands the purpose behind his job and the important part it plays in the larger scheme of things, the greater interest he will have in his work, for you've helped make him *somebody.*

3. "*Offer a person emotional security,* if you want to get the best results from him," says Wendall Phillips, a production foreman for a midwestern tire and rubber company. "If you constantly threaten a person and cause him to worry about losing his job, demotion, suspension, or a penalty of some sort, you can never get him to work at his full potential. You cannot order a person to do something by using fear or threats and expect to get the best results. Fear always leads to hate, and when a person hates you, he'll never willingly obey your commands."

As an experiment, use these three methods I've just given you for a few weeks. Use praise instead of criticism, let people know how important their jobs are, and offer them emotional security instead of using threats to get them to do what you want. You'll get results far beyond your highest expectations. You'll be amazed at the cooperation and support that you'll be able to get from your people.

Six Guidelines for Issuing Clear, Concise, and Positive Orders That Are Easy to Understand

Your order can be oral or written. The choice will depend upon what's to be done and how complex the task is. To issue clear, concise, and positive orders that are easy to understand, follow these six guidelines:

1. Fit your order to the job to be done.
2. Make your order fit the person.
3. Use simple words and simple terms.
4. Concentrate on a single point.
5. Use oral instead of written orders whenever possible.
6. Use these three pointers for written orders.

1. *Fit your order to the job to be done.* You don't need a ten-page memorandum to say, "Okay, start the motors," to the morning shift. But if you're working on a technical project, a carefully written step-by-step plan is a must.

Don't confuse all your previous detailed planning with the final order you give. An extremely complex plan can be put into operation with a simple order. For instance, the written documents that were prepared for the invasion of Normandy in World War II would completely fill a room of more than 200 cubic feet clear to the ceiling. Yet General Eisenhower kicked off the invasion with a simple 23-word sentence that said, "You will enter the continent of Europe and undertake operations aimed at the heart of Germany and the destruction of her armed forces."

That simple order launched more than 4,000,000 men, 5,000 naval vessels, 5,000 fighter planes, and 6,000 bombers into the battle for Europe. Hundreds of staff officers drew up the detailed plans for the operation. But in the end, all those forces, millions of men and thousands of ships and planes, were set into motion with that one simple sentence. My point is you should issue your actual working order in as few simple words as possible.

2. *Make your order fit the person.* Not only should you make your order fit the job to be done, but you must also make your order fit the person who's going to do the job. The experience, background, education, intelligence, and position of the person receiving your order will all play a part in how you word what you say.

However, even the most educated person will be happy to get his instructions in the simplest words possible. Your best bet is to use the clearest, most concise language you can to avoid mistakes and misunderstanding. If you must use technical or scientific terms, do so, but surround these words with simple ones like *make, work, do, push, pull.* Then you'll get your message across with no trouble at all.

3. *Use simple words and simple terms.* I want to expand my previous point even more here for it is such an important one. I have actually seen people go out of their way to use big words to drive another person to a dictionary. Perhaps they wanted to appear wise and well-educated, but I know their primary objective was just to show off. For example, I once knew a company executive who loved to use such words as *obfuscate,* for instance. If confusion was his goal, he succeeded, for the word *obfuscate* means *to cloud, confuse, darken,* or *muddle.*

Instead of using simple verbs like *make* or *do,* he used *construct, fabricate, accomplish, perform, consummate,* or *effect.* He never *started* anything. Instead, he always *initiated, commenced,* or *inaugurated* everything. He never *sent* a message; he always *forwarded, transmitted,* or *communicated* it. Nor did he *send out* information; he *circulated* it, *promulgated* it, or *disseminated* it. Nor did he ever use such small words as *if, so, for, but.* He felt these were below his dignity. He always made certain to replace them with *in the event that, therefore, on behalf of.*

You don't have to use big words when you write or talk. Small words move with ease where big words stand still—or worse yet, bog down and get in the way of what you really want to say. There is not much, in all truth, that small words will not say and say quite well.

The simplest writing is always the best writing because it's the easiest to understand.

4. *Concentrate on a single point,* don't scatter your fire. Even though there might be a multitude of details to be taken care of, these will all fall into place quite naturally if your order has but one specific final objective.

So don't clutter up your mind with trivia that confuses or clouds the main issue. Keep it as simple as possible. Farm out the details to your subordinates for them to do. That's what they should be getting paid for.

5. *Use oral instead of written orders whenever possible.* There's no point in wasting time and effort to put an order in writing if you can get the results you want with an oral order. For instance, a great many orders are issued orally on the spot to correct a mistake. If you see something wrong in your area of responsibility, I'm sure that's what you'll do, too. You might then issue a written directive later on to prevent repetition of that mistake.

How do you know when to issue an order verbally or when to put it in writing? Wanda Carter, a company personnel director, told me this: "If your order is going to change established policy or procedure, then it has to be put in writing, no matter how simple it is. An oral order should be used mainly to correct a basic mistake the person is making. If that oral order changes an existing policy, then it has to be confirmed in writing as soon as possible to prevent any future confusion or possible misunderstanding."

6. *Use these three pointers for written orders.*

(a) Use your own language. Don't freeze up when you pick up a pen. Use the same kind of language you'd use to tell your neighbor about the fish you caught last week down at the lake. Add whatever technical terms you need, make the rest simple one- and two-syllable words, and you'll get your message across loud and clear without any trouble at all.

(b) Develop your own style. Don't try to impress someone by writing a letter or an order the way you *think* other people want it written. There's no such thing as a standard letter to follow as an infallible guide. That's why government writers are so hard to understand. They copy someone else's style right down to the letter, mistakes and all. Develop your own distinctive style. Let your writing reflect your personality so vividly that everyone will know who wrote the order even if you forget to sign it.

Let me give you a couple of examples here of both good and poor styles of writing. The poor styles I have taken directly from government publications, for I think federal bureaucrats are the worst violators of all, although I've seen some mighty close seconds in big corporations.

Poor Style: Sound attenuators eliminate the heavy equipment operator's ability to detect danger signals or apprehend vocalized instructions.

Good Style: When heavy equipment operators wear ear plugs, they cannot hear sounds of danger, nor can they hear or understand oral orders.

Poor Style: An exit is that portion of a means of egress which is separated from all other spaces of the building or structure by construction or equipment as required in this subpart to provide a protected way of travel to the exit discharge. Exit discharge is that portion of a means of egress between the termination of an exit and a public way.

(This is actually taken from a federal Occupational Safety and Health Administration publication.)

Good Style: An exit is a way out of an enclosed space. (That, by the way, is the definition in my dictionary.)

(c) **Don't worry too much about grammar.** The way a word is used is more important than the way a book on grammar says it should be used. Besides, you don't have to be a grammarian to recognize a good sentence. After all, the first requirement of grammar is that you focus your reader's attention on the meaning you want to convey. If you take care to make your meaning clear, your grammar will usually take care of itself.

Three Methods You Can Use to Check for Understanding

You can check for understanding in several ways. You can have people repeat your oral orders to you. You can have them ask questions if they don't understand. You can ask them questions to see if they understand what you want. Let me discuss each of these separately now.

1. *Have your oral orders repeated to you.* I can think of absolutely no exception to this rule. The first time you break it, so help me, things will go wrong. If people don't understand your instructions, it's a cinch you won't get the results you want.

So make this a hard and fast rule to follow. Oh, I know that once in a while a person will become irritated when you ask him to repeat your order. He will think you're insulting his intelligence. There's an easy way around that. All you need say is, "Would you mind repeating what I've just said? I want to double-check myself to make sure I didn't leave anything out, or that I didn't give you the wrong information." That will solve the problem at once.

2. *Have them ask you questions when they don't understand.* Normally, if a person doesn't understand what you want, he'll ask you to clarify it for him.

But if you're giving instructions to a group, don't assume that everything's understood just because no one asks you a question. Many times, a person will have a question, but he doesn't want to expose his ignorance in front of the others. If you suspect that's the case, then move on to the third method which is to . . .

3. *Ask questions yourself to make sure your order is understood.* For instance, you could ask, "How do you plan on tackling this problem, Marcia? What are your own ideas on how to handle this, Steve?"

Or you could use an approach like this:

"Do you understand why this part goes on first?"

"Do you see why this small ring goes on last?"

"Do you know why the temperature has to be kept at a constant sixty-eight degrees?"

How to Get the Maximum from Your Orders

If at all possible, disguise your orders as suggestions or requests. You see, if your people have any initiative whatever, you'll get far better results by using suggestions than by giving direct orders. The average person doesn't respond too well to direct commands unless he's in the military, and even then, that's no guarantee.

I have always been able to get extremely good results by *asking* a person to do something or by *suggesting* that he try it a certain way. You can use such expressions as "Why don't you try it this way? What is your idea on this? Would you be good enough to . . . I wish you would . . . do you think you can . . . when do you think you could have it done?"

"Many times the best way to get a job done that you want is to let the other fellow think it's his own idea," says Dan Zeigler, a production foreman for a tool and die company. "If you want to get something done without a lot of static and backtalk, the best thing to do is to plant the idea in someone else's head in such a way that he'll come to think of it as his own. Then you know it'll get done for he'll want to carry out *his own idea*."

A good way for you to practice this technique is to use it on your children and your spouse. Experiment a bit. Pick up some experience around the home and you'll soon be ready to go out and play the game like an old pro.

Developing the *Aura of Command*: Six Guidelines

Certain individuals seem to have the knack of assuming command of a situation, no matter what it is. Why is this? Because such a person is used to accepting full responsibility for his actions. He immediately takes charge even when he lacks the authority to do so. Since most people do not care to accept responsibility, especially for a bad situation, they are only too glad to defer to someone who takes over the position of leadership.

That's the first thing to keep in mind when you are developing your own *aura of command*. *If you have the courage to make decisions and accept responsibility for your actions, you'll find that people will always defer to you.*

You need not say a single word, for you'll be surrounded by an aura of command and authority that, even though invisible, is still so easily recognizable you can almost touch it. People will automatically look to you for leadership whenever a problem comes up. Here are six simple guidelines you can use to learn how to accept responsibility so you can develop your aura of command.

1. Seize every opportunity that offers you increased responsibility.
2. Do every job you're given to the best of your ability.
3. Accept honest criticism and admit your mistakes.
4. Stick to what you think is right; have the courage of your convictions.
5. Take full responsibility for the failures of the people under you.
6. Assume complete responsibility for your own actions—for your failures as well as for your successes.

When you follow these 6 guidelines to develop your aura of command,

You'll Gain These 4 Valuable Benefits

1. People will instantly do what you ask them to do.
2. They will turn to you for advice and assistance.
3. You'll gain the reputation of being a born leader.
4. Your orders and commands will always be obeyed without fail.

How to Project Your Aura of Command to Others

You can project your aura of command to others without saying a single word. Your entire physical bearing can be used to project the power of your personality through body language. Your posture should be erect, your head up, your chest out. You must show alertness and vital energy in all your actions.

If you have confidence in yourself and act as if it were impossible to fail, people will gain strength from your example. Your appearance and manner must depict confidence sometimes even beyond what you actually feel. By controlling your voice and gestures, you can exert a firm and steadying influence over those around you.

People always have the highest regard for the boss who remains calm in times of trouble. But they look down on the one who panics at the first hint of something gone wrong.

You increase people's confidence when you can view a bad situation with a cool and calm presence of mind. By such a positive attitude, you seem to take the burden on your own shoulders. You give them the feeling that there is a way out of the dilemma and the problem can be solved.

People will have confidence in your strength, courage, and ability to set matters right. You will project an aura of command that makes them not only give way to you on sight, but also obey without fail every command you give.

Let me summarize for you here the seven techniques you can use to insure that your orders and commands will always be obeyed without fail.

1. The first requirement is to *make sure that the need for an order actually exists.*

2. The second requirement is to *know exactly what you want before you ever issue an order.*

3. The third requirement in giving commands that will always be obeyed without fail is to *let a person know exactly how he will benefit by carrying out your order.*

4. To get a person "in the mood" to follow your orders, use one or all of these three simple methods:

(a) Use praise, recognition of efforts, reassurance of worth.

(b) Make a person's job interesting and worthwhile.

(c) Offer a person emotional security.

5. To issue clear, concise, and positive orders that are easy to understand, use these six guidelines:

(a) Fit your order to the job to be done.

(b) Make your order fit the person.

(c) Use simple words and simple terms.

(d) Concentrate on a single point.

(e) Use oral instead of written orders whenever possible.

(f) Use these three pointers for written orders:
    (1) Use your own language, not someone else's.
    (2) Develop your own distinctive style.
    (3) Don't worry too much about grammar.

6. You can check for understanding of your orders and commands by (a) having your oral orders repeated to you; (b) having people ask you questions when they don't understand; (c) asking questions yourself to make sure your order is understood.

7. To get the maximum results from your orders, disguise your commands as suggestions or requests.

And now on to the next chapter, where you'll learn how to correct a person's mistakes so skillfully that you can make it sound like a compliment to him.

You might wonder why a chapter like that is included under business conversations that order, command, or direct. The answer is quite simple. To correct a person's mistakes, you must give him the proper order that will change the wrong procedure and make it right.

chapter 7

How to Correct
a Person's Mistakes
So It Sounds
Like a Compliment:
A 16-Step Program

You'll find that a great deal of your business conversation having to do with issuing commands and giving orders will be spent in correcting a person's mistakes and telling him what he's done wrong.

But you cannot use criticism of a person to correct his mistakes. That will never work. As I've said quite often in the preceding chapters, criticism destroys. It ruins friendships and creates enemies. It destroys love and marriages. Criticism tears down a person's self-respect, dignity, and self-esteem. In the end, criticism destroys people. I cannot think of one single thing that criticism does that is of any value whatever to anyone.

"But wait," I can hear you say. "What about the times I have to correct the mistakes of one of my subordinates? Then I have no choice. I have to criticize him. If I can't use criticism, how will I ever be able to correct the error?"

I will agree only partially with what you just said. True, there are times when you will need to correct a person's mistakes. But that's all you need do. *Correct the mistake, but don't criticize the person for making it.* The dividends you'll receive when you do it that way are tremendous. Let me tell you right now about some of . . .

THE ENORMOUS BENEFITS YOU'LL GAIN WHEN YOU LEARN HOW TO SAY IT WITH FLOWERS

When you can correct a person's mistakes without criticizing him for making them,

1. Your subordinates will do a far better job for you. They won't make the same mistake twice in a row. They'll be only too glad to do what you ask them to do, for they'll appreciate being treated with kindness and courtesy as ladies and gentlemen.

2. Your people will work with initiative, ingenuity, and enthusiasm. You'll motivate them to do their best for you. As a result, performance, production, and profit will all improve and increase because things will get done right the first time.

3. Individual and group discipline and morale will both improve. People will work together as a team with high spirit and enthusiasm— with conviction, purpose, and direction toward a common goal.

4. Your subordinates will respect you and have full confidence in you. They'll trust your judgment and accept your leadership. People will give you their willing obedience, loyal cooperation, and whole- hearted support.

5. You'll be able to fulfill several of his basic needs and desires. For instance, you'll give him a feeling of importance when you don't tear him apart for his mistakes. You'll reassure him of his worth. You'll give him a true sense of belonging to the team. He'll still have his self-respect, dignity, and self-esteem intact, and finally, you'll give him the valuable feeling of emotional security.

Sixteen Techniques You Can Use to Gain These Benefits

1. How to Call Attention to a Person's Mistakes Indirectly

Your first goal should be to correct the mistake so that it will not happen again. Sometimes you can get that done by using only this first technique. If you can, that's wonderful.

When you see something wrong, when you see a mistake being made, simply walk over to the group and ask, "What happened?" That's all. The cardinal rule to remember here is to leave out all personal remarks. Do not try to blame anyone. When you ask, "What happened?" you get rid of personalities completely. You focus on the mistake itself, and only on the mistake. Let me give you an example so you can see how well this technique can work for you.

"Here's how I use this method," says Ralph Anderson, a safety inspector with a farm implement manufacturing company. "I might say, 'That's odd—we never had any trouble with this machine before— *what happened?* This is the first accident like this—*what happened?*'

"By asking what happened, I'm not blaming anyone. I'm not hunting for a culprit or looking for a guilty party. I'm simply looking for facts to keep the problem from happening again. And it works. Even when the person who's at fault admits his error, it takes off the sharp edge; it gets rid of the bite. Just compare these two statements for yourself:

What happened? *Who* did it?

"You can feel the difference between the two questions. One is asking only for facts. The other is looking for a scapegoat."

You can figure out for yourself how to use this technique in your own operation, whatever it is. The two important words to use are: *What happened?* When you use them, people will open up and talk. They'll tell you what went wrong, where the problem is. All you need do is listen. Then you'll get all the facts you need to correct the mistake. Most of the time, you won't need to take any corrective action at all, for if you don't criticize and find fault, people will correct their own mistakes.

2. Why You Need to Get All the Pertinent Facts First

Too often, the boss will jump to conclusions without getting all the facts first. You'll never solve a problem or correct a mistake that way. Your people will be reluctant to tell you anything at all if you approach the problem like that. They must understand that all you want to do is correct the mistake, not punish some individual. If you are more interested in performance than you are in punishment, people will cooperate with you and open up.

Sometimes, however, they won't come out and give you all the straight answers, no matter how hard you try to get them to talk. In that case, double-check your own actions. I've found that when people clam up and refuse to talk, usually the boss is at fault. His subordinates are afraid to say anything, fearing the consequences.

Perhaps the mistake came from your poor instructions, improper orders, bad rules, misassignments. Remember, you can pull some boners, too. But rare is the employee who has the courage to tell the boss when he's wrong. Too often, this can invite devastating retaliation. Let me show you by example how you can best avoid this situation.

"Whenever one of my subordinates has the guts to tell me I'm wrong, I know I've found a person who's capable of accepting greater responsibility, no matter what his present job is," Joe Mixon told me. "So many people are afraid to do that. Of course, much depends on the boss's attitude.

"If they think they're going to catch it for saying anything about your being wrong, they won't say a word. That's why I always let my people know that all I want to do is correct the mistake, not punish anyone. My policy with my employees is *don't tell me what I'd like to hear—tell me what I have to hear.*"

If you'll practice that same policy yourself with your people, you'll have no trouble at all in getting all the facts you need to correct the mistake and solve the problem, even if it's yours.

3. How to Decide Whether a Formal Counseling Sessions Is Necessary or Not

If the mistake can be corrected on the spot, chances are there's no necessity to call someone into your office for a formal counseling session. However, if, in your opinion, the mistake will be repeated unless you talk directly to the person responsible for the error, then you have no other choice. You must call him in and talk *with* him. Please note that I have emphasized that you talk *with* him, not *to* him. There is a tremendous difference between these two approaches.

A great many times, the person's attitude will dictate whether or not a formal counseling is required. If the individual has a sour outlook, if he has a don't-give-a-damn or couldn't-care-less attitude, or if he has it in for the boss or the company for no reason at all, you must take action to *help* him.

You don't have to destroy him in the process. Offer advice, counsel, and guidance in such a way that he'll scarcely realize that you're finding fault with his work. Ninety-eight percent will respond favorably when you treat them this way. Only a rare few will remain stubborn and recalcitrant. Even they can be persuaded to see things your way eventually if you have the patience to wait them out.

4. How to Pick the Right Time and Place

I learned a long time ago that if my boss came down to my office to discuss something, no major problem was involved. However, if he called me to come to his office, and it wasn't to be a routine meeting with others present, I knew that something really serious was going to be covered.

You can use the same approach here. If your counseling session is an extremely serious matter, then the only place to hold it is in your office where your authority is clearly evident.

However, if the counseling session is for some minor matter, then any place, even the company cafeteria where you can discuss things over a cup of coffee, would be fine. However, complete privacy is a must, as is quiet. If you and your employee have to shout at each other to be heard, there's always a chance for further misunderstanding. Yell at a man and he can misinterpret noise for anger.

Another point to be considered is the time. Unless it's an emergency that has to be dealt with immediately, pick the best day of the week. I have never liked Friday for a heart-to-heart talk. There's too much risk of a person brooding all weekend over what you say and coming back to work the next week still sour over what happened.

Nor do I like Monday. That's a bad time because no one's really into the swing of things yet for the week.

I personally like Tuesdays. That way I can let a person know by a wave of the hand, a pat on the back, or a cheery "Hello" for the rest of the week that I carry no ill will or hold any grudge against him.

5. Why You Must Never Lose Your Temper When Counseling an Employee

If you lose your temper, it's no longer a counseling session to help an employee correct his mistake. It's nothing but a hot-tempered argument between two angry persons. You won't even be able to remember the purpose of your interview.

If you can't see any other good results except for your temporarily feeling better for having blown off steam, don't do it. You're a human being, not an overheated car radiator. Don't let your personal feelings and opinions creep in. That's the "Jones, you ought to shave your beard" kind of criticism and it's completely useless.

That's criticism of an individual, not correction of his mistake. It will go in one ear and out the other of your employee, that is, if you're lucky. The one thing your subordinate will remember is that you lost your temper and that you chewed him out unmercifully when he didn't have it coming. He'll never forgive you and you'll have gained an enemy instead of a friend.

You must be in a cheerful, positive mood yourself to hold a counseling session. If you're upset about something, or a personal problem is bothering you, postpone the interview with your employee. If you don't, he can easily interpret your attitude as being directed toward him.

6. Why This Is the Only Way to Begin

Don't tear a person apart the moment he enters your office. Nor should you enumerate all his faults one after the other as if you were ticking off a grocery list. No one lives who can take that kind of treatment for long.

Instead, tell a person how good he is, how pleased you are with his work, how glad you are he's in your company, what a terrific job he's doing, all *except for this one small point you want to talk over with him.*

The key to this technique is to *praise a person at the same time that you're pointing out his error.* Kind words help establish a friendly cooperative atmosphere. Praise and compliments open the other person's mind to you and make him receptive to your remarks. You can use comments like this to get him to gracefully accept your correction of his error. Let me give you some examples:

"Tom, that was certainly a fine progress report you submitted. You covered all the main points. However, there is just one thing I want to take up with you. . ."

"Annie, you're doing excellent work. But there's one idea for self-improvement I'd like to discuss with you. . . ."

"Hank, I know you've been looking for ways to improve your work procedures. I've noted one thing you're doing that's causing you a problem so I'd like to suggest. . ."

"Mary, your typing is outstanding. You make very few errors and your work is clean and neat. Your spelling is exceptionally accurate. However, I did find one small mistake in this letter. It's not an earth-shaking one, but it does change the exact meaning of what I wanted to say. . ."

"Tim, your report card really looks terrific. I'm really proud of your work. Your history grade is the only one that's off a bit, but I know you can bring it up, too, when I see how well you did in your other subjects. . ."

Remember that all of us hunger for a word of praise. Everyone likes a compliment. As Mark Twain once said, "I can live for two months on one good compliment." *So praise first before you correct the mistake and praise again afterward, too.* Practice that old-fashioned Golden Rule in all your counseling sessions. Use a lot of TLC. It helps.

7. How to Take Your Own Inventory

After you praise the person, continue your counseling session by taking your own inventory so he'll feel more at ease with you. You don't have to list all your mistakes for the past year to use this technique. Do as Bettina Gregory, an office manager, does. Here's what she says:

"I start out by saying, 'Marie, I've made the same mistake myself, and probably a lot more times than you have, too. Here's what I did to correct it.' Then I tell her how I managed to do it—which is really an easy way of letting her know what I want her to do—and then I ask her if she'll try it my way. What else can she say except that she will. When I handle it this way, the average person identifies with me, gets my point at once, and has no hard feelings about it either."

I, too, have used this same technique for many years now. It works extremely well with everyone, even with people who think they know all the answers. I recommend it highly.

8. Why You Should Let Him Tell His Side of the Story First

Give the person plenty of opportunity to present his side of the story. Most people are extremely anxious to let you know exactly what happened, why, and how. They want to make sure you understand and will talk readily if you just give them the chance to do so.

If a person does seem reluctant to speak, ask him some leading questions. Keep asking *why . . . why . . . why.* Or say, "And then what happened? And then what did you say? And then what did you do? What happened next?" When you ask questions like these, you give the person a chance to unload and you'll be in a much better position to discover the real reason for his mistake. Then you can take the proper action to keep that error from reoccurring.

9. How to Weigh All the Evidence and Facts Carefully

Before you call a person in for a formal counseling session, you should have gathered enough facts to warrant it. However, more information may now come to light that wasn't available before. It could be that after you hear your employee's side of the story, no further corrective action will be necessary. His statement may indicate that the problem has already been solved. If this is so, close your interview promptly and pleasantly.

If you handle this properly, your employee need never know he was suspected of some specific mistake. Let me show you how Gordon McCall, a department foreman, handled his own particular situation.

"Whenever I'm in doubt and have to call a person in to talk with him, I start out by telling him of a problem I have. Then I ask him for his advice or his idea on how to solve it.

"For instance, one time I was having a tremendously high rate of small tool pilferage in my department. I narrowed my suspects down to four. I called them in one at a time and talked to them about my problem. As an excuse for having the person in my office, I told him I needed his help and I wanted his expert advice on how to solve this problem. I implied that I knew who the person was, but that I didn't know exactly how to handle the situation without hurting the individual. I said I wasn't interested in punishing anyone, but I just wanted the pilferage stopped.

"I talked to each person the same way. The thefts stopped. I don't know to this day who was guilty, but I don't really care. It might have been one of the men I interviewed—maybe not. If not, the factory grapevine carried my message to the guilty party. The point is, not only was my problem solved, but some person's job and reputation were saved, too."

10. Why You Should Discuss Only One Mistake per Interview

A lot of people have a tendency, during a formal counseling session, of overloading the person with every mistake they can think of since he's been working for the company.

For instance, say you call a person in to point out *one* mistake. He agrees with you and seems willing to cooperate, so you decide to give him both barrels while you have him on the run. You even bring up mistakes he's already corrected and that you should have forgotten long ago. Make it a standing rule that when a mistake has been corrected, it is never to be brought up again.

Stick to only one mistake at a time. Next week or next month, after he's solved his most pressing problem, talk to him about something else that's bothering you. By that time, it might no longer be a sore spot.

I would caution you about one thing. If you bring a person in too often to discuss his mistakes, check yourself to determine your reasons. Are you really talking about mistakes, or are you picking on him and nagging him?

11. Why You Must Be Specific About How to Correct the Mistake

If you want your counseling session to be effective, you must be specific about how the mistake can be corrected. The person must know exactly what he's doing wrong and precisely how he can correct his error. Your whole interview will be wasted if you don't let him know what he can do to improve his performance.

I can well recall the time my son, Bob, came home from his high school shop class all upset. He insisted he was going to drop the course. Finally, I got the whole story out of him.

His instructor had criticized a project he was working on by saying, "Oh, Bob, that's no good at all." But he didn't follow through with any concrete suggestions about how to make things right. So Bob was crushed. Not only was his work wrong, but now he didn't know how to correct his mistakes.

So be specific about how to correct the error. Tell the person exactly what he's doing wrong and show him how he can correct that mistake. Most people are anxious and willing to do the right thing when they know what the right thing is.

12. Why You Should Fit the Penalty to the Offense

Hopefully, your formal counseling session will be penalty enough, and nothing further will be needed. However, if some sort of punishment is necessary, such as a written reprimand, for example, remember that the primary purpose should be to correct the mistake and to keep it from happening again—*nothing more*. Don't be vindictive about it.

I've found that a good method to use is to let the person choose his own punishment. Ninety-five out of a hundred will give themselves a more severe sentence than you would have. Then you can become his benefactor by reducing the punishment you didn't even give him.

For those few who give themselves too light a sentence, tell them you're sorry, but that wasn't quite what you had in mind. Tell them what the punishment has to be and stick to your guns. If you're fair and treat everyone equally, the average person will accept his punishment with good grace.

13. How to Close Your Counseling Session on an Up-Beat Note

Don't end your counseling session on a sour note. Mix some honey with the vinegar. Leave a person with the idea that he's been helped, not kicked. Praise him again at the end of your interview. Emphasize how valuable his contribution is to your company. Give him a verbal pat on the back so you can finish on a friendly note. His last memory of the meeting should be that pat on the back, not a kick in the seat of the pants.

14. How to Get Your Employee to Constantly Improve

It's ever so easy to get your employee to constantly better himself. All you need do is praise the slightest improvement and praise every improvement. Do you have a daughter or a son? If you have, and he's still in those tender years of grade school, watch his face the next time he brings his report card home to you.

Suppose you look at it and say, "Johnny, you didn't do well in reading, did you? In fact, that's a pretty miserable grade! I'm ashamed of you!" Watch his reaction. His face will drop; there'll be tears in his eyes. But you can bring the sunshine back in his face when you say, "But your grades went way up in spelling and arithmetic. I'm really proud of you!"

If you want to get the best out of your people, praise the slightest improvement and praise every improvement. As a far wiser man than I once said, "I am anxious to praise but reluctant to find fault. If I like something, I am always hearty in my approbation and lavish with my praise."

15. How to Give Your Employees a Good Reputation to Live Up To

If you practice the preceding technique constantly, this one will become automatic. Whenever you praise a person, he will always want more. You'll be giving him a reputation to live up to when you compliment him for his good work. If you set a high standard for him, he'll know when he misses it. You won't have to tell him. He'll know when the praise stops. If you set no standard for him to live up to, he'll aim at nothing for he'll have no goals.

16. Follow Up with Further Action If Necessary

If another interview is needed to correct the same mistake, harsher methods will be required. In the first interview, all you need do is *plant the seed*. In the second one, it's time to *plow out some weeds*. If you still need a third interview, then it's high time to *harvest the crop*. And if a fourth one is needed, then you just don't have a green thumb, my friend.

Before I give you a final checklist to let you see if you've handled things properly, let me quickly list these 16 techniques that I've just discussed to refresh your memory:

1. Call attention to a person's mistakes indirectly.
2. Get all the pertinent facts of the case first.
3. Decide whether a formal counseling session is necessary or not.
4. If it is, pick the right time and place.
5. Never lose your temper when counseling an employee.
6. Always begin your counseling session with praise.
7. Take your own inventory to make the person feel more at ease with you.
8. Let him tell his side of the story first.
9. Weigh all the evidence and facts carefully.
10. Discuss only one mistake per interview.
11. Be specific about how to correct the mistake.

12. Always fit the penalty to the offense.

13. Close your counseling session on an up-beat note.

14. Get your employee to improve by praising the slightest improvement he makes.

15. Give your employees a good reputation to live up to.

16. Follow up with further action such as another interview if necessary.

A Final Checklist for You

1. Did you treat the other person as you'd like to be treated yourself?

2. Did you answer all his questions without leaving him in doubt about some of your answers?

3. Did you weigh his case on its individual merits without bias or prejudice?

4. When you gave him the answer, were you proud of the understanding and tolerance you showed in your decision?

5. Did you do everything you could to help him solve his problem or to correct his mistake?

6. Did you correct the mistake without criticizing the person?

7. Did you remember to praise him in the beginning and again at the end of your interview?

8. Are you truly proud of what you said to the person and how you said it?

If you can truthfully answer *yes* to each of these 8 questions, you're in good shape. You've truly learned how to say it with flowers.

PART III

Business Conversations That Are Used to Exchange Information

Business conversations that are used to give information to others can be divided into two main types:

    1. Those that tell a person how to do something.

    2. Those that tell a person how he's doing.

I will not discuss the first type, for there are far too many highly specialized occupations that completely defy discussion in general terms.

However, I will cover the procedures you can use as an employer or manager to let your employees or subordinates know how they're doing or how they're getting along.

Remember, too, that your employees can let you know how you're doing when you ask them for their opinions. I also want to give you the most reliable way to find out what's going on in your organization. These three subjects will be discussed in Part III, as will body language which can be used to send a message without using a single word.

chapter **8**

How to Make
the Average Employee
a Superior One
by What You Say to Him

"Why don't they let me know what's going on?" "Why don't they tell me what they want?" "Why can't they make up their minds?" "Why is it always hurry up and wait?"

Have you ever heard comments like these before? I'm sure you have. So have I, too many times. And when I hear them, I know that I'm not keeping people properly informed as I should.

You see, there's absolutely no reason to run an organization, be it a company or a department, in such a way that people have to ask questions like these. Every single person has the basic right to work and to think in the clear.

He should be told the *why* and the *wherefore* of whatever he is expected to do, as well as the *what* and the *how*. An employee's efficiency, morale, confidence, and enthusiasm will depend largely upon how well the boss keeps him informed.

For example, if you have the bad habit of constantly brushing off your subordinates, not keeping them properly informed just because you think it's not important for them to know, then you're doomed to work in an information vacuum yourself. If you don't keep your people informed, you can be sure they'll never tell you anything you need to know either.

But if you do believe in the importance of giving your people full information in a straightforward manner, and then do exactly that, you'll always get back much more than you give. In fact, when you do this . . .

YOU'LL GAIN THESE FOUR EXTRAORDINARY BENEFITS

The Well-Informed Employee Is Always the Best Employee

The person who knows the big picture, who knows exactly how his own job fits in, who knows what you honestly think of him and his work, is a far better employee than the one who's constantly kept in the dark.

The well-informed employee is always a much more effective employee. He will have a positive attitude toward you and the organization. He can also understand what the company is doing and why when he knows its long-range objectives. A full understanding of the company's future goals will help him establish his own.

Keep Your People Informed to Encourage Their Initiative and Enthusiasm—Their Teamwork and Morale

If you want your people to do their best for you, then keep them well-informed about their individual progress. Each person wants to know exactly what you expect from him. He also wants to know how well he has done—what you think of his work. He appreciates a word of praise and a pat on the back for a job well done.

If you keep your people well-informed about their individual progress—if you let them know exactly where they stand with you— you'll encourage their initiative and enthusiasm. You'll improve their efficiency and raise their morale.

Keeping People Well-Informed Will Eliminate Rumors

Keep your people well-informed and you'll get rid of vicious rumors that can cause a person to worry about his job security, a reduction in force, a loss in pay, demotion, and the like.

To tell the plain truth is the only way to stop unfounded rumors and idle gossip. This alone will get rid of many imagined conditions that can cause friction, misunderstanding, dissatisfaction, frustration, and fear among your subordinates.

Keep Your People Well-Informed to Gain Their Respect, Confidence, Willing Obedience, Loyal Cooperation, and Full Support

These are some tremendous dividends you can gain for yourself by the simple act of telling the truth and letting a person know what's going on. But it's true. When you are open and frank with a person, when you tell him the straight truth, when you hide nothing from him, he will respect you and have confidence in you. He'll be willing to carry out your orders to the letter and do the job properly for you. He'll give you his loyal cooperation, wholehearted support, and be an asset to your organization.

TEN TECHNIQUES YOU CAN USE
TO GAIN THESE BENEFITS

How to Let People Know Exactly Where They Stand with You

"Most employees worry about what the boss thinks of them and the way they do their job, especially when he stands behind them and watches their work without saying a single word," says Ed Andrews, a warehouse foreman. "Wouldn't you feel that way, too? Well, your subordinates are no different than you are.

"If you don't believe me, just try it sometime. Watch a person do his job. Don't say anything at all. Just stand there and watch him work. Do you know what will happen? You're going to make him so nervous, he'll start making mistakes. He can't help himself; he's worried, wondering why you're watching him work without saying a single word. He's afraid the axe is about to fall simply because of the way you're looking at him.

"So I don't make my people guess. I don't play games with them. I tell them the truth; I level with them. If a man isn't doing his job properly, I tell him. But if he's doing a good job, then I let him know that, too. I find I can get better results when I keep people fully informed about their progress on the job."

Not only should you let a person know orally exactly where he stands with you, just as Ed Andrews does, but you should also have some sort of performance review that you can use to rate your employee periodically in writing. Keep a written record of how well a person does his work. Let him see your written report and have him sign a statement saying he's read it. If you ever need to let someone go for cause, you'll soon find you need documentation to prove your case.

To help you get started, here's a checklist I've used successfully over the years to rate people who've worked for me. If the person you're rating is in management—a supervisor, for instance—then use the statements that apply to him and to his job.

If the person is labor—a production employee, for example—you can do the same. This list is not final by any means. You can add or delete items as you see fit. You can also use it as the basis to make up a checklist of your own. (Incidentally, it's a good one to use to rate yourself, too, if you're honest about it.)

How to Rate a Person's Performance: An 18-Point Checklist

You can assign numerical values to each point. For instance, if a person has done the best job I've ever seen, I give him a *4*. If he's above average, I assign him a *3*. If he's just average, he gets a *2*. If he's below average, he rates only a *1*.

Since there are 18 items in the checklist, the highest possible score would be a *72*, but I doubt if you'll ever have anyone who'll achieve that. I never have. If he's above average on most items and the best on others, his score will run somewhere between *54* and *72*. If he's average all the way and gets a *36*, then he's no doubt reached the top level of his abilities, and stands little chance of further advancement. However, if he's below average all the way and earns only an *18*, you should consider getting rid of him.

PERFORMANCE REVIEW CHECKLIST

1. Knows his job
2. Can always be depended on in all things
3. Is preparing himself for advancement and promotion
4. Looks for new ideas; supports worthwhile changes
5. Accepts correction of his mistakes gracefully
6. Is persistent—keeps at it until he succeeds
7. Sticks to major points—doesn't get lost in trivia
8. Is effective in "selling" his own ideas
9. Resists pressures from below, above, outside
10. Tells people what they have to hear—not what they want to hear
11. Is self-reliant and has confidence in himself
12. Weighs the facts carefully and objectively before making a decision
13. Does not make snap judgments
14. Makes allowances for human frailties; does not criticize others
15. Conducts himself by a proper code of ethics
16. Keeps his head in an emergency; does not panic
17. Is highly respected by his associates
18. Is an effective negotiator

How to Tell a Person When His Work Is Not Satisfactory

Don't wait until it's time for a person's written performance review to tell him you're not satisfied with the way he's doing his job. That's not fair to him at all. If you don't tell him what he's doing wrong, he'll never have the opportunity to correct his mistake.

When you see him making a mistake, correct his error immediately. Don't nag or harass him. Just tell him the truth. Show him where he's in error and let him know you don't expect to see that same mistake again. Also let him know you expect him to find ways to improve himself. To soften the blow, tell him how he can expect to benefit when he corrects his mistake.

For instance, if you know an employee is coming in late several times a week, let him know right away that you're aware of this failure of his. Tell him you expect him to correct this fault and that it will be an item for consideration and your personal attention on his next performance report if he doesn't. Or worse yet, continued violations like this could result in his being let go. If he corrects the mistake, never mention the matter again. Consider the problem solved and the case solved. Don't beat a dead horse to death.

Why You Should Always Praise a Person for a Job Well Done

"I never realized how important it was to praise a person for a job well done until I started losing some of my best people to big corporations," says Lloyd Chapman, the owner of a small Oklahoma oil company.

"I always figured that as long as I paid my people even better than some of the bigger companies did, that was enough. It just never occurred to me that a person wants to hear you say 'Thanks' once in a while, too. I thought getting paid a good salary was thanks enough.

"Now I know that everyone wants to hear exactly how well he has done. From the lowest-paid worker in my place right on up to the top dog, everyone appreciates a word of thanks and a pat on the back for a job well done. And you know something? I even appreciate hearing it from my own people, too!"

You've heard me say this for several chapters now. I'm glad to see that I'm not the only one who realizes how important praise is to people. If you like the way a person does his job, then tell him so. Don't make him guess or keep him in the dark. When you praise him, you'll be able to make him more enthusiastic about his work. One of the best ways to motivate a person to do a better job is to show him your appreciation for what he's already done for you.

How to Praise a Person Properly

At first glance, this doesn't seem too hard to do. In fact, it would seem as easy as pie to praise a person. But there's such a thing as overkill. By that I mean you ought to avoid such superlatives as "the very best . . . without parallel . . . impossible to top . . ." and the like. The person could suspect your sincerity if you're too flowery.

For instance, I once received an army commendation medal. The citation used such words as "superior . . . outstanding . . . exemplary . . . without equal . . . unsurpassed . . . highest possible . . ." and so on. I didn't recognize myself. I thought I was reading about someone else.

You'd be much better off to praise a person using words that come naturally to you, perhaps such phrases as "Good work, George . . . excellent job, Sally . . . thanks a lot for doing a bang-up job, Al." People will be much more likely to believe you when you use your own language.

Now I'm not implying you should hand out compliments sparingly or grudgingly. All I mean is that you should be completely sincere when you praise a person's work. Say what you mean and mean what you say.

If a person is doing his level best and comes through for you in a pinch, you don't need to gush all over him like an oil well. Just let him know that you do appreciate his efforts a great deal. Sometimes you're better off just saying, "Thanks a million, Tom. You're aces with me."

As I've told you before, except for a rare few, there are no magic words as such. How you say it is what makes what you say work magic for you with others.

How You Can Make an Employee Feel Like a VIP

"A good way of making a person feel like a VIP, a very important person, is to build up the value of her work," says Arline Elliott, the owner of a women's wear store. "Tell her how essential her job is to your organization and how important she is to you."

I agree with Arline. Most people really need to feel that their jobs are the most important ones in the place, that their positions have a real status. When you give that status to their positions, you make them feel like VIPs. Almost all of your employees, including the janitor, need to feel essential to you and your efforts before they'll ever start clicking for you.

Still another way of making people feel like a VIP is to bring them up-to-date constantly on new developments and future projects. Let them know ahead of time when changes are going to be made. As members of your team, they're entitled to know what's going on, too. Give them the feeling that they know everything the boss knows. This makes them feel important; it feeds their ego.

Why You Should Brief Your Assistants at an Early Stage on Planned Changes

I realize that some plans can't be discussed far in advance with all your people. They should, however, be gone over as much as possible with your major subordinates before you take final action. You can make them responsible for passing the information on down to their own people.

Such advance information will give people an all-important sense of participation. Not only that, since they will be taking part in helping you make your plans, they will be anxious to make sure they succeed. They will feel a sense of personal responsibility. As a result, they will carry out your plans with vigor and enthusiasm.

Another excellent reason for keeping your subordinates informed about future changes is that you'll cut out rumors by doing so. For instance, when rumors fly around about expansion of the organization, people aren't too worried about losing their jobs. But when they feel there's even the remotest possibility of cutting down on the operation or consolidating various departments, they do worry about the future. Then they definitely worry about losing their jobs or being demoted. And the more they worry, the worse becomes the quality of their work. To prevent all this from happening, keep them informed at all times. Let them know what's going on.

How to Prevent or Eliminate Misunderstandings

A great many misunderstandings and hard feeling can come about from a simple lack of information. For instance, John Green gets a two-week paid vacation. But George Black, who works right beside him, gets three weeks off with full pay. There's no problem, if John has been told and remembers that when he's been with the firm for 10 years just as George has been, then he'll get a three-week paid vacation, too.

Sam Brown feels he's been mistreated because he bought some tires for his car from the company and they charged him cost plus 10 percent. Sam thought he was being cheated, but he hadn't listened closely enough during his initial briefing as a new employee. He'd heard only the one word—*cost*. He'd completely missed the phrase: *plus 10 percent.*

Most of the time complaints like these come from a simple lack of information. Sometimes supervisors are at fault for not telling the employee what's going on. At other times, employees are wrong for not paying closer attention to what's being said, not reading the bulletin board, and so on. And sometimes, they simply forget.

Whatever the reason, see that the complaint is resolved and the misunderstanding straightened out promptly and satisfactorily by passing the correct information along to the unhappy person.

If a Planned Company Change Affects a Person, Let Him Know

You don't have to reveal company secrets to practice this technique, but you do have an obligation to let your people know if any planned changes will affect their jobs, their income, or their future. Do this, and you will fulfill a person's basic need for emotional security.

For instance, if changes in your company will create a new position in a department other than your own for which one of your people is qualified, tell him about it. He's entitled to the chance to better himself. Usually, new positions like this are open for bidding by employees, but you'll make a person feel more important if you personally encourage him to apply for the job.

Even if you handicap your operation temporarily by losing a good person, you'll benefit in the long run. And if he doesn't get the job, at least he will be grateful to you for having encouraged him to try for it. Even if he misses, he'll appreciate your trust and confidence in him, and he'll do an even better job for you than before.

If a Planned Change Does Not Affect a Person, Let Him Know That, too

Just as it's important to let a person know when certain planned changes are going to affect him, it's just as important—in fact, sometimes even more so—to let him know when contemplated changes are *not* going to affect him. Here is a glaring example of how things can go wrong by not following this simple rule.

"Seemingly out of a clear blue sky, last summer we started getting all kinds of complaints from our production employees," says Kenneth Gordon, the industrial relations manager for a large electric appliance manufacturer. "They grumbled about bad lighting, poor ventilation, excessive heat, noise, etc. As each problem was satisfactorily solved, they would come up with still another one.

"This was highly unusual for our employees, for we've always enjoyed friendly and cordial relationships with them, so I called in one of the people who's been with us a long time to find out what was really at the bottom of all of these complaints.

"Well, as Ruth told me, their real problem was the fear that they were going to be the victims of automation and lose their jobs. You see, we'd had a professional leasing firm in to survey our place with the idea of selling the building to them and then renting it back on a long-term lease. That way we could free a lot of capital for expansion purposes instead of having it tied up in our physical plant.

"But the sudden and unexplained presence of a lot of strangers with pencils and notebooks had aroused our employees' suspicions. They were certain that they were going to be replaced by machines. Once the reason for all the strangers was explained, the complaints stopped."

You can get this kind of static unless you go all out to keep such misunderstandings from happening. If things like this suddenly happen to you, remember that a few well-placed questions from you to your employees can often quickly clear the air. Of course, the best way to do it is to tell them what's going on first. That information will keep the problem from coming up.

If you haven't been taking the time to keep your people informed as you should, use these techniques that I've given you in this chapter for the next couple of weeks or so and you'll be most happy with the results you get.

Let me list these techniques for you once more so you will have them all together in one convenient place for quick and ready reference.

1. Let people know exactly where they stand with you.
2. Use a checklist to rate a person's performance.
3. Tell a person when his work is not satisfactory.
4. Always praise a person for a job well done.

5. Learn to praise a person without using flattery.

6. Make your employee feel like a VIP.

7. Brief your major subordinates at an early stage on any planned changes.

8. Prevent and eliminate misunderstanding by keeping people well informed.

9. If a planned company change affects a person, let him know.

10. If a planned company change does *not* affect a person, let him know that, too.

You'll find that keeping your people informed will encourage their initiative and enthusiasm—their teamwork and morale. Your employees will become more effective in their work and do a better job for you. When you keep your people informed, you'll gain their respect, confidence, willing obedience, loyal cooperation and full support.

These are excellent benefits, gained just by letting people know what's going on and keeping them informed.

Have Your People Tell You What You Have to Hear

This chapter has been aimed primarily at showing you how to keep your own employees informed, but I want to conclude it by saying that the flow of information has to go up as well as down to be completely effective.

One of the most important things your employees can ever do for you is to tell you the truth, too—to let you know what's actually going on in your own shop.

I learned this lesson from an old foreman who told me, "Don't let your employees tell you what you *want* to hear. Let your wife do that. Make them tell you what you *have* to hear. That's the only way you can be sure of hanging onto your own job."

His advice has proved valuable to me over the years. I know it can be valuable to you, too, so I'm going to cover that subject in the next chapter where I'll give you the techniques you can use to gain information from your employees that will benefit you.

chapter 9

Eight Techniques for Gaining Information from Employees That Will Benefit You

One of the main purposes of having a conversation with your employees or your subordinates is to gain information that will be of benefit to you. How can you gain that information? By asking your people for their suggestions and recommendations, their advice, and their help. Let me give you an example of how well that can work for you.

The other morning I read in the paper how the employees of one of the big three automobile manufacturers stood and cheered as the first new model rolled off the assembly line. A company spokesman said that they had instituted a new management-employee program that stressed cooperation and involvement. He said that the company had used 135 employee suggestions to improve their new model car.

When you, too, ask your employees for their opinions and advice,

YOU CAN GAIN THESE 4 FANTASTIC BENEFITS

They'll Feel as Though They're Really Part of the Team

When you ask a person for his ideas and opinions, you're letting nim know that he's both wanted and needed. No one wants to be a nonentity or just another clock number on the payroll. Every single person in your organization wants to be part of your team. Everyone wants to feel that he belongs. That's one of the 14 basic desires that every person has.

When you ask your employees for their advice and help, you give them that individual identity they want so much. You make them members of the team. They'll work much harder for you when they feel they're making a major contribution to the success of your organization.

You Can Identity People of Above-Average Ability

One of the best ways to pinpoint people of above-average intelligence and ability in your organization is to establish a creative climate and atmosphere. When you ask for specific solutions to definite problems, you automatically set up hurdles and obstacles that test your people's maximum potential. Ask for their advice and help and you will discover employees with above-average ability who can help you solve your problems.

Your Employees Will Put Their Imagination, Initiative, and Ingenuity to Work for You

If you're the big boss, you can offer a reasonable financial reward to the person who comes up with a concrete solution to a certain stated problem. When you do that, you are making it quite plain to your people that their ideas are really wanted. In fact, you are actively soliciting their assistance when you offer them a monetary reward. Use that incentive and your employees will put their imagination, their initiative, and their ingenuity to work for you. They will use their brains overtime to come up with answers to your problems.

You'll Give People a Feeling of Importance

Although it's important to offer a tangible and concrete financial reward to the person who comes up with a useful and usable suggestion, you'll find that giving him a feeling of importance will also be of great benefit to you. That's another one of the 14 basic desires that every person has. For example, you can give him a letter of appreciation or a certificate of achievement along with the financial reward. It can be framed, hung on the wall, retained and remembered long after the money is spent and gone.

EIGHT TECHNIQUES YOU CAN USE TO GAIN THESE SUPERB BENEFITS

How to Get Yourself in the Right Frame of Mind

The first thing you must do to be able to ask your employees for their help and advice is to get yourself in the right frame of mind so you will accept their suggestions when they offer them to you. Don't let your position as a manager or your status as an executive get in your way. It can, you know, for after all, you are the boss; they are your subordinates. Theoretically, at least, that makes you smarter than they are. But that's not always true.

"You can't ask for a person's help if you're more concerned about your position than you are with what he has to offer you," says Charles

Foster, the founder and owner of a large restaurant chain in the southeastern part of the United States. "Status can become a real obstacle if you judge the value of a person's ideas by his education, the way he expresses himself, the kind of job he has, the way he dresses, and so on.

"I can think of all sorts of recommendations I didn't accept in the past simply because I didn't see how George, the bus boy, or Sam, the dishwasher, could possibly come up with any worthwhile ideas because of the menial positions they held.

"Today I know better. I've learned that all sorts of excellent ideas for improvement most often come from the person who's actually doing the job. Just because I happen to be the boss doesn't mean I have a monopoly on brains. Now I'm willing to listen to anyone who can help me run a better operation, so I can give the best service possible at the least cost to my customers."

How can you, too, forget your status and your position and get into a receptive frame of mind yourself? Well, first you can make a good start by doing away with those meaningless "time of day" exchanges with your employees when you tour your place. Stop and really talk to a person for a change. Ask him questions about how to improve your present procedures. Get him to open up by asking him for his ideas on your operation.

When you ask for a person's advice, his help, or his ideas, you must really mean what you say. Be sincere. Don't do it with tongue in cheek. Don't ask for advice if all you want is reassurance that your way is right. If you really are sincere about asking your people for their help, they'll know. They'll appreciate your trust in them and your confidence in their abilities. And they'll want to help you solve your problems, too.

How You Can Stop Wasting Money on Efficiency Experts and Management Consultants

Steve Harrington is the president and chief executive officer of a furniture manufacturing company in Asheville, North Carolina. I met him on a vacation trip I took through the mountains of the Carolinas one summer. Let me tell you what he told me:

"I used to hire efficiency experts and management consultants to the tune of several hundred dollars every time we had a problem we couldn't seem to solve for ourselves," Steve told me. "But no more. Here's why I stopped doing that.

"About two years ago we added several new items of furniture to our line. This meant we had to make a lot of changes in our production lines and we seemed to create more and more bottlenecks that slowed our whole system down.

"It was really a big headache to us. Our stock inventories were falling faster than we could replenish them. We were losing valuable production time. Our employees work on an hourly wage plus incentive pay depending upon production, and they were losing money. Tempers were short; morale was low and discipline was going out the window. Quality control was turning back twice as much production as usual.

"It seemed that no one could come up with any answers to solve our problem, so I called in an efficiency expert to see if he could help. He spent about a week in the plant and came up with a solution that worked. I was quite well satisfied for he'd solved my problem for me. That is, until one day as I was walking through the plant, one of my oldest and most reliable employees, Frank Kephart, stopped me to ask a question.

"'You know that guy you had in here about a month ago to iron out your production line problems for you?' he asked.

"'Yes, Frank, of course I remember,' I said. 'But why do you ask that?'

"'Well, I was just wondering how much money you wasted on him,' Frank said. 'You see, when he came here he went around the place talking to everyone and asking them for ideas on how to solve your problem. The one I recommended to him is the one we're using now. *I'd have told you about it for nothing if you'd just asked me.*'

"Frank's remarks got me to thinking, so I checked back through and looked at the number of times and the reasons I'd called in outside help to solve my problems. Then I asked my employees a lot of questions about their visits, too.

"Come to find out, most of those so-called efficiency experts and management consultants weren't really so smart after all. Ninety-five percent of the time the answers they gave me were coming right from my own employees. I could've had those same answers for nothing if I'd just had enough sense to ask my own people for their help and advice.

"You can bet I don't call in any outsiders any more to solve my business problems. Now I use the money that I used to pay those experts to offer a reward to my own employees for coming up with usable ideas and money-saving suggestions."

Maybe right now you're not the big boss so you can't pay your subordinates cold hard cash for their helpful suggestions, but you can reward them in some other way for their good ideas. For instance, when it comes time for a promotion, you know your boss will be asking for your recommendation. This is one way you can reward a person. Or see if you can get the authority to give a person a day or so off with pay as a reward for an idea. Use your imagination and come up with some suggestions of your own to make to your boss. Perhaps he'll reward you, too.

How to Make Your Subordinate Feel It's His Problem, too

Each one of us is more interested in his own problems than he is in someone else's problems. For instance, I know perfectly well that you are more interested in your problems than you are in mine. And your employees are more interested in theirs than they are in yours. So if you want to get your employees interested in your problem— *then you must make your problem their problem.* Here's how you can do that:

When you ask John for his advice and counsel in solving your problem, when you acknowledge your ignorance and ask him to help you or show you how to do it, you challenge his ingenuity. The moment he becomes interested in helping you solve your problem, it automatically becomes his problem as well. Let me give you an example of this technique:

"One of the toughest problems I had to solve when I took over the management of this store was getting my department heads to cut costs," says Ellen Simpson, the manager of a Baldwin Discount Center in the midwest. "But that's why I'd been sent to this store in the first place: to cut costs and overhead and increase net profits or else. This store was showing the least profit of all the Baldwin Discount Centers and the owners wanted some definite corrective action taken to change that.

"The previous manager had tried preaching, sermonizing, pleading, appealing to honor, duty, and loyalty, but with absolutely no results. So when I took over I didn't use any of those methods. I didn't preach or scold.

"I just told them that unless we could cut costs and start showing a profit, this store was going to be closed and *we'd all be out of a job. That one statement made my problem their problem immediately.*

"I gave each department head the responsibility for reducing his overhead costs in his own area. I told him to get ideas from his own subordinates and that we would reward each person whose idea was used.

"Before long I was flooded with all sorts of suggestions on how to save money on utilities, warehousing and storage costs, customer delivery service, packaging and shipping, even postage and telephone charges.

"Within six months we had reduced our operating costs by 28 percent and the store was showing an acceptable profit. And all because I made my problem their problem when I told them we'd all be out of a job if we didn't succeed."

You can use this same technique when you make your problem your employees' problem. Set up your own employee think tank and give them your headaches to solve. Whatever you do and however you do it, *remember the fastest way of solving your problem is to make it their problem, too*. Just be sure to reward them when they do solve it for you.

If you can't fatten a person's paycheck when he helps you solve your problem, then do as Captain James Roberts, a U.S. Army basic training company commander, does. "I can't raise a man's pay when he comes up with a good, usable idea," says Captain Roberts. "After all, his pay is controlled by Congress, just as mine is. But I can reward him in other ways, and I do. I can give him a letter of commendation or appreciation; I can recommend him for promotion the next time there's a vacancy; I can give him some time off—a three-day pass, for example. The point is, I give him the best reward I can and he appreciates it."

You can do the same, no matter what your job is, whether you're a foreman, a supervisor, or the big boss himself. Give your people the best reward you can for their help in solving your problems. They'll appreciate it and they'll keep on doing their best for you.

How a Company Was Saved from Financial Ruin by Its Employees' Suggestions and Recommendations

As will happen sometimes, this company, a Michigan manufacturer of car mirrors for the automobile industry, was forced to turn to its employees for help because of adverse financial circumstances. But even when the financial position of the company improved, the president was wise enough to see the advantages of retaining the system.

One of the biggest Detroit customers of this company had put it on the line. Either the company had to lower its prices, or the buyer would go somewhere else to find a new supplier of their car mirrors.

One of the machine operators on the assembly line knew a method that would reduce his crew of five people to four and help save money. But he hesitated to offer his idea to the company when the employees were asked for help in reducing costs. After all, he might be the one the company would decide to let go.

So he approached management this way. He would give his cost-cutting ideas to the company if they would promise that no one would lose his job as a result. The company agreed to his condition. They also extended the same guarantee to any employee who could come up with suggestions on how to reduce production costs. Let me tell you now about some of the benefits that everyone gained.

1. Every employee can have as high a pay raise as his cost-cutting idea will pay for.
2. Every employee gets monthly bonus checks that can go as high as 20 percent of his base pay.
3. The company is prospering. Employment has almost doubled since this program was started.
4. The company's main product sells for 15 percent less than it used to in spite of inflation.

Employees are happy and satisfied. They have learned, and so has management, that everyone profits when they all cooperate and work together as a team toward a common goal.

An analysis of this example and the previous one shows that when these employees were asked for their advice and help, 12 of their 14 basic needs and desires were satisfied. Let me list them for you, so you can see for yourself how valuable this technique can be for you in conversations with your employees:

1. *Financial success:* money and all the things that money will buy. (By saving their jobs in these two examples.)
2. *Recognition of their efforts* by management and their fellow employees for their cost-cutting ideas.
3. *Group approval* for their efforts by fellow employees and management as well.
4. *Ego-gratification, a feeling of importance* for having contributed to the company in its time of need.
5. *A sense of roots or belonging* to the organization. Hardship creates fellowship.
6. *The opportunity for creative expression* when asked for new ideas and suggestions by management.

7. *The accomplishment or achievement of something worthwhile.*

8. *The desire for new experiences* was realized as original ideas were put into practical application by the company.

9. *A sense of personal power* was gained as each employee realized how much the company depended on him.

10. *Liberty and freedom* to offer new ideas to the company.

11. *A sense of self-respect, dignity, and self-esteem* was heightened when their ideas were accepted.

12. *Emotional security,* which is based upon many factors, including job security, freedom from worry, anxiety, and fear, was achieved by all the employees.

You can see from this how advantageous it is to ask your employees for their suggestions and recommendations, their advice and their help. It gets the results you want and brings you a mountain of benefits. That kind of conversation with your employees is well worthwhile.

How Asking for Help Will Encourage Individual Initiative

Although it's wise to form groups of people so they can work together like a think tank to help you solve your problems, you should also encourage each person to come up with a better way of doing his own specific job.

First of all, if you want your individual employees to come up with some work improvement ideas, you must let them know that you'll listen to their suggestions.

Tell them you realize they know more about their own jobs than anyone else. Explain to them that you know there's always room for improvement and that you're counting on them to pinpoint those areas for you.

It's always best to ask specific questions so you can isolate definite areas that need improvement. For instance, you could ask questions like these:

"How can we cut down on the time between order and delivery for our customers, Mary? Any ideas on this?"

"What's your own personal opinion as to the cause of this quality problem, Frank?"

"How can we get rid of this safety hazard on your job, Tim?"

If you hear an employee complaining about some procedure

being a waste of time or costing too much money, encourage him to think constructively about how he would change it. Ask him to come up with some possible improvements or to show you a better way. Let him know that you really do want to hear his suggestions when you ask for them by offering a suitable reward if his methods work.

By giving your employee some concrete problem to solve, you'll encourage and stimulate him to do his best thinking for you. You'll give him something to use his brains for. That's when a person comes up with his best ideas—when he really has to, when he has something that has to be solved or else. It's hard to get the brain in gear if you don't give it something to work on, some problem to solve, some question to answer.

How to Keep the Lines of Communication Open

Don't make it hard for the person to submit his ideas to you. Don't get him all tangled up in rules, regulations, office procedures, and red tape by making him put everything down in triplicate on some complicated suggestion form your clerk has devised. Remember, you're asking an employee for a favor when you ask him to give you his ideas. Do him the favor of making it easy for him to do so.

"There are several methods you can use to make it easy for your employees to submit their ideas directly to you," says Helen Miller, director of education and training services for a large chemical products company. "First of all, design a simple one-page printed form that will help the person get all his facts together in one place.

"It should be worded in such a way that he'll be able to answer the *who, what, when, where, why* and *how* about his idea. If a sketch or drawing is needed, make the services of your drafting department available to him.

"Some companies use suggestion boxes. We ourselves like the *open door policy*. That is, we establish certain hours during the week when our doors are open to employees so they can discuss their improvement ideas with their superiors. We've found that this one-on-one procedure gives us the best results."

You can keep an open door as Helen Miller suggests, or you can make individual appointments with your people to discuss their ideas. An appointment with the boss makes a person feel important; it proves you are really interested; it shows that you consider the person's ideas vital to your company.

How to Follow Through on a Person's Idea or Suggestion

A person's idea is the most important thing in all the world to him. Don't disappoint him by dragging your feet, putting it off, or forgetting it.

Get someone to go to work on the idea at once. Evaluate it. See if it will work or not. Find out if it's really an improvement. And let him know what's going on, too. Keep him informed; don't leave him in the dark.

Tell him if his idea is receiving serious consideration. If you've run into some unexpected problem with it, let him know that, too. After all, it is his idea. He might be able to come up with some concrete answers for these new complications. At least, he'll know you're working on his suggestion and that alone will make him happy.

When you keep him informed of all you're doing, that is proof positive that you do take new ideas seriously. He'll do his best to come up with more and even better suggestions for you in the future.

How to Reward a Person for His Suggestion or His Idea

You like to get proper credit and recognition for what you do. So do your employees. If you forget or neglect this part, you might as well forget about asking your subordinates for their suggestions and their ideas. You won't get any.

So be quick to show your appreciation for what he's done by presenting him with the appropriate reward: a bonus, a raise, a promotion, a letter of appreciation, a certificate of achievement.

When you reward an employee for his efforts, you will raise the standards of every single person in your organization. You'll stimulate everyone to try and come up with some useful and usable ideas of improvement.

So ask your subordinates for their advice and help, their suggestions and ideas. You'll get lots of dividends when you do. You'll be able to reduce operating costs. You can better meet your competition. You can increase profits. You'll find better ways of doing things. Everyone in your organization will be working closer to his maximum potential. All this will come just from what you say and how you say it to your employees.

In a nutshell, then, here are the techniques you can use to gain valuable and useful information from your employees that will benefit you:

1. Get yourself in the right psychological frame of mind to accept suggestions and recommendations from your subordinates.

2. Make your subordinate feel that it's his problem, too. Then he'll be glad to help you solve it, especially if the solution is going to benefit him.

3. When you ask for help, you will encourage individual initiative and ingenuity.

4. If you want to gain information from your employees that will benefit you, then make sure to keep the communication lines open. Have an open door policy.

5. Always follow through on a person's idea or suggestion.

6. Be sure to reward a person in some way for his suggestion or his idea.

If you've never used these techniques in your conversations with your employees before, put them into practice now. You'll be amazed at the good results you can get when you ask people for their ideas and their opinions, their suggestions and recommendations. You'll find that this is the best way of making conversation with your employees pay off for you. It beats talking about the weather or politics and makes conversation with them well worthwhile.

In fact, you might find yourself saving the money you used to spend on efficiency experts and management consultants, just as Steve Harrington, the furniture manufacturing company president and chief executive officer I told you about earlier in this chapter, did. Or your company might even be saved from financial ruin by your employees' suggestions and recommendations, as was the Michigan manufacturer of car mirrors for the automobile industry. Those two benefits alone make these techniques worthwhile.

chapter 10

The Only Reliable Way
to Find Out
What's Going on
in Your Own
Organization

Do you want to find out what's going on in your own department or your own company? Then listen to your employees with an open mind. Do you want your people to respect you? All you need to do is let them talk to you about their personal problems, their worries, and their fears. Do you want a person to level with you—to tell you the whole truth? *Then give him the courtesy of listening to what he has to say.* To listen carefully and attentively is one of the highest compliments you can pay to anyone.

When you learn how to properly use the silent skill of listening, especially to employee gripes and complaints,

YOU'LL GAIN THESE 4 BIG BENEFITS

1. You'll Get to Know and Understand Each Employee Better

What irritates a person can be a key to his personality. If he objects to reasonable rules and regulations, he may be a malcontent and a potential troublemaker. If you know this, then you're way ahead of the game. If, on the other hand, his complaints are usually justified and not too frequent, he's probably a well-adjusted individual. You should consider what genuinely bothers a person in your assessment of his overall value to you.

When you know and understand each employee better, you will not only find out what upsets him, but you'll also discover what really turns him on. You can determine where his true interests lie, what his real value is to the company, how he can be motivated to do a better job for you. When you encourage a person to talk freely about himself, and listen intently to what he says, you'll get to know and understand him better, and that's a mighty big benefit for you.

2. Even Though You're in Management, Your Employees Will Like You When You Listen to Them

One of our most famous United States Supreme Court Justices once said, "To be able to listen to others in a sympathetic and understanding manner is the most effective technique you can use for getting along with people and tying up their friendship for good."

It's just human nature for your people to like you when you listen to them attentively. Let me ask you this: Have you ever disliked a person who listened with intense interest to your ideas and opinions? Or, on the other hand, have you ever really liked someone who wasn't courteous enough to listen to you? Well, your employees are no different than you are. They're human, too, so they'll not only accept you, but they'll even like you when you listen to them and pay attention to what they say.

3. Listen to Your Employees; They'll Know You're Really Interested in Them

I know of no faster way to turn a person off than to pay no attention to him or to his problems. By the same token, you can turn him on when you show him how interested you are in what he says. A good way to show your interest is to ask questions like these: "What did you do then? What happened after that? Then what did you say?"

Even the most reluctant and bashful person will open up and talk when you show your interest in him this way. So concentrate 100 percent on what he is saying. Focus all your attention on him. Listen to him with all the intensity and awareness you can command, for listening lets your subordinate know you're really interested in him.

4. You'll Find Out What Your Employees Really Want When You Listen to Them

People will tell you what they really want if you will just take the time to listen to them. So forget yourself and what you want for a change. Concentrate completely on what they want from you and what you can do for them.

As you'll learn later on in Part IV in Chapter 14, *to find out what people want and then to help them get it is the most important secret of salesmanship.* It is also the foundation of all successful human relationships.

Practice this principle and you, too, can find out what your employees really want from you so you can help them get it. You'll help yourself at the same time, for you'll have a much smoother running organization when your employees are happy and satisfied. All you need do to get them to open up and talk is simply to listen carefully to what they say.

TECHNIQUES YOU CAN USE TO GAIN THESE WONDERFUL BENEFITS

Why Listening to Employee Complaints Is Your Responsibility

Perhaps you think you shouldn't have to listen to an employee's complaints. After all, you tell yourself that you're too busy with your own problems: cutting costs, meeting quotas and deadlines, increasing production, improving quality, attending meetings. Not only that, you say that's why your company has an industrial relations manager, a personnel section to handle gripes, an employee relations counselor your people can go to with their complaints. Sorry, but I can't agree with you. Nor does Neil Butler, a company employee relations manager.

"Listening to the complaints and gripes of an employee is one of the most important responsibilities that every supervisor has," Neil says. "The employee relations department is the company's final line of defense, not the first line of defense as so many supervisors think. It's where the last ditch effort is made to satisfy an unhappy employee who has a beef with the company. If we can't satisfy him, his complaint will probably become a formal grievance to be filed by the union with management.

"Every attempt should be made to take care of an employee's complaint at the lowest possible level. The person's immediate supervisor is most familiar with the problem and he should try to come up with a satisfactory answer. If he cannot, then he should go to his foreman for help in solving his subordinate's problem.

"Here in our plant, when a person comes to our office with a complaint, we want his immediate supervisor to come with him. In fact, when the problem can't be solved at a lower level, we expect the supervisor to take the initiative in bringing the employee to see us.

"That's what we'd like to see happen. But it's not an ironclad rule and it doesn't always work that way. Sometimes, the employee prefers not to have his supervisor with him. So our door is always open to anyone who has a complaint or a problem—with or without his immediate supervisor.

"I can usually tell what's wrong, though, when an employee comes in to see me by himself. His supervisor thinks he's too busy or too important to listen to the person's troubles. When too many people show up from the same department with complaints, I know the real problem doesn't lie with the employees. It's their section chief, their supervisor, or even the department foreman who's at fault."

The Only Way to Get Accurate and Reliable Information from Your Employees

If you want to get accurate and reliable information from your employees so you can find out what's really going on in your own organization, you must learn to ask questions, questions, and still more questions. Never, never dominate the conversation by doing all the talking yourself if you want to find out where your people stand on a certain point. You must ask questions and then listen to the answers. To get information, all you need do is ask another question whenever the person stops talking. Just prime the pump; let him work the handle. To help you make use of this highly effective technique, I want to give you . . .

A 6-Point Checklist for Asking Questions That Get Answers

1. *Your questions should have a specific purpose.* One question might be used to emphasize a major point, another to stimulate thought, and still another to arouse interest and make your employees more alert. If you yourself will ask, "Are there any questions?" then you'll give people the opportunity to clear up any misunderstandings and to voice their own opinions.

2. *Your questions must be understood by everyone.* They should be phrased in language and terms that are familiar to all your employees. Questions must be worded in such a way that your listener will have no trouble at all in understanding exactly what you mean. If your question creates another question in your listener's mind, it's worse than useless. "Please tell me exactly what you want me to do" is an age-old plea of employees to their supervisors.

3. *Your question should emphasize only one point at a time.* Avoid asking two questions in one or asking a question in such a way that other questions are needed to bring out the information you want. The words, "This *one* thing I do," are as valid today as when the Apostle Paul wrote them to the Philippians nearly two thousand years ago.

4. *A good question asks for a definite answer.* Don't let your employees bluff you or get away with vague nonspecific answers that tell you nothing. Ask your questions in such a way that definite answers are required, and don't give up until you get them.

5. *It should discourage guessing.* Never word your question in such a way that your listener can guess at an answer and satisfy you. His answer should be based on information and facts, not imagination

and fancy. There will be times when you'll be asking for a person's candid opinion, but subjective thinking has to be based on objective facts.

6. *The best question always asks "Why?"* The why can be either spoken or implied, but it should always be there. Too many supervisors are content with an answer of *yes* or *no*, even when that answer tells them nothing. If a person says "Yes," ask him *why*; if he says "No," ask him *why*. That little three-letter word is one of the most valuable question words you can use to get accurate information and to find out what's really going on in your own organization.

Why You Must Make the First Move Yourself

By that I mean you must let your employees know that you are willing to listen to them. If you don't, you'll never find out what's going on in your own organization. There is no better way to raise morale and win the regard and respect of your employees than to really listen to their gripes and complaints. To pay close attention to a person's problems shows that you are truly interested in him, that you respect him, that you feel he does have something worthwhile to tell you.

"The supervisor who knows his or her people best listens to their complaints," says Kathy Wright, an office manager with a large insurance company. "She has to. Otherwise, she'll never really know or understand them. I encourage people to talk by asking them questions about themselves, their families, and their outside interests. As they get used to talking with me about these subjects, they become more willing to discuss their work, their problems on the job, what they don't like about the company, and so on.

"The only sure way to actually learn what makes a person tick—and why—is to give him or her your undivided attention so you can really listen to what he or she says. This is especially true when the person is presenting a complaint to you."

To be an effective listener, you must use great patience. I know there will be times when you'll be so busy that you think, *just one more complaint from someone and I'll blow my stack!* And that's exactly when another one of your people will come to you with a personal problem.

His complaint may not seem like much at all to you, but it's the most important thing at the moment to your employee, or he wouldn't have come to you for help. So ask him to sit down and talk it over with you. You may have to get him started, but get him to talk his problem out; let him get it off his chest. Many times he will discover his own solution simply by talking about it with another person.

True enough, this could even take up some of your off-duty time, but it's a must if you want to have a smooth-running organization. Remember, an employee can't possibly function properly on the job when something is bothering him or when he's worrying about a personal problem.

So whenever you feel you're too busy to talk with someone, please remember this: *Rejection hurts; attention heals.* It's really just that simple.

How You Can Become a Better Listener

University studies of management in more than 100 firms showed that managers and executives spent no less than 40 percent of their time listening to their subordinates. Yet those managers retained less than 25 percent of what they heard. To help you do a better job than that, I want to give you . . .

TEN TECHNIQUES TO HELP IMPROVE YOUR LISTENING ABILITIES

1. *Give your wholehearted attention to the other person.* Listening with everything you've got means putting aside your own interests, preoccupations, and problems, at least temporarily. For those few moments, concentrate 100 percent on what the other person is saying. Focus all your attention on him. Listen with all the intensity and awareness that you can command.

2. *Really work at listening.* Listening is hard work. When you listen intensely, your heartbeat quickens, your pulse rate increases, and your blood circulates faster. Even your body temperature rises slightly. You yourself will know whether you're really working at listening or just faking it.

3. *Show an interest in what the speaker is saying.* One good way to show interest is to look directly at the person. Establish eyeball contact and hold it. Show by your alert posture and intense facial expression that you are deeply concerned with what he's saying. Whatever you do, don't fiddle with objects on your desk or clip your nails.

4. *Resist distractions.* If the conversation takes place in your office, tell your secretary you don't want to be disturbed. Shut the door, cut off the telephone, turn off the radio. Give the speaker the best

opportunity to tell you what you need to know. If you don't, he might react the way I did once in a doctor's office in Omaha, Nebraska.

My wife and I were receiving a final report from a high-priced neurosurgeon about her physical condition. He was interrupted three times by phone calls from his secretary. The fourth time the phone rang, I picked it up, and said, "The doctor is out. He won't be back for 30 minutes. Don't call again before 2:30!"

5. *Practice patience.* Patience is largely a matter of waiting, watching, listening, sitting silently until the person who's speaking is completely through. If he's your employee and you're his boss, chances are the tempo of his thinking is slower than yours. If it weren't, your positions might be reversed. So understand why he's slower in expressing himself than you are. Have patience with him.

6. *Keep an open mind.* Remember that you're listening to your employee to get information from him. If his ideas don't coincide with yours, that doesn't mean you're right and he's wrong. Most innovations in business and industry come from the rank-and-file worker as managers of large and successful companies will be quick to tell you.

7. *Listen for ideas.* A good listener watches for ideas, concepts, and principles. A poor listener tends to get lost in trivia and details. If an employee has an idea to speed up production and eliminate waste, keep your eyes on that objective. Don't fret if you can't remember all the technical details by heart. That can come later.

8. *Judge the content, not the delivery.* I once worked for a man who'd been a college English professor. That bothered me for quite a while, until one day he said, "Look, Jim, I'm not grading you on your grammar, sentence structure, or choice of words. I'm interested only in *what* you're telling me, not in how you're saying it."

So don't worry about a person's personality or his style of delivery. You should be interested only in finding out what he knows. Judge the content, not the delivery.

9. *Hold your fire.* Many times a listener spends most of his time trying to figure out how to rebut the speaker, rather than actually listening to what's being said. Forget your pet theories. You might learn something brand-new and profitable if you teach your ego to "hold its breath."

10. *Learn to listen between the lines.* I've mentioned this subject before, but it's important enough to bring it up again. Lots of times you can learn more by what the other person doesn't say than by what he does say.

The speaker doesn't always put everything he's thinking into words. Watch for the changing tone and volume of his voice. Sometimes you'll find a meaning that's in direct contrast to his spoken words. Watch the facial expression, mannerisms, gestures, body movements. To be a good listener means you must use your eyes as well as your ears. Right now, I want to give you . . .

Seven Tell-Tale Body Language Signs to Watch for

In the next chapter I will discuss body language in more detail, but here I want to give you 7 tell-tale signs that are important to you when you're listening to one of your employees:

1. *Eyes.* No matter what his mouth says, his eyes will tell you what he's really thinking. If the pupils widen, then he's heard something pleasant. You've made him feel good by what you've said. If his pupils contract, then just the opposite is true. He's heard something he dislikes. If his eyes narrow, you've told him something he doesn't believe so he feels he has cause not to trust you or what you say.

2. *Eyebrows.* If he lifts one eyebrow you've told him something he doesn't believe or that he thinks is impossible. Lifting both eyebrows indicates surprise.

3. *Nose and ears.* If he rubs his nose or tugs at his ear while saying he understands, it means he's puzzled by what you're saying and probably doesn't know at all what you want him to do.

4. *Forehead.* If he wrinkles his forehead downward in a frown, it means he's puzzled or he doesn't like what you've told him. If he wrinkles his forehead upward, it indicates surprise at what he's heard.

5. *Shoulders.* When a person shrugs his shoulders, it usually means he's completely indifferent. He doesn't give a hoot for what you're saying or what you want.

6. *Fingers.* Drumming or tapping the fingers on the arm of the chair or the top of the desk indicates either nervousness or impatience.

7. *Arms.* If a person clasps his arms across the chest, it usually means he's trying to isolate himself from others, or he's actually afraid of you and is trying to protect himself.

How to Calm Down an Angry Person Just by Listening

I learned this technique from a master in the business, Roy Feldman, a top employee relations manager. I've asked him to tell you exactly how he does it.

"When an angry employee comes through my door with a complaint, I handle him like a VIP," Roy says. "I treat him as if he were the president of the company or a majority stockholder. I have him sit down. I make him comfortable, offer him a cup of coffee. I do everything I can to put him completely at ease.

"After he's settled down, I ask him to tell me his story. I tell him I want to hear it all from beginning to end. Then I listen to what he says without interrupting him or saying a single word. That's the first thing he wants—someone who will listen to him—someone who will lend a sympathetic ear to his problem.

"When he's all through, I tell him I can sure understand how he feels. I say that if I were in his position, if the situation were reversed, I'd feel the same way he does.

"Now I've taken a lot of the steam out of him simply by listening to him and by telling him I understand how he feels. He wasn't prepared for that, so he calms down even more. Instead of finding that I'm his enemy, he suddenly finds I'm his friend. He came in prepared to do battle with me, but now he finds he has no one to fight!

"Next I ask him what he wants me to do about his complaint. This really floors him because most of the time an executive doesn't *ask* his employee what he can do for him, he *tells* him what he's going to do. But we don't run our employee relations program that way. We don't tell an employee with a complaint what we're going to do— *we ask him what he wants us to do for him.*

"I've had people look at me in astonishment and say, 'Gee, Mr. Feldman, I honestly don't know. I hadn't thought about that. I just wanted someone to listen to my side of the story for a change. You've done that, so that's enough. I'm satisfied.'

"Sometimes they tell me what they want me to do. Ninety-five times out of a hundred, I find that they ask for far less than I'd have offered. Then when I give them more, they are really impressed with the generosity of both management and the company.

"Either way, when they leave, they're fully satisfied. In both cases, they supplied themselves with their own answers, so they're bound to be completely happy with the end results.

"Actually, my job is easy. All I do is listen. Then I ask him what he wants me to do. When he tells me, then I help him get what he wants."

Mr. Feldman's way of handling employee complaints follows the principle I've told you about already, and that is to find out what the other person wants and then to help him get it.

To help you put this technique to work for yourself, I want to give you . . .

TWELVE GUIDELINES FOR HANDLING EMPLOYEE GRIPES AND COMPLAINTS

1. *Make it easy for them to come to you.* You don't have to be overly chummy, but you shouldn't be cold and distant with your employees either. The important thing is to free your subordinate from the fear that his complaint might antagonize you and create a bigger problem for him than he already has.

2. *Get rid of red tape.* I have absolutely no use for government officials who use red tape to keep from making a decision or giving a person an answer. Don't clutter up your grievance procedure with cumbersome rules that defeat your purpose. Keep it plain and simple. You want to get to the problem and its solution in the least amount of time possible. A good way to do this is to keep your door open at all times to your employees.

3. *Explain your grievance procedure to everyone.* It does no good to keep your door open unless your employees know why it's open. Pass the word along—let them all know—keep everyone informed. State clearly and precisely how an employee should present his complaint and say what will happen when he does. Explain your procedure, step by step, so that everybody will understand it clearly.

4. *Help a person voice his complaint.* Sometimes an employee may not be skilled in putting his grievance into words. If he feels that the successful correction of his problem will depend on his verbal ability, he may give up even before he starts, and bottle up his discontent inside where it will fester and continue to grow into an open sore.

5. *Always grant a hearing to an employee with a complaint.* No matter how trivial his complaint might sound to you, it's important to him, so always give your employee the chance to air his gripe and get it off his chest.

6. *Practice patience.* I know you're busy and you have many other things to do. But be patient; hear the person out. If you don't, next time you hear him it could be at a formal arbitration hearing. Then

you'll have to listen whether you want to or not and it will be even more expensive and time-consuming.

7. *Ask him what he wants you to do.* Here's how you can turn a complaint into a benefit for you. Just ask, "What would you like me to do to help?" This one question will do more to oil the rusty relationship between management and labor than any other that you might use.

8. *Don't make hasty or biased decisions.* You must not make your decisions with the biased view of management, but with the wisdom of an impartial judge. Nor should you make hasty or snap judgments. If you need more time to get more information, take it. A wise decision is more important than a hasty one.

9. *Get all the facts first.* Sometimes you'll need to hear someone else's side of the story first before you can make your decision. If this is necessary to get all the facts, do so, no matter how much time it takes. But don't use this as an excuse to put things off.

10. *Let the employee know what your decision is.* Once you've made your decision, let the person know what it is. Tell him yourself. Call him back to your office if need be. Don't pass the word to him via your clerk or secretary. Do that and he'll know for sure that you weren't really interested in his case after all.

11. *Double-check your results.* Later on, check back with your employee to make sure his grievance has been taken care of to his complete satisfaction. Follow up and he will know that you are really interested in his welfare.

12. *Be concerned.* There's not much use paying attention to a person and listening to his complaints unless you honestly do care, unless you really do want to help, unless you won't feel right until you do. I can't tell you how to work this step. It has to come from inside.

If you've been having trouble solving your employee problems or handling their complaints, use the techniques I've given you for a few weeks. You'll be deeply gratified with the end results when you do.

chapter 11

How to Use
Body Language
to Project the Power
of Your Personality

As I told you previously, there can be some overlapping in the various types of business conversations. And so it is with body language. Body language is often used to subtly inform another person how you feel about something. It can also be used in the art of persuasion. But one of its most valuable uses is in projecting the power of your personality.

In the last chapter I gave you a few body language signs to watch for in conversations with your employees. And you are already familiar with two other body language signals: the frown that displays dissatisfaction or anger, and the smile that portrays joy and happiness.

In this chapter I want to give you the techniques you can use to project the power of your personality. You will also learn to recognize these unspoken signals when someone else uses them on you, not only in business, but also in your social conversations as well.

THE IMMENSE BENEFITS YOU'LL GAIN FROM THIS CHAPTER

1. You can project the power of your personality to others by your physical appearance and demeanor. For instance, an erect posture with your head up and chest out shows you have supreme confidence in yourself by your self-assured manner and bearing. As a result, others will have full confidence in you, too.

2. The way you look at a person can control a bad situation and get things back to normal quickly without your having to say a single word. I'll give you an example of how to use that power later on in this chapter.

3. You can use body language to discipline your employees and get them to do a better job for you. Your physical presence alone is enough to stimulate people to get to work. To see and be seen is a cliché, but it never fails to get results for the boss.

4. You'll gain the reputation of being a "born leader," when you use body language to project the power of your personality. People will automatically turn to you for assistance and advice.

5. When you know how to read another person's body language, you'll easily learn his secrets. He won't have to tell you what he's thinking; you'll know. This knowledge will give you a distinct advantage over him.

THE POWERFUL TECHNIQUES YOU CAN USE TO GAIN THESE BENEFITS

Why Nonverbal Communication Is So Important to Understand

Nonverbal communication is freer from deception than verbal language. We find it easier to lie with words than with our bodies. For instance, have you ever tried to keep your hands still, or keep from biting your lips, or not sighing when you were extremely nervous or worried about something? Impossible, wasn't it? No matter what you said, your body told others what you were really feeling.

When someone is talking to you, you usually look at his face first to see if his expression goes with what is being said. Then you listen to the tone of his voice to see if there is a hidden meaning somewhere. Finally, you actually listen to the spoken words. Even if the spoken words are cynical or sarcastic, you will accept them as a joke if the speaker's face is jovial and happy.

For instance, my children always knew that if I said Robert instead of Bob, Lawrence instead of Larry, Teresa Lynne instead of Terese in a louder than normal voice, they had done something wrong and a serious conversation was about to take place. You are communicating nonverbally not only when you use gestures, but also when you change the volume or tone of your voice.

If you feel that nonverbal communication is not important to understand, then please consider this: University studies indicate that over 90 percent of the meaning of any message is transmitted nonverbally. That being so, it becomes extremely important to you not only to know how to use body language yourself, but also to be able to read another person's body signals.

How to Look the Part of a Commanding and Powerful Personality

To have the look of power and command so that people will always give way to you on sight, you need not be six feet tall or built like a professional athlete. The way you carry yourself is the key. I have seen tall physically strong men turn and run in battle, while small short ones stayed and fought the enemy with courage. Power comes from within, and is primarily a matter of attitude.

Of course, there are certain physical characteristics you can develop that will help you project the power of your personality: a steady unflinching gaze, a tone of voice that implies complete self-confidence and commands immediate obedience, and above all, a solid presence that lets people know you are exactly where you ought to be.

If you show confidence in yourself and always act as if it were impossible to fail, people will gain strength from your example. Your physical appearance and manner must depict a confidence sometimes even beyond what you might actually feel. By controlling your voice and gestures, you will be able to exert a firm and steadying influence on your colleagues as well as your own employees.

People always have the greatest respect for the leader who remains cool in the midst of trouble. But they have no use whatever for the one who panics at the first sight of something gone wrong.

You can increase people's confidence in you when you view a tough situation with a calm and cool presence of mind. By assuming such a positive attitude, you appear to take the entire burden on your own shoulders. You give your employees the feeling that there is no need to worry and that the problem can be solved.

Your people will have confidence in your strength, courage, and ability to set matters straight. You will be able to project the power of your personality so that they will quickly obey every one of your commands without fail.

How to Use the Steepling Technique to Project Your Power

Smart people who know how to project the power of their personalities often make a steeple with their hands. Watch a group of people during a business meeting. As the boss listens to a subordinate's suggestion, he will often steeple. This shows he is seriously thinking about what the other person is saying. As his thoughts become deeper and more profound, he may steeple in a higher and higher position until the steeple nearly hides his face.

Medical doctors, psychiatrists, and psychologists are all avid steeplers. The implication is that they are deep thinkers and extremely intelligent and important people. Use the steepling technique and people will draw the same conclusions about you. This technique is a powerful adjunct you can use, not only to project your own power, but also to turn off another person's play for power.

How to Create Your Own Space Bubble to Establish Your Turf

In companies and corporations, the general rule of thumb is that the more powerful you become, the larger the area you can call your own. Low-ranked employees may work together in groups in one large room. Their supervisor might have only a glassed-in cubicle from which he can both see and be seen by his subordinates.

A young executive can be blessed with a private, although small, office. As a member of the power elite, even if you're a junior one, you will be entitled to that.

No matter how small your office is, you can expand your own space bubble of power by placing visitors' chairs against the farthest wall as far away as possible from your desk. Another person should never be able to *invade* or *encroach* upon your territory by putting his arms on your desk.

If you have the authority to select the furniture for your office, always pick soft easy chairs or a low sofa for your visitors. When you are sitting in the power position behind your desk, and your visitor is slumped down or sprawled out in an easy chair or low sofa, he is immediately at a disadvantage. It's much easier for you to retain the upper hand psychologically when your visitor is sitting in a weaker position.

How You Can Use Body Gestures to Your Advantage

You already know how to use the steepling technique to project the power of your personality. Another way you can project power is to appear completely relaxed and at ease.

For example, in an interview, the power person is relaxed and at ease in his posture and manner. He can choose to sit, stand, even stroll around while talking to the other person. If a man, he might even straddle a chair or put his feet up on the desk. If a woman, she can place her hands on her hips and spread her feet slightly to project her power.

But the person being interviewed is powerless to do any of these things. He is limited to sitting up straight, usually on the edge of the chair, in a completely motionless position.

You can also project the power of your personality by maintaining a neutral facial expression. At a high-level meeting of business executives, the ranking individual rarely smiles, even when greeted cordially by others. Less powerful people will usually smile throughout the entire meeting.

How to Use Your Eyes to Invade Another Person's Territory

A powerful person is accustomed to staring down another individual as a way of invading his territory. Usually, if the boss stares at an employee, the employee will lower his eyes and only glance up now and then to sneak a quick look at his superior.

There's a trick to this staring technique. *Never, never look directly into the other person's eyes.* You can't win if you do that. Instead, pick a spot in the middle of his forehead just above the level of his eyebrows. Keep your eyes glued to that one spot and no one will ever be able to stare you down. Eventually, the other person will have no choice but to lower his gaze.

How Body Language Can Clearly Reveal a Person's Inner Thoughts and Feelings

A person doesn't have to say a word to let you know what he's thinking or how he feels. His hands, eyes, mouth, and body can give away how he really feels inside.

Hands can indicate fear and anxiety in a number of ways: fingers twitching or drumming the knees, clinging hands, palms wet and clammy, hands visibly nervous when holding a cigarette, clenched fists, hands gripping the arms of the chair until the knuckles turn white.

Eyes can reveal fear by shifting back and forth, refusing to meet the other person's gaze, or by excessive blinking. The mouth shows fear when one bites his lips or licks them or has a tightly clenched jaw. The body held stiff and rigid indicates a deep-seated anxiety; so does excessive perspiration or constant deep breathing with heavy sighs.

The male abdomen is also used in body language. In courtship, a man will tighten his abdominal muscles and pull in his belly to display his strength and virility. When he is depressed, he will often over-relax these muscles and let his stomach sag visibly downward. The degree of tension of the abdominal muscles will tell a great deal about the emotional and mental status of a man.

One way to tell if a person is really listening to you or not is to watch the position of his head while you are speaking to him. If he is your employee and is really attentive to what you're saying, he'll usually tilt his head to one side. Less powerful people often do this when they are listening to instructions from their superiors.

The less powerful person, as your employee is, for instance, will also mirror exactly the body posture of the more powerful person. If you lean forward and cross your arms, he will soon do the same. If you cross your legs, so will he. If you look anxious while speaking to him, he will soon show body language signs of anxiety, too.

How a Schoolteacher Can Stop Trouble Without Saying a Word

Eugene B. Lynch, a university psychologist and educator, not only knows how to stop trouble in a classroom without saying a single word, but he also passes along this information to other potential teachers in his courses.

"Maintaining order and discipline in the classroom is often the biggest job the teacher has," Dr. Lynch says. "If the instructor will use my system, he can eliminate between 70 and 90 percent of classroom disruptions. When used properly, discipline is almost invisible. Let me give you an example of that:

"A teacher tells her class to begin working on arithmetic problems. But in a few moments, Johnny decides he'd rather do something more pleasurable.

"Seeing this, the teacher walks over, leans over Johnny with her hands planted squarely on his desk, looks him straight in the eye, tells him quietly to get back to work, stares at him for a full count of three, and then leaves. Johnny suddenly develops a deep interest in arithmetic.

"Close physical proximity is one of the most important elements in maintaining discipline," Dr. Lynch goes on to say. "So is a quick response to disruption. A lot of teachers think that if you ignore the problem, it will go away. But that is simply not true. Immediate corrective action is necessary to retain control of the class.

"So respond quickly. From then on it's mostly body language, facing the child directly, having a tone of voice and a facial expression that shows you mean business. Eyeball-to-eyeball contact is also extremely important. The use of body language also helps the teacher keep his mouth shut. When he doesn't talk, he can't end up with his foot in his mouth or make a fool out of himself in front of all the other students."

If you will note, the close physical proximity that Dr. Lynch mentions is an invasion of the student's space bubble. This serves to deflate his ego, and makes him more susceptible to direction by the teacher.

How to Project the Power of Your Personality on the Phone

Although you cannot use the body language of your hands or eyes over the phone, how you use your voice and the words you use can still vividly project the power of your personality. For instance, you should never refer to yourself by your given name. If you call someone on the phone, don't say, "This is Joe." Don't even say, "This is Joe Davis." Instead, say, "This is Davis." The use of first names encourages unwanted familiarity. In power circles, familiarity is an invasion of privacy. It punctures your space bubble. Be courteous and polite, of course, but keep people at arm's length from you.

When answering the phone, don't use your title. To do so implies that you can't get by without it. Don't say, "This is *Mr.* Davis, or *Superintendent* Davis, or *Doctor, Professor, Major,* or whatever. Just say, "Davis," or "Davis speaking." When introducing yourself to someone, simply say, "I'm Davis," or "My name is Davis." That's enough.

If you are a woman, follow exactly the same procedure. This places you on the same level as your male colleagues. Never refer to yourself as *Miss, Ms.,* or *Mrs.* This invites too many chauvinistic remarks, especially about the title, *Ms.*

Telephone selling, or telemarketing as it is also called, has increased greatly since the early seventies when the cost of driving a car went up drastically. Many companies and corporations today use the phone instead of the traveling salesman to get orders and to do business; and so do retail firms.

I usually get anywhere from two to four telephone calls a day from local stores wanting to sell me something. Most of these calls are made when I'm eating supper, watching television, reading the newspaper, whatever, and I don't want to be disturbed by anyone. It takes a powerful personality with a terrific message on the other end to get my attention. He has to offer me a great big benefit of some sort right away to get my interest.

Many of the calls I receive sound like this: "I'm going to be in your neighborhood tomorrow checking on (water purity, roofing, sidewalks, siding, whatever). Could I drop by and see you so I can show you what I have to offer?"

My answer to this is that I'll not be home. That kind of call offers me no benefit whatever. The only benefit appears to be to the caller. In other words, it will be convenient for him to call on me since he's going to be in my neighborhood anyway.

As Elmer Wheeler, one of America's greatest salesmen, once said, "Your first ten words are more important than the next ten thousand." His statement is especially applicable to telephone selling.

So if you want to be successful in telemarketing, you must grab the person in the first few seconds by offering him a benefit he can't possibly refuse. There is simply no other way to get him.

Why You Should Eliminate These Words from Your Vocabulary

Certain words and phrases automatically place other people above you when you use them. You can bring yourself up to their level immediately by eliminating these words completely from your vocabulary.

I refer specifically to the use of the words "Sir" and "Ma'am." Never use these words either alone or in the phrases so often heard: "Yes, Sir . . . No, Sir . . . Yes, Ma'am . . . No, Ma'am."

The use of *Sir* and *Ma'am* immediately places you on a lower level than the other person whether you realize that or not. These two small words imply *submissiveness* rather than courtesy and respect. You can still be courteous and show respect for the other person without being submissive. For example, if your boss asks if you've completed a certain task, don't answer with "Yes, Sir!" Say instead, "Yes, Mr. Jones. I have."

Don't reply with only *Yes* or *No* when answering a question. It sounds too curt and brief and borders on being insolent or discourteous. Answer *Yes* or *No* in a short sentence just as I showed you in the above paragraph. If the person to whom you are speaking has a title, use that, too, in the place of *Sir* or *Ma'am*. For instance, you can say, "Yes, Doctor, I have . . . No, Professor, I have not."

How to Interpret Body Language in Social Activities

It is very important for you to be able to interpret body language at social activities, especially in business or at office parties to keep yourself from making the wrong move or stepping on the wrong person's toes.

For instance, if your boss and some of the other top brass have formed a little circle that excludes all others, don't try to invade their area uninvited. You can easily recognize when they don't want others to be included in their conversation if they are sitting on a couch and the two at each end are "bookended," that is, turned inward to enclose the person in the center and with their backs to the outside. This serves to lock out intruders, for the implication of this kind of grouping is, "This is a closed discussion . . . keep out . . . you are not invited."

If they are standing in a group, elbow to elbow in a "circle the wagons" posture, it also means they want to be left alone. Sometimes one man will put his foot up on a coffee table to prevent any outside intrusion into the group. Men will also tend to protect a woman by placing her in the middle of the circle or by placing themselves between male visitors and the female.

If men and women are forced to sit very close together, face to face, and they are not on close intimate terms, they may cross their arms and legs protectively and lean away from each other while talking, almost as if they had bad breath.

Six Final Tips on How to Project the Power of Your Personality with Body Language

When you want to communicate equality with your associates (this is especially important to a woman), you can use these simple but powerful body language signals. These are also valuable to project the power of your personality to your subordinates or to your boss as well, or to assert your status as an executive or a manager.

1. *Don't smile unless you are genuinely happy.* This does not mean you have to walk around with a frown on your face as if you were carrying the weight of the whole world on your shoulders. It means exactly what it says. Don't smile unless you are really happy. A neutral facial expression best conceals your inner feelings and emotions.

2. *Don't allow other people to interrupt you.* If someone does interrupt you, even if it's your superior, simply say, "I'm sorry, but I wasn't finished," and then resume speaking at once where you were cut off. This is usually enough to stop the other person dead in his tracks unless he is abnormally obtuse.

3. *Don't restrain your body gestures.* If you need to use your hands

or arms to make a point, do so. The only thing to avoid here is pointing your finger at someone as if you were accusing him of some wrong. This turns everyone off completely.

4. *Look people straight in the eye.* I've already told you that the trick to this is staring at a spot in the middle of the forehead just above the eyebrows. This is one of the most effective techniques you can use to make the other person back off. If he's trying to argue with you, saying nothing but staring at him this way will cause him to become nervous and flustered. You can make your point without ever saying a single word.

5. *Use your space bubble effectively.* Many young executives fail to do this and then wonder why their personal private space is always being invaded. The proper placement of office furniture is often the key here.

6. *Be completely relaxed.* I don't mean that you should be sloppy about your dress or careless about your appearance. The key to being relaxed is self-confidence. If you know your job, you don't have to be nervous and filled with tension. You can relax and really enjoy your work.

This concludes Part III on how to use business conversations that transmit information to others. In Part IV, I will take up *Business Conversations That Use Persuasion.* There you'll learn how to use persuasion to get people to accept your ideas, buy your products, or simply do what you want them to do.

PART IV

Business Conversations That Use Persuasion

If you want people to accept your ideas or buy your product or simply do what you want them to do for you, it's persuasion, not force, that will get the job done.

Businesspeople, salespeople, preachers, teachers, politicians—all these professionals use persuasion to get people to do what they want done. In Part IV you'll learn their secrets so you can get others to carry out your desires, too.

Of course, persuasion is not limited to business conversations alone. Wives use it on their husbands all the time to get what they want and vice versa. Parents use it on their children and children use it on their parents.

Persuasion is a valuable tool that you can use in many social situations, so no matter who you are or what you do, this particular section will be of great value to you.

chapter 12

Using Persuasion to Get People to Do What You Want

Exactly what is the art of persuasion? Most salespeople and psychologists will tell you that it's getting another person to do what you want him to do. But that's not enough. True persuasion is getting the other person to *want* to do what you want him to do. There is a tremendous difference between these two ideas. Let me give you a brief example to illustrate this point.

To get a person to do what they want him to do, most people will appeal to logic, common sense, and good judgment. For instance, a real estate salesman does that when he tells the prospective buyer all the advantages of owning a *house*. When he does that, he's appealing to the person's mind.

But the really smart real estate salesman will appeal not only to the potential buyer's mind, but he will also make his sales pitch to the person's heart by telling him the benefits of owning a *home*. And the salesman who sells a *home* will outsell the one who sells *only a house* every time. Why? Simply said, it's because the head never hears 'til the heart has listened.

Let me give you another quick example. Did you ever hear a person say, "I'll do what you want, but my heart isn't in it." If he says that to you, it means he hasn't been emotionally convinced to do what you've asked him to do. To win a person completely over to your way of thinking, you must appeal to his feelings as well as to his mind.

So if you want to persuade people to do things your way, if you want to influence them, if you want to control their actions, then just remember this one thought and you will never go wrong:

THE HEAD NEVER HEARS 'TIL THE HEART HAS LISTENED

When you use this idea as a basis along with the specific techniques I'll give you in this chapter, you'll succeed every time in persuading people to do what you want. How can I be so sure of this? Because I've used this system all my life and it's never failed me yet.

That's how sure I am. And when you use this principle along with these techniques, too,

YOU'LL GAIN THESE 4 EXTREMELY WORTHWHILE BENEFITS

1. You'll have no trouble at all in persuading a person to accept your idea, your proposition or your point of view.

2. You'll be able to sell an individual easily on your product or your service or in just doing what you want him to do.

3. A winning, positive, and outgoing personality will be yours. As your skills in persuading others improve, your confidence in yourself and your own abilities will increase and multiply.

4. You'll be able to get others to think and act favorably toward you. You'll gain the ability to persuade others to always want to do what you want them to do.

TECHNIQUES YOU CAN USE TO GAIN THESE DESIRABLE BENEFITS

How to Find Out What People Want Before You Start

In the first chapter I told you about the 14 basic learned needs or desires that all people have. Just in case they've slipped your mind for the moment, let me sum them up for you here in one short simple sentence like this:

> Every normal person wants to know how to be loved—how to win money or fame or power—and how to stay healthy.

I also said that it was up to you to find out exactly what a person wants most of all so you could help him get it.

How can you best do that? By paying complete and full attention to what he says so you can find out exactly what he wants or to discover what he really needs. When you pay attention to a person this way, he will also pay attention to you and to what you want. And only then will you be able to persuade him to your point of view.

The reason for this is quite plain. You see, rich or poor, young or old, happy or unhappy, each one of us has a deep desire—yes, even a craving—for attention.

Let me give you a few quick examples of this: For instance, a crying child tugging at his mother's skirt is demanding her attention.

When she gives him that attention he needs so much, he'll stop crying and behave.

What does the straying unfaithful husband want and need most of all? Ninety-five percent of the time he's seeking the attention his wife has not given him. When she gives him the attention he needs, he'll stop wandering and stay home.

The nagging wife, the unfaithful husband, the runaway teenager, the rebellious child, the hypochondriac in the doctor's office, the patient on the psychiatrist's couch, even the rioter in the streets—all these people are crying out for someone's attention.

Just look about you and you'll easily see for yourself plenty of examples of people demanding attention, even in your own family. I have a granddaughter who wants to make absolutely sure I'm looking when she does something special for me. To make sure of my attention, Jessica will look at me from the corner of her eye and say, "Now watch me do this, Grandpa . . . Grandpa, are you watching me?" And she's only three years old!

Remember that your listener is human, too. He also wants your attention, so give it to him. Pay attention to him and to what he says so you can find out what he wants and what he's most interested in. When you do that, you make him important, not only to you, but also to himself, and that's a mighty big persuader to use.

When you give a person your undivided attention first, he will automatically give his full attention to you and to what you want from him. Does this technique of paying attention to him first work? It most certainly does; it always has and it always will. It's a fail-safe procedure. Let me give you a few concrete examples of that.

When you give your undivided attention to people to find out what they want and then help them get it, you'll succeed in whatever you're doing. I don't care what your goal is; whether it's getting someone to chair a meeting, teach a Sunday school class, make a fund-raising speech, persuade a group to take action, win a bunch of skeptics over to your point of view, convince a purchasing committee that you have the best product; you'll be successful if you pay attention to people first and find out what they want before you ever start.

A Technique You Can Use to Persuade People to Pay Immediate Attention to You

You can use a variety of methods to persuade people to listen and pay attention to you. For instance, you could use a startling statement . . . an authoritative quotation . . . an unusual anecdote . . .

a strong example. However, I prefer by far the use of the leading question that promises your listener a benefit, for it is without doubt the most effective approach you can use. Here are some quick examples of this potent technique:

1. How'd you like to make some easy money?
2. How'd you like to increase profits 25 percent?
3. Want to meet a handsome man tonight?
4. How'd you like to cut production costs in half?
5. Want to get rid of that tired worn-out feeling?
6. How'd you like to be proud of your floors?
7. Want to get more MPG from your car?

No matter what your specific circumstances are, use the kind of question that promises your listener an immediate benefit just for listening to you and he'll be forced to give you his full and undivided attention.

Not only can you offer your listener a benefit with the leading question technique, but you can also get him saying "Yes" at once, and that's ever so important in persuading him so that he'll want to do what you want him to do.

You see, when he says "Yes" to your opening question, it establishes a positive mood. This makes it much easier for him to continue to agree with you.

Nine Benefits You Can Gain by Using the Leading Question Technique

1. *With leading questions, you can control the initiative in the conversation.* You actually lead the other person's thinking along the path you want it to take when you ask him leading questions. You point his mind in a specific direction so he'll give you the answer that you want.

2. *Leading questions increase your listener's interest.* A person's attention span increases when you can get him to talk by asking him leading questions. The more he talks, the more you learn about him and what he wants most of all.

3. *When you ask questions, you stimulate a person's thinking.* Questions make your listener more alert and attentive to what you say. He becomes anxious to learn more. Many times, your idea becomes his idea and he wants to take credit for it.

I've seen managers and supervisors use questions time and again to get what they wanted by letting the other person think it was all his own idea in the first place.

4. *Questions help reveal your listener's attitude.* When you know what a person's thinking is and what his innermost feelings are, you can slant your approach to meet his individual needs and desires. You'll know which one (or more) of the 14 secret motivators you ought to stress to persuade him to want to do as you desire.

5. *Questions let you know if you're getting your point across or not.* Attention is always lost when understanding is gone. One of the best ways to find out whether your listener understands you or not is to ask him questions.

His answers will let you know how good your conversational methods and techniques are. At the same time, his answers will indicate where your approach needs to be improved.

6. *You can reinforce and emphasize major points of interest.* Retention of major points of emphasis is made easier by frequent repetition. When you ask questions on a specific point, it is plain to see you are stressing that idea. Your listener's answers will reinforce those major points of interest.

7. *Questions give the person a feeling of importance.* When you ask questions, you give a person the chance to express his own opinions. That makes him feel important and fulfills one of his basic desires by feeding his ego. When he knows that you are interested in what he says, and that you respect his opinions and ideas, then he'll respect your opinions and ideas, too.

8. *Questions help a person recognize what he actually wants.* Remember Ted J., the insurance agent I told you about back in Chapter One who quadrupled his sales by plugging the person's ability to control and dominate his family even after his death? Ted did that by helping people recognize what they actually wanted from insurance. Help a person discover what he really wants most of all and you'll be in complete control of the conversation. He'll do whatever you ask as long as he knows he can get what he wants as a result of that action.

9. *To find a person's most vulnerable point, ask questions.* Your listener's weakest spot is your main key to success in persuasion. When you find his most vulnerable point, don't hesitate. Attack without delay. Concentrate on it; exploit it immediately. You can use it to get your own way without fail every single time.

When you review this chapter on how to use persuasion to get people to do what you want them to do, you will see that I have emphasized the importance of asking leading questions to get what you want over and over again. But if you want to find out exactly what your listener wants most of all—if you want to know precisely how you can help him get what he wants so that you, too, will benefit as well—you'll see that the only sure way to do this is to ask questions, questions, and still more questions.

When you get in the groove of constantly asking questions instead of talking just to hear the sound of your own voice, you'll find that the conversation flows more smoothly and that it's much more exciting and stimulating. Not only that, you'll discover it's highly profitable to you as well.

Asking leading questions that promise a benefit, then, is the surest way of getting a person to pay attention to you. Questions, rather than statements, can be the most effective way to make a sale, win a person over to your way of thinking, and persuade him to do what you want.

Why You Should Start with Questions That Are Easy to Answer

You should always start with questions that are easy to answer so your listener will relax and feel at ease when he talks with you. People enjoy giving answers they know are right, for it gives them a chance to show how much they know and that makes them feel important.

This is especially true if your listener is a stranger and you want to sell him something—say, a house or a new car. He'll really be on guard with you in the beginning. Mistrust is characteristic of almost all of us when we're doing business with someone we don't know.

Your listener doesn't know whether you'll be hard or easy to talk with. The first few things you say will help him decide that. As Elmer Wheeler (who was often called "America's number one sales-man" and whose "Sizzlemanship" methods have been used by most of the country's top corporations) always said, the first ten words were more important than the next ten thousand.

If you're hard to talk with, your listener will become evasive and withdrawn. When you press harder to make your point or your sale, he'll withdraw even more. This becomes a vicious cycle that ends up with no agreement at all or with a "no sale" sign on the cash register.

But if you will start out with easy questions, his nervousness and fear of you will soon disappear. He'll answer your questions with confidence. You ask him more easy questions. He relaxes even more. Soon you're engaged in a pleasant, fruitful, and beneficial conversation.

For instance, a lawyer never presses the witness for an answer to the crucial question the very first thing. A real estate salesman asks first about the number of children, what kind of house the prospect lives in now, how long it takes him to get to work, whether he prefers living in the city or the country, that sort of thing. A personnel manager interviewing a job applicant asks questions about a man's family, hobbies, likes and dislikes to put him completely at ease before he starts digging for hard facts about education, past experience, and his other business qualifications.

You, too, have to warm up your listener first so he will feel comfortable with you. You can't approach him with the bureaucratic iciness of an internal revenue agent and expect him to cotton to you just like that. It can't be done. So just relax and be comfortable. Make it easy for both of you and you'll be able to get what you want.

A 5-Step Procedure You Can Use to Persuade a Person to Your Point of View

1. *Tell him immediately how he's going to benefit.* No matter what your proposition is, your listener always wants to know right off what's in it for him. If you don't tell him that in the first five or ten seconds, you might as well stop talking.

So let the other person know at once what he's going to gain by listening to you. Don't make him guess. Tell him exactly what the benefits are. Don't be vague and nonspecific or talk in circles or generalities. Be concrete, definite, and specific about the advantages that can soon be his when he does as you ask him to do.

Just for openers, you could show him how he'll save time, money, and inconvenience by using your product or service. A reverse way of doing this would be to show him how much he'll lose if he doesn't accept your offer. However, this sort of tactic plays directly upon his fears so it's best used as proof or backup for the major benefits you're offering him.

2. *Tell him about someone else who benefited.* No matter how good your product or your service is, no matter how good your approach or how convincing your argument might be, nothing is ever equal to proof like this: "You know Tom Smith who lives over on Walnut Stret just a few blocks away from you? He was in the other day and bought

this same exact model from me. So I don't want you to take my word for it. You can ask Tom. In fact, I wish you would, for he will tell you how good it really is."

Proof of how satisfied someone else is with your product or your service is one of your most useful tools in persuading people. Never neglect this valuable technique. Always use it.

Successful mail order salespeople never send out a sales letter that doesn't have some kind of testimonial to back up their claims. The time will never come when a testimonial that has the ring of truth about it will not be a potent factor in dispelling all doubt in the mind of a hesitant customer. So bring on your witnesses for proof.

3. *Show him how to gain the same benefits.* After you've shown him how someone else gained the benefits, show him the techniques he can use to gain those same benefits. One of the best ways to do this is to use a demonstration or a practical application or both.

A demonstration is always used by the best salespeople. It is a sure-fire way of keeping your listener deeply interested in what you're doing. Products like cars, washing machines, dryers, vacuum sweepers, radios, TVs, and so on, lend themselves extremely well to the demonstration technique. Abstract services such as insurance, religion, fund drives, success motivation courses, health services, and the like are usually harder to demonstrate and persuade people so they often require audio-visual aids like records, tapes, charts, diagrams, and illustrations.

4. *Tell him what it's going to cost to gain the benefits.* In this step, you tell your listener exactly what it's going to cost him to gain the benefits you've been telling him about. Again, let me emphasize that you must be specific and concrete, especially in this step, for in most cases you are now reaching for his pocketbook. Vagueness implies that you have something to hide and that you can't be trusted.

If you're selling him something on the time payment plan, don't tell him fifty dollars a month is all he'll need and then start adding on the sales tax, the excise tax, and the carrying charges. Break it down for him and make sure he understands how much of his money is going where and for what. Give him the bottom line without beating around the bush. He'll appreciate your straightforward frankness and honesty.

5. *Ask him to take action.* After you've told your listener all about the benefits, how someone else gained them, how he can gain them for himself, and how much it'll cost, ask him to take action. Leave out this one vital step and you'll never persuade anyone to do anything.

A salesman calls this step the "close," and the most successful ones start closing a sale with the opening sentence of the conversation.

One of the best ones I've ever seen work this technique is Charlie Ryan. He sells washing machines and dryers for a big appliance company. Don't think for a moment that Charlie is "just another washing machine salesman." His income is in a healthy five-figure bracket.

Charlie stands beside the escalator exit right at the corner of his department. He asks every woman who comes down the escalator the same question: "How'd you like to have a brand-new washing mchine installed in your home today?"

"I save a lot of valuable time that way," Charlie says. "Almost every woman will say 'Yes' to that question. If she does, then I say, 'Let me show you how to do that.' I turn and walk straight to my demonstrator. If she follows me, I know she's interested and start demonstrating the new washing machine right away. While I'm doing that, I tell her how she's going to benefit by owning it. If she doesn't follow me, I simply go back to the escalator and start all over again with the next woman who comes in."

There are six salesmen in Charlie's department. He talks to more prospects than anyone else and sells more washing machines than any two salesmen put together. Charlie is aggressive; he knows his product. He tells his prospect immediately how she can benefit, and he tries to close the sale with his opening sentence. You can easily use the same procedure to persuade people to do what you want with just a little practice. All it takes is a bit of courage.

How to Overcome Your Listener's Objections

There are a variety of methods successful salespeople use to overcome their prospect's objections. However, one of the best ones you can use is the "Yes, but . . ." technique.

This is a polite but firm procedure. You agree with your listener, but you immediately point out why he should do as you ask anyway. "Yes, I know my product costs a bit more, Mr. Jones, but it lasts twice as long, the resale value is much higher, and the peace of mind you'll have while you own it are well worth those few extra dollars you are spending now." (A well-known television manufacturer uses this sales pitch very successfully.)

Before I conclude this chapter, I would like to recap for you the techniques you can use to get people to do what you want them to do every time.

1. If you want to be sure of succeeding, find out exactly what a person wants before you start.

2. If you want to persuade your listener to give you his full and undivided attention, use a leading question that promises him a benefit.

3. When you ask your listener leading questions, you gain the following benefits:

   (a) You control the initiative in the conversation.

   (b) You increase your listener's interest in what you're saying.

   (c) You stimulate a person's thinking.

   (d) Your listener's attitude is revealed to you.

   (e) You'll know whether you're getting your point across or not.

   (f) You can reinforce and emphasize major points of interest.

   (g) You'll give the person a feeling of importance.

   (h) You help a person recognize what he actually wants.

   (i) You can find your listener's most vulnerable point.

4. To get the results you want, start with questions that are easy to answer.

5. To persuade a person to your point of view, use this 5-step procedure:

   (a) Tell him immediately how he's going to benefit.

   (b) Tell him about someone else who benefited.

   (c) Show him how he can gain the same benefits.

   (d) Tell him what it's going to cost to gain those benefits.

   (e) Ask him to take action.

6. To overcome your listener's objections, use the "Yes, but . . ." technique.

Let me wrap up this chapter by saying that you must first always find out what a person wants before you start. Then you tell him what's in it for him by using emotional words that appeal to his heart. Finally, you ask him to take action. Use these techniques that I've given you here and you'll always be able to persuade a person to do what you want him to do.

chapter 13

The Secret of
Dealing with
Resistance
and
Overcoming
Objections

When you add the secret of dealing with resistance and overcoming objections to your arsenal of conversational techniques, you'll discover that you're well on your way to becoming a powerful and masterful personality.

Perhaps you haven't yet realized the progress you've actually made. If you will stop and think about it for a moment, you'll find that you are becoming a completely different person, one who commands new talents, power, influence, and respect, all as a result of your conversational skills and expertise.

However, you will at times encounter people who will offer strong resistance to you. Not everyone will immediately do what you want them to do without question. So it will be up to you to find ways of dealing with their resistance and overcoming their objections so you can convert them to your way of thinking.

The real key to success in dealing with your listener's resistance and overcoming his objections is to appeal to his heart. Offer him certain emotional benefits that will enable him to fulfill his basic needs and desires. In this chapter, I will show you exactly how to do that. When you use the technique that I'll give you here,

YOU'LL GAIN THESE 6 SPLENDID BENEFITS

1. People will always do what you want them to do.
2. They will follow your instructions to the letter and obey your orders without question.
3. You'll be able to easily put your ideas and proposals across to others.
4. You'll get cooperation and teamwork from everyone.
5. You'll get your own way every time.
6. You'll gain the power to influence and control people by what you say.

TECHNIQUES YOU CAN USE TO GAIN THESE SENSATIONAL BENEFITS

Getting your message across to someone so he will do what you want him to do is as dependent upon his listening level as it is upon the words you use. If you use short, simple, and concrete words of one and two syllables, and at the same time avoid cumbersome, vague, and abstract words, then you can be sure that your listener will understand you. But just understanding is not enough. Your success in overpowering his resistance and overcoming his objections will also depend upon his listening level.

You see, whenever you talk to someone, he will be hearing you on only one of these three listening levels: *the nonhearing level . . . the semi-listening level . . . the thinking or comprehension level.* Let me discuss each one of these now in detail with you.

1. *The nonhearing level.* At this level of comprehension, you're not even registering with your listener. In fact, it's inaccurate to call him a listener, for he's not paying any attention to you at all. His mind is concentrating only on what he wants to think about and what he himself is interested in.

A wife often finds that her husband uses this level to carry on a so-called conversation with her, especially in the evening after he's eaten and settled down in his favorite easy chair in front of the television set.

If he's reading the paper, he might even lower it once in a while to look at his wife, and even talk occasionally, saying such things as, "Yes, dear, that's right . . . I see . . . then what did she say?" But he really isn't listening to her at all.

2. *The semi-listening level.* At this level, your listener is at least able to remember part of what you've been saying. If you were to stop suddenly and ask him what you've been talking about, he'd no doubt be able to repeat your last sentence or so or at least tell you what your last idea was.

However, he really hasn't absorbed what you've been saying. As soon as you stop talking, your ideas immediately disappear from his mind for he's not thinking seriously about them at all.

3. *The thinking or comprehension level.* This is the level you want your listener to reach so you can put your ideas across and get him to do what you want him to do.

How can you tell when his mind has reached the thinking or comprehension level? When he asks you questions, voices objections, and offers resistance to your proposition. So don't be upset or worried when he does these things. This is precisely what you want to have happen.

You see, when your listener presents a counter argument or voices an objection, this shows he's interested in what you're saying. He wants to know more. If he were not interested, then he wouldn't ask you anything. Your next step, then, after you've raised your listener's mind to the thinking level, is to deal with his resistance and overcome his objections. Here's how you can do that:

How to Overcome Your Listener's Objections: The First Technique

In Chapter One I told you about Byron Kent, the insurance salesman who researched hundreds of interviews to find out why people bought or failed to buy insurance. He discovered that in more than 60 percent of cases, the first objection raised against buying insurance was not the real reason at all.

He found that a person almost always has two separate and distinct reasons for doing anything: one reason that sounds good to his listener, and another one that he keeps secret and hidden to himself.

You should always make sure that you find the hidden or real reason for your listener's resistance. To find the deep or hidden reason for a person's objections, simply keep asking one or all of the following three questions:

1. Why or why not?
2. And in addition to that?
3. Is there any other reason?

You must be persistent about this. Eventually, the real reason will come to the surface. Usually, you'll hear comments something like this: "Well, to tell you the truth," or "Well, if you really want to know why . . ." When you hear phrases like these, you'll know that the real objection is coming next. The moment you know the real reason for the person's resistance, you can move on to the next technique so you can overcome it.

How to Overcome Your Listener's Objections: The Second Technique

The best way to overcome your listener's objection is to turn it into a benefit for him. Let me show you how Fred Martin, a lubricating oils salesman, does this:

"One of the major objections a prospect usually raises is that although the product is good, the price is too high," Fred says. "Now when your prospect offers this kind of an objection, you can react in one of two ways.

"You can take his objection as an insurmountable obstacle or as a complete defeat, pack up your sample case, and leave. But that's a quick way to starvation.

"Or you can take his objection and turn it into a benefit for him so you can make a sale that might not otherwise be made. My answer to 'The price is too high' objection goes something like this:

"'Mr. Prospect, a cheap product costs you twice the price because you'll have complaints, mishaps, and you'll lose valuable customers. I'm offering you the best product that money can buy at a fair price.

"'Into it go the highest quality materials and processes that add up to top-notch performance for your customers. The high-grade performance of my product is a result of years of experience and know-how in the oil business.

"'My company produces its lubricants at the least possible cost and sells them at the lowest possible price. If a less expensive method of production could be developed, my company would be the first to use it so the price could be lowered to you.'

"If the prospect still hesitates, I say, 'You must make the final decision, of course, but I hope you realize that buying cheap to save money is like stopping a clock to save time.'

"This last remark really makes my prospect stop and think. It results in a sale more often than not."

How successful is Fred in converting objections into benefits so he can make more sales? Well, he moves three times as much oil as any other salesman in the company and he's in line for promotion to general sales manager.

Now you may not be a salesman, but you can use this conversational technique of changing an objection into a benefit in almost any sort of situation you can think of. For instance, does your wife object to going on a fishing or camping trip in the mountains for your annual vacation? You won't get anywhere by arguing with her about it. All you'll do is increase her resistance to what you want to do. Figure out how to turn her objection into a benefit for her and you'll get your own way every time.

By the way, if you're the wife and you want to go to the Bahamas or Acapulco for your yearly vacation and your husband objects, you'll have to offer him some benefits to get him to go. If you know how to satisfy a man's basic needs and desires, you'll win every time. He won't stand a chance, especially if you offer love and romance as a benefit.

How to Overcome Your Listener's Objections: The Third Technique

Logic, reason, and common sense are simply not enough to deal with a person's resistance, overcome his objections, and convince him to see things your way. To completely overcome a person's objections so you can get your own way every time, you must appeal to his emotions rather than only to his mind.

Now let me give you a specific example of how the emotions of the heart can completely overcome the rational logic and reasoning of the mind. Take love, for instance:

How many times does a girl marry the man her parents did not want her to? Even my own wife did that! Mother had her eye on the young banker or the doctor who had money, a promising career, social status, and a prominent position in the community. Or maybe Dad had picked the brilliant young attorney who seemed headed straight for the governor's mansion.

But daughter married the milkman . . . the farmer . . . the shoe salesman . . . the rock musician . . . the garage mechanic . . the grocery clerk . . . the waiter in the restaurant. Why? Well, Mom and Dad had picked their daughter's potential husband with their heads. Daughter had picked him out with her heart. The moral of this little story is quite simple:

People are ruled more by emotions than by logic and reason.

As I told you in the last chapter, the head never hears 'til the heart has listened. Now this is not to say that daughter was wrong, even though in view of today's high divorce rate, you might think so. I'm not saying that anyone is right or wrong. I'm only telling you why people do the things they do and what motivates them.

A person doesn't have to be in love to be emotionally involved. Check back on your own life and see how many of your own decisions—other than falling in love—were made on an emotional basis. If you didn't make most of your decisions that way, then you're a lot different from most of us.

Almost everything the rest of us do—buying cars, clothes, even changing jobs or moving to a different house—is done on impulse; the way we *feel* about a certain thing at a particular time, logic and reason be damned, no matter what the consequences. When a woman makes decisions like this based on her emotions, it's called *feminine intuition*. If a man does it, it's usually called *instinct*. Whatever it is, it's what we usually do. It's the way we make decisions.

So if you want to deal with a person's resistance and overcome his objections, appeal to his emotions. You should always appeal to his good judgment by all means; always give a person a logical and sensible reason for doing what you want him to do, so he can justify his actions to other people when they ask.

But if you really want to overcome a person's objections, if you want to get action from him, if you want to get your own way every time, then appeal to one of his basic emotional drives. Then you'll be sure of winning.

How to Overcome a Person's Objections by Asking Him Questions

You can use questions for more than just getting information from your listener. You can use them to break down the barriers of your listener's resistance and overcome his objections. Questions can also be used to change a person's position, sway his way of thinking, or get him to make a firm commitment to you.

This kind of questioning is truly a conversational art. It can be used successfully in all sorts of situations. Just suppose, for example, that you're trying to sell a product or a service or an idea, or simply get the other person to see things your way.

Somewhere along the line, whenever it seems most appropriate, you can ask him, in effect, "If I show you how or where you can benefit, will you buy my idea (or service or product or whatever)?"

Now your listener either has to say "yes," or he has to tell you why he doesn't want to go along with your idea. Either way you force his hand in the matter, so he has to bring his thinking out into the open for you to see. You could not have done this without your skillful use of questions.

You see, if he says "yes," you're in good shape. All you have to do then is close the sale. If he says "no," he still has to tell you why he cannot go along with you or why he cannot accept your idea. You are now in a position to deal with his resistance and overcome his objection by changing it into a benefit for him.

So in your conversations with others, get in the habit of talking less but asking more and more questions. When you say something, try to word it in such a way that you'll get a reaction to your statement so you can tell what the other person is thinking.

When you're trying to get another person to adopt your line of thinking or to see things your way, you cannot ask indiscriminate questions just at random. This accomplishes nothing; it does not serve to bring two minds closer to any sort of an agreement.

Ask yourself first: "Exactly what specific information do I need from this person to be able to sell him on my idea?" Then word your questions properly so you can get the information that you need.

This will take practice. You will not learn this technique in five minutes. It will require a lot of thinking on your part to come up with the right kind of questions. However, it'll pay you rich dividends. The most successful people in the art of persuasion have mastered this technique of asking questions to get what they want. In fact, this ability is a major factor in putting yourself across with people, no matter what your objective is in doing so.

So learn how to ask questions and lots of them in your conversations. It's a simple and easy way to deal with a person's resistance and overcome his objections so you can get what you want. Use this technique; you'll find that it will work like magic for you.

A Guaranteed 6-Step Technique for Winning Every Argument

Almost every day, some circumstance will come up where you need to get another person to accept your viewpoint or to see things your way. Whether you accomplish that or not depends largely on which of the following methods you use:

The first method—and the one that most people use to try and win an argument—is force. If you use force in an attempt to overpower or intimidate your opponent, your argument will turn into nothing more than a shouting match and an ego battle.

But this is a complete waste of time. You cannot win an argument by forcefully ramming your ideas down the other person's throat. The only way you can ever really win an argument is when you get the other person to change his mind.

To win an argument every time, you must work *with* human nature, not *against* it. If you want a person to see things your way, don't force your ideas on him. He must accept your ideas from within himself—from inside his own mind. Your ideas must become *his* ideas before he will ever accept them. When he has convinced himself that your viewpoint is correct, he will change his mind voluntarily. When he sees things your way, when he makes your viewpoint his viewpoint, you'll win your argument; but not until that happens.

You can get a person to accept your ideas only when you appeal to his emotions as well as to his reason, logic, and common sense. As I've already told you, the head never hears 'til the heart has listened, but that's such an important concept it's well worth repeating several times. You cannot possibly win an argument until that happens. Here, now, are 6 guidelines you can use to win every single time:

1. *How to retain control of the argument at all times.* Don't jump the gun and try to win by stating your side of the case first. If you do, you'll reveal your position and expose your vulnerable points. When you try to get your licks in first, you allow the initiative to pass to your opponent. You must retain control of the situation yourself.

Although it might sound paradoxical, the best way to do this is to let him state his argument first. Don't interrupt. Let him talk himself out so he will exhaust himself mentally.

It is an extremely good idea to get the person to repeat some of his key points or his sore spots. Letting him get it all off his chest helps immeasurably. If you can get him to repeat his complaints several times, he literally drains himself emotionally. That makes it much easier for you to win when he's mentally fatigued.

2. *How to probe and explore his argument.* Unless the person is ready to receive a particular idea, he is not likely to accept it. Lead him on an objective fact-finding survey of his position until you find a weakness in his argument.

When you do find such a weakness, use it for your opening statement to persuade him to your point of view. When he sees that weakness for himself, he will become much more receptive to your ideas.

That's why you should always let him talk first. You get his ideas out into the open where you can probe them for weaknesses.

The moment he realizes there are some holes in his argument, the more willing he will be to accept your point of view.

3. *How to know when to take action.* It's no use for you to attempt any action until you know the person is receptive to change. Listen for comments like these: "I could be wrong on a point or two . . . I'm willing to listen to reason . . . I've never looked at it that way before . . . I could be mistaken on this one small detail . . ."

When you hear expressions of self-doubt like these, it's a clear signal to you that it's time to take action and present your side of the case.

4. *How to state your side of the argument.* The tendency is always to use the old forceful methods to win an argument. Using force seems to be built right into us and is part of our makeup. But you must discipline yourself to avoid this bad habit of trying to show the other fellow up. Even if you out-talk him to the point he can say nothing in rebuttal, *you still will not win until he accepts your viewpoint as his very own.*

It's a proven fact that the best way to state your case is to do so moderately, accurately, and with sincerity. Be enthusiastic, but don't let your enthusiasm carry you away emotionally so that you exaggerate or make too forceful an approach.

5. *Don't be greedy.* Most people who use force to argue try to prove the other person completely wrong on every single point. They insist on winning 100 percent. This is a mistake. A skillful person, who uses persuasion rather than force to win an argument, will always be willing to concede something to his opponent or to give ground on some minor matter.

So be flexible. Compromise a bit; bend with the wind. Politicians do that to survive. The smart ones live on; the stubborn ones do not. So give in here and there on small points. Just follow this next rule and you will always be safe: Give ground on trifles—never on principles. All you need is the wisdom to know the difference between the two.

6. *Help the other person save face.* Not being greedy or not insisting on winning your case 100 percent helps the other person save face. But you can do much more than that. Here's how:

Many times your opponent realizes he's wrong. He's already changed his mind and wants to agree with you, but unfortunately his ego gets in the way of his good judgment. His pride prevents him from admitting his mistake. If you find your opponent in that spot, open the door for him. Help him find a way out of his dilemma.

One way you can do this is to suggest that he might not have had all the facts when he made up his mind. You might say something like this, "John, if you didn't know about this, I can see why you made the decision you did. I'd have done the same thing myself."

Even if John did have all the facts, he will grab at this lifeline you've just thrown him. All he need do is say he didn't have that fact and he's out of his corner. You've achieved your goal. You've helped him save face.

When you help a person save face and keep from destroying his pride, you'll gain a friend who'll support you all the way. When that happens, count yourself lucky. Friends like that are hard to come by.

Before I move on to the next chapter, I want to wrap this one up for you in this quick summary.

To deal with your listener's resistance and overcome his objections, use the following techniques:

1. To find the deep or hidden reason for a person's objections, keep asking one or all of the following three questions:

   (a) Why or why not?
   (b) And in addition to that?
   (c) Is there any other reason?

2. Turn his objection into a benefit for him.

3. Appeal to his heart as well as to his head.

4. Ask questions in such a way that your listener is forced to agree with you.

5. Use this 6-step technique for winning every argument:

   (a) Let the other person state his side of the case first.

   (b) Probe and explore his argument for weak points.

   (c) When you hear expressions of self-doubt from him, you know it's time to state your side of the matter.

   (d) State your case moderately, accurately, and with sincerity. Remember you can never win until your listener accepts your viewpoint as his very own.

   (e) Be willing to compromise on minor matters. Give ground on trifles—not on principles.

   (f) Help the other person save face.

chapter 14

The 10 Secrets of Persuasion That Successful Super Salespeople Use

You may not realize this, but everything you do requires salesmanship in one way or another. No matter what you do for a living, there's always an idea or a product or a service waiting to be sold to someone. And selling requires persuasive conversation.

We are all constantly selling ourselves in some way, literally from the cradle to the grave. A baby sells its mother (by crying) on the idea of eating. A boy sells his father (by perseverance) on the idea of buying him a bicycle. A man sells his boss (by increased job efficiency) on the idea of a pay raise. The congressman sells the voters (by exhortation) on sending him back to Washington for another term. The old man tries to sell his God (by prayer and Bible study) on the salvation of his soul. The person doing the selling is either a good salesman or a poor one, depending on how well he does his job.

I want to use this chapter to help make you into a better salesperson through the conversation you use. To do that, I'll give you ten techniques that super salespeople use to become successful. When you use these trade secrets,

YOU'LL GAIN THESE PHENOMENAL BENEFITS FOR YOURSELF

1. *You can improve your own sales performance,* when you learn the techniques that super salespeople use to get to the top of their profession. If you're not in sales work, that's all right, too. You can use these same techniques in your church or social activities to take charge. And you can use them on your spouse to get him or her to see things your way and to do what you want.

2. *You'll be able to sell your ideas to others.* Getting a good idea is one thing. Getting the right person to accept it is quite another. No matter how good your idea might be, it's useless unless you can sell it to the ultimate user. The techniques in this chapter will show you how to do that, and that's a mighty big benefit for you.

3. *You can get your own way every time* when you can sell other

176

people on your ideas or on your way of doing things. You can use these sophisticated sales techniques on tough bosses, obstinate customers and clients, stubborn authorities, and anyone else who's been keeping you from getting what you want.

4. *You'll become a master in the art of persuasion.* The power of persuasion is one of the finest forms of selling. When you reach the point at which you can persuade your prospect to buy something he doesn't even want, you've become a super salesman and a true master in the art of persuasion.

TEN TECHNIQUES YOU CAN USE TO GAIN THESE AMAZING BENEFITS

How You Can Get Your Prospect to Say "Yes" Immediately

Although all 10 of these techniques are highly important, successful super salespeople place this one right at the top of the list.

Jessica Masters, a highly successful mutual fund saleswoman in a business that's often regarded as strictly a man's world, says that it's extremely important to get your prospective client to say "yes" immediately.

"I word all my questions to a new prospect so the only possible answer he can give me is "yes," Jessica says. "For instance, I might say, 'Would you like to have your investment risk reduced to the absolute minimum?' Of course, the answer always has to be 'yes.' How could it be anything else? Then I might follow up my first question with, 'If I can show you how you can gain the maximum return on your investment along with that minimum risk, would you be interested?' Again, the answer has to be 'yes.'

"You can use many other ways to phrase your questions to insure getting a 'yes' answer. The important thing is getting the prospect to say 'yes' so continually that when the final buying decision has to be made, the word 'yes' just falls out of his mouth automatically."

You can use this same technique on your wife, your husband, your children, your friends and associates, anyone. Just get the other person to say "yes" at the beginning. Keep him from saying "no" by the way you word your questions.

A "Yes" answer establishes not only the right psychological frame of mind, but also the proper physiological conditions in his body. All the body processes, both physical and mental, are in an accepting, relaxed, and open attitude when a person says "yes."

By the same token, just one single "No!" changes all these psychological and physiological processes into a fighting and defiant mood of rejection. All the body's systems—glandular, muscular, neurological—prepare themselves for combat. If your wife or husband, your children, a prospective client or customer, or your boss says "no!" to you at the very beginning, it requires a near miracle to change that person's negative attitude to a positive one.

So plan your approach to get an affirmative answer from the person at the very start of your conversation. If you want to win people over to your way of thinking, if you want to make a sale or win a friend, then get the other person to agree with you immediately. You'll get your own way every time when you do. This technique is one of the trade secrets of super salespeople. Use it; it will give you unlimited powers of persuasion and that's really the name of the game.

Discovering the Real Reason Behind the Person's Objection

In previous chapters I've told you that people will usually have two reasons for doing or not doing something: One reason that sounds good to the listener, and another reason that he keeps hidden all to himself.

At that time I also said that one of the best ways to drag that hidden reason out of a person was to keep asking, "And besides that . . . in addition to tnat," or "Isn't there some other reason you object to this? Is this your only reason for not accepting my offer?" This method of questioning is extremely valuable to you when you're trying to convert a reluctant prospect into a solid customer.

But there are still other methods you can use when you want to get information, not only from a prospective client or customer, but also from other people such as the members of your own family or from your employees or associates. The most powerful word in the English language that you can use to keep the other person talking so you can learn what you want to know from him is a simple little three-letter one, *why*? Let me give you an example so I can show you how well this technique works:

A friend of mine, Arthur Harper, for years now has told me he didn't believe in life insurance. So I was really surprised the other day when he said he'd bought a $100,000 policy from a young man the week before. When I asked him how in the world this could have happened, here's what he said:

"When this young man came calling on me, Jim, I told him I didn't believe in life insurance," Arthur said. "But instead of arguing with me as all the other salesmen had done before, he simply looked me straight in the eye and asked, 'Why?'

"Well, I explained to him why, but every time I stopped for breath, he'd ask, 'Why?' and the more I talked, the more I realized there was something the matter with my reasoning. Finally, I convinced myself that I was wrong, so I bought some insurance from him.

"That young man didn't sell me anything. He just kept asking me 'Why?' I sold myself and he made the profit. Smartest salesman I've ever met."

As I've said, you don't need to be in business or in sales to use this highly effective "why" technique. You can use it in church, PTA, your club, or in any other social activity you can think of to persuade people to your way of thinking. It will always work; I can assure you of that.

So use this "why" technique yourself the next time you want someone to do something and they're hesitant at first. They'll actually end up convincing themselves that what you're asking is the right thing for them to do. It's one of the easiest ways I know of to persuade people to your way of thinking.

How You Can Use This Important Sales Secret Yourself

I've already told you previously that to find out what the other person wants and then to help him get it is not only one of the most important secrets of selling, but that it is also the number one rule in all human relationships. To prove that point to you, I want to give you an example of how it can be used in all walks of life. I am indebted to Walter Parkhill for telling me this story.

"A few years ago, I was elected superintendent of our church Sunday school," Walter told me. "I felt that the immediate need of our church school was for a larger teaching organization so I asked our minister to give me five minutes to talk to the congregation after our Sunday morning services.

"Now I could've stood up and complained that this job of superintendent had been shoved off on me—after all, how many times had I heard that complaint before from previous holders of that office—but I didn't. I knew I'd have a far better chance of getting what I wanted from the congregation if I talked about the things they wanted. So here's what I said to them:

"'I want to talk to you for a few moments about some of the things you want for your children. You want them to come here to

Sunday school where they can meet other good children and learn more about life from the truths of this great Book. You and I want our children to keep from making some of the mistakes I have made, and possibly even some of you have made. Now how can we do this?

"'First of all, we need a larger teaching staff. We now have only 6 teachers in our Sunday school, and that includes our minister. We need at least 20. Some of you may hesitate to teach because you feel you don't know enough about the Bible. I felt the same way when I took over a class a year ago. Let me tell you this: You'll learn more about the Bible in 6 months by teaching the children for 30 minutes or so each Sunday morning than you'll ever learn in 6 years by just reading it all by yourself.

"'You husbands and wives can study and prepare the Sunday school lessons together. It will give you something to do in common besides watching television. And it'll bring you a lot closer together than those TV programs ever will. When your children see you taking an active interest, they'll become more interested, too. You all have the talents and ability to do this. I don't know of any better way to improve and multiply your talents than through this wonderful work of teaching a child to live a better life. I know that is exactly what you want for your own children.'

"Do you know what happened? We got 25 new teachers that morning, five more than I'd asked for! In fact, we had more teachers than there were children to go around at first. So we started a house-to-house canvass in our neighborhood to invite more children to come to our Sunday school classes. After the children started coming, their parents began to follow. We reached the point where our original building was full and overflowing so last year we built a brand-new church! All this from talking to people for 5 minutes about what they wanted most of all and then showing them how they could get it."

How to Sell Benefits Instead of Features

An inexperienced salesperson will often make the mistake of trying to sell a product's features rather than its benefits. What's the difference between a feature and a benefit? Simple. Let me show you that by a couple of examples. The squelch control on a CB radio is a *feature*. Since it gets rid of static and background noise so you can hear the other party better, that's a *benefit*. A 30-inch blade on your lawnmower is a *feature*. The time you save in cutting your grass with that blade is a *benefit*. Another way of saying it is that a feature is something that the product has. What that feature will do for you is the benefit.

Sears Roebuck is a master of the art of using features to sell benefits. Sears teaches its salespeople to offer the customer such benefits as comfort and convenience, safety and security, a feeling of importance and pride of ownership, good health and freedom from pain, a material gain or a savings of time, money, and effort.

But before a salesman can offer any benefit to the customer, he has to know his product inside out. He has to know which feature offers which specific benefit. If he doesn't, he won't be working for Sears for very long. Sears must be doing something right. They're the biggest, most successful retailer in the entire world and they've held that position since 1966.

Now you have a fistful of benefits that you can offer your listener, too: the attainment of those 14 basic needs and desires every person has that I told you about in Chapter One. Figure out which of those basic desires he can achieve by doing as you ask, show him how to get them, and you'll win him over to your way of thinking with no trouble at all. You can persuade him to do what you want every single time.

How to Concentrate on a Single Point and Not Scatter Your Fire

"One of the secrets of persuasion that smart salespeople use is to concentrate on a single point and not scatter your fire," says Doris Daniels, a real estate broker from Kansas City, Missouri. "Let me give you an example of exactly what I mean by that.

"Several years ago, some developers wanted to build a shopping mall out east of Independence just off of Interstate 70. They asked me to locate a suitable site of at least 80 acres for them.

"I found the perfect place, some undeveloped land owned by three brothers and a sister, all of whom lived and worked in the city. It had been left to them when their parents died. None of them could farm it and all of them wanted to sell it, but they'd never been able to agree on a single price. When I found this out, I knew at once that this was my one single point on which I had to concentrate to get them to sell their land.

"I got an option from each one of them: four options at four different prices. Then I called them all together to discuss the matter. 'Your prices are all too high,' I told them. 'Here's what the developers are willing to pay you for that land. If you won't agree to that price, then they'll go somewhere else.'

"I pointed out that this was the first time they'd had an offer for the land and that if they passed it up, it would probably be the last one for a long time to come.

"Then I said that unless they could agree on a single price, they'd never be able to sell that land for as long as they all lived. This was the one major obstacle I had to overcome so it was the one point I concentrated on.

"They had to agree on a single price before they could ever sell. Once I made that point crystal-clear to them, then the rest was easy. Today, there's a beautiful shopping mall where before there was nothing but wasteland, all because I concentrated their attention on that one single point."

You can do the same. You'll find it's much easier to persuade others to do as you want when you concentrate on a single weak point and don't scatter your fire all over the place.

How to Keep from Losing the Sale After It's Made

"Too many sales can be lost because salesmen talk too much," says Sherman Wilson, an agency manager for a large well-known insurance company. "Once you've closed your sale, stop talking. Get the money or the signature or whatever you need and then, to put it quite bluntly, *shut up!* Otherwise, you're liable to unsell your sale."

Sherman's company has a simple three-point rule for its salespeople to follow: (1) Get in. (2) Get the sale. (3) Get out!

Talking too much and losing your listener is a bad habit many people besides salespeople have. Some preachers have the same problem. I know that from my own childhood. You see, my father was always extremely critical of a minister who kept on preaching after his sermon was finished, especially if he went beyond high noon.

My father loved to fish on weekends and had he had his own way, he'd have been sitting on the river bank early Sunday morning. However, to keep peace in the family, he took us all to church, and waited until Sunday afternoon to pursue his first love.

One particular Sunday on the way home from church, my mother asked him how he had enjoyed the sermon. It was the wrong day to ask. The minister had been unusually wound up, the sermon had run to nearly half-past twelve, and my father was going to be late getting down to the river.

But with a patience with which I've never been blessed, he turned to her, and said, "He said more than he had to talk about!"

So be smart. Don't let people say this about you. Know when it's time to quit and then do so. In fact, sometimes it's even better to quit before you're through so you can leave something to talk about the next time.

Selling the Right Person on the Right Product

You'll save much time when you concentrate your efforts on the right person. Time is important to all of us. It's a successful salesman's most valuable asset. He'll never waste it by giving his sales pitch to someone who can't make the buying decision. There's a saying among successful sales people that goes like this: *Sell the secretary on seeing the boss; sell the boss on buying your product.*

There are exceptions to this rule, of course, just as there are exceptions to any rule. For instance, if the secretary is going to use the equipment you're selling, then get her on your side first. Sell her and let her sell the boss. Let me give you a specific example of that technique:

"I called on this particular company only to find that the boss was out of town," Roger Peterson, a young typewriter and office equipment salesman, told me. "But rather than waste the trip entirely, I demonstrated our new typewriter to his secretary so she could learn its advantages for herself.

"Later on when I called back, the boss told me he had already reached a tentative agreement with another company.

"'But your secretary knows that my typewriter will save her time and energy and turn out better work than any other,' I told him. 'Please ask her for yourself.'

"So he called his secretary in for verification of my remarks. She was so enthusiastic in her endorsement that he forgot all about his tentative agreement and bought a dozen new typewriters for the company from me."

This technique will work in other situations as well. For instance, when I got married more than 40 years ago, it was still the custom to introduce the prospective in-laws to each other on some pleasant Sunday afternoon so they could size each other up and find out about their religion, their politics, their drinking habits, and their economic and social status.

On one such occasion when my future in-laws were meeting my

parents for the first time, my mother took me aside in the kitchen and said, "You're trying to sell the wrong person, son. Her mother's already sold on you. You don't have to soft-soap her any longer. Now go after her father. He's the one you need to convince, for he makes the decisions in that house—not her. She just came along for the ride."

Use This Technique and You Will Always Succeed

Another characteristic of the top-notch salesperson is to keep coming back time after time even though the prospect continually says, "No."

"How many times do you call on a person before you finally give him up?" I once asked Craig Lambert, a top-notch hardware salesman out of Atlanta, Georgia.

"It depends upon which one of us dies first," Craig said.

Craig then went on to tell me that if he is convinced a prospect is worth calling on, he will keep calling as long as that person is there. "I once made 40 calls on one man before he gave me an order," Craig said. "Finally, he told me that he could not keep from buying from me. When I asked him why he said that, he replied, 'Your persistence has paralyzed my resistance!'"

You can use the same technique to get results, too. Just keep calling back until you get what you want. Sooner or later your persistence will paralyze your listener's resistance, too.

The Best Way to Clinch a Sale

This procedure will work like magic for you whenever there is paperwork to be signed. If no contract is called for, make one up anyway.

Have the contract all ready with your prospect's name, address, the amount to be paid. Every single thing must be completed so all the individual needs to do is sign his name.

When the person starts telling you all the reasons he cannot accept your proposition, don't argue with him. And don't fold up your tent and walk away. Just hand him your pen and point out the big "X" where his signature goes.

Do you think this method is too presumptuous? Well, it is not. You'll be glad to know that you'll never make anyone angry by using this procedure. The magic of this technique is that you concentrate a person's mind on signing—not on refusing.

You crowd out all the reasons he thinks he should not until his mind becomes filled with all the reasons that he should. His thoughts tend always to be translated into positive action.

Why You Should Always Leave the Person with a Good Taste in His Mouth

Before you part company, stress again all the benefits the person is going to gain from his transaction with you. The best business is repeat business. The one-time sale where you have to make a new customer each time is a tough business to be in.

Let me ask you this: After you've bought a new car, how many salesmen have ever contacted you again? I've bought a number of new cars in my life, and of all those salesmen, only one ever bothered to get in touch with me afterward. The truth is, when I'd take my car to the dealer where I'd bought it to be serviced, most salesmen would run and hide to avoid hearing a possible complaint from me.

Let me give you a little tip about doing business with people. Never forget a customer—never let a customer forget you. Another way of saying it is, *the best way to get new customers is to take care of the old ones.*

So always leave the person with a good feeling toward you. You might have to come back to the same well more than once for a drink of water. If you do, you won't have to work nearly as hard the second time.

In summary, here are the ten secrets of persuasion that all successful super salespeople use:

1. Word your sales talk so your prospect has to say "Yes" immediately. Never ask him a question that requires a "No" answer.

2. Keep digging until you find out the real reason behind a person's objections.

3. Find out what the other person wants and then show him how to get it.

4. Sell your prospect benefits—not features.

5. Concentrate on a single point—don't scatter your fire.

6. Don't lose your sale after it's made by continuing to talk.

7. Sell the right person on the right product. For example, sell the secretary on seeing the boss; sell the boss on buying your product or your service.

8. Never give up. If you think a prospect is worth calling on, keep going back until he says yes to you.

9. The best way to clinch a sale is to get your prospect's signature on a contract. The magic of this technique is that you concentrate his mind on signing—not on refusing.

10. Always leave the person with a good taste in his mouth. Then you won't nave to sell him all over again the next time you call.

If your profession is selling and things have been a bit rough for you, practice these ten techniques for the next several weeks and see for yourself the change they can make in your life. You'll be deeply gratified with the tremendous results that you get. Not only will you have more confidence in yourself, but your income will go up, too. I guarantee it.

chapter 15

How You Can
Use Persuasion
to Gain People's
Complete Cooperation
and Full Support

Cooperation from others is one of the major factors of success, no matter what profession or occupation you're in. One of the first things a person learns when he goes to work is that all business is a cooperative enterprise. You must cooperate with someone and offer to do something for him if you want him in turn to cooperate with you and do something for you.

And this basic fact of human relationships doesn't apply only to business or earning a living. It applies to your entire life, to everything you do. In your personal life, in your family relationships, in your church, civic groups, school, community affairs, whatever—you must cooperate with someone, and they must cooperate with you and support you if you are to accomplish whatever you set out to do.

What it boils down to is that you simply cannot succeed in life without the complete cooperation and full support of other people. If you want to get ahead in this world, no matter what you do, you must get other people on your side first. And that's what this chapter is all about.

BENEFITS YOU'LL GAIN WHEN YOU COOPERATE WITH PEOPLE *FIRST*

1. People will respect you and have confidence in you.
2. They'll give you their willing obedience, loyal cooperation, and full support.
3. When people support you, they'll accept your leadership without question.
4. They'll work with initiative, ingenuity, and enthusiasm.
5. They'll work together as a team with high spirit and morale— with conviction, purpose, and direction toward a common goal.
6. You'll make them feel they belong where they are.
7. They'll work as hard as you do to get the job done.

TECHNIQUES YOU CAN USE TO GAIN THESE GREAT BENEFITS

A Method of Persuasion You Can Use to Gain Cooperation

There is no deep, dark, or hidden mystery about how to win the cooperation of other people. It simply comes down to this: If you want to gain the complete cooperation and full support of others, then you must give them your cooperation and support first. If you'll look at the benefits I said you could gain from this chapter, you'll note I emphasized that you had to give your cooperation to people first to achieve them.

Now successful people know you must always give before you can get, for when you do, you always get back more than you give away. So if you want to get cooperation and support from people, your most persuasive tool is to give them your cooperation and support first. You can easily tell if you're doing that in your own business. If the people who work for you are prompt and cheerful, filled with enthusiasm, enjoy their jobs, and are willing to put in an extra hour or so when it's required, or when you ask them to do so—you can be sure you're doing the right thing.

But if you're not giving your people your complete cooperation and full support first, you can always tell that quite easily, too. They'll be just as disinterested in cooperating with you and supporting you as you are with them. They'll drag into work late, be indifferent about their jobs, and run for the time clock even before the whistle blows. If that's the way your people act, don't ask them for anything extra. You won't get it.

So remember, *you must always give before you can expect to get, and you always get back exactly what you give away, but the return is usually multiplied many times over.*

This idea is so important, it should be practiced every day in your contacts with others—your employees, associates, customers, clients, friends, even your own family—if you want to be successful and enjoy your success all at the same time.

Five Ways to Win and Hold the Confidence of Others

If you want to persuade people to support you and cooperate with you, you must win their confidence first. There is no better way to win and hold a person's confidence than to tell him the whole truth. By the same token, there is no quicker way to lose his confidence and trust than to lie to him. So if you want to persuade people to have confidence in you and trust you, follow these five simple guidelines:

1. *Practice absolute honesty and truthfulness at all times.* I can think of no exception whatever to this rule. Of course, this doesn't mean you should intentionally insult a person or hurt his feelings by telling the truth. If you can say nothing good about a person, then do exactly that: say nothing. Just take inventory of your own defects, not someone else's. If you're like most of us, that will keep you quite busy enough.

2. *Make your word your bond.* If you want people to have full and absolute confidence in you, then your word must be your bond. To make sure you always keep your word, keep these three simple points in mind.

   a. Never make a promise you cannot keep.

   b. Never make a decision you cannot support.

   c. Never issue an order you can't enforce.

3. *Be accurate and truthful in all your written statements.* Your signature on any document or letter is just as important as what you say to a person face-to-face. When you sign a check, your signature is your certification that you have money in the bank. Your signature in your work and your business must carry the same weight.

4. *Stand for what you believe to be right.* Have the courage of your convictions, no matter what the consequences. Never compromise your standards; never prostitute your principles. If you are ever tempted to compromise, then place honesty, your sense of duty, your personal honor and integrity above all else.

5. *Be ready to accept the blame if you are wrong.* If you are wrong, have the courage to say so. Always be willing to take the blame if you are at fault or if you've made a mistake. Most people are willing to take the credit, but few will accept the responsibility for an error.

Here's a Sure-Fire Method to Gain a Person's Trust

The most important thing a trial lawyer can do in presenting his case in court is to bring on his witnesses. Naturally the judge and jury feel that the lawyer is prejudiced in his views. If he is the prosecuting attorney, he sees things differently than if he were the defense. So most things a lawyer says are taken with a grain of salt. He has to prove his case to win the confidence and support of the jury. He does this by calling his witnesses to the stand to verify that what he says is true.

You can also use witnesses outside the courtroom to persuade people and to establish the confidence of others in what you say and do. It's the most reliable way of doing business. Let me give you a specific example of how best to use this technique to win the support of others.

One winter, when my wife and I were still living in the midwest, we decided to spend several months in Arizona. We had a travel trailer to live in, so I wrote to a dozen different parks in Phoenix and the surrounding area requesting information about their services and facilities.

Seven of the 12 sent back beautifully printed colored brochures and form letters telling me what they had to offer. Four of them didn't answer. The twelfth one sent me a brochure, too, but he also enclosed a personal letter with the names and addresses of people in Missouri who'd spent their winters with him before. Two of those names were people who lived right in my city of Springfield.

"Please call or write to any of these people," the letter said. "They can tell you far better than any brochure what I offer and whether you'd enjoy staying with us or not." You know where we spent the winter, of course.

Why This Method of Persuasion Is So Highly Effective

Persuasion takes many forms. One is teamwork. If you want people to cooperate with you, support you, and back you to the hilt, then you must be part of the team, too. You must be willing to share the same hardships, the same discomforts, and in some cases, the same dangers they do. This is especially true if you work in a modern industrial plant.

If you think today's industrial plants are not dangerous to work in, then you've never been inside a modern steel plant, a textile mill, or a rubber factory. Modern machinery, although highly efficient, can be deadly dangerous in spite of all the safety precautions. I've seen enough workers with missing fingers, hands, or arms to know.

I'm not suggesting that you should run a mixing mill, a drill press, or a rubber calendar if that's not your job. But I am saying that if you have an air-conditioned office while your employees must of necessity work in sweltering heat cooled only by ventilating fans, then you can cooperate and show your support for your people by getting out there and sweating with them side by side once in a while.

No one will expect you to spend eight hours with them that way. That's not your job and your employees know it. But a simple act of cooperation like this will establish a bond between you and your subordinates that you'll never be able to gain in any other way. You won't need to use words to persuade them to cooperate with you and support you. Your actions can be the most persuasive technique you can ever use. Let me give you a specific example of what I mean:

"I never go through the plant but that I stop and lend a hand somewhere to someone," Ben Watson, an assistant rubber plant manager, told me. "For instance, there's always a skid that has layers of rubber stuck to it. It's tough to get one layer off and into a mixing mill, so whenever I see a millman sweating and tugging away at a stubborn piece of rubber, I stop and help him for a minute.

"Maybe it doesn't really help him that much, but that's not the point anyway. We rub elbows, I get my hands dirty and sweaty, and we both part with a big fat grin for each other. That's why I stopped to help in the first place."

Ben's method of lending a helping hand to gain people's cooperation and support is especially good to use when you're setting out on a new project and people are a little backward about getting started. If you pitch in first, they'll be persuaded to cooperate with you, support you, back you to the hilt, and follow your lead.

Only one small note of caution is in order here, and that is: When the boss gets too involved in the work, then he's no longer the boss. So keep that one thought in mind. Before you get in too deep, be sure you have a way out.

How to Get People to Support You Even When You're the Boss

When you're the boss and need people to help you do the job, you can usually get it done in one of three ways:

1. *You can give a person a direct order* to do something. Even if that person is your employee and has no other choice than to do as you say, this is normally the least desirable of the three methods, for you will usually get only the bare minimum results.

2. *You can ask a person to help you do the work,* using your already established procedure. This is better than the first method, but it still leaves a great deal to be desired. This technique is often called

"cooperation," but that word can be grossly misleading. For instance, management always says it cooperates fully with labor. What this usually means is that management furnishes the methods while labor provides only the means. But that's not cooperation at all. That's only giving lip service to the idea.

3. *You can ask a person for his ideas* on the best way to get the job done. This is by far the most desirable method you can use. You can use it to persuade a person to give you his full cooperation and support. He'll back you to the hilt and do whatever you say when you ask him for his opinions and advice.

Why the Participatory Management Technique Is So Effective

Asking an employee for his ideas on how to get the job done is often called *participatory management*. It is a highly effective technique to use, for when you ask a person for his opinions and advice on how to do the job, you've made him feel important and that's one of the 14 secret motivators that turn people on.

Making people feel important is a highly persuasive stimulant and incentive to produce. As a friend of mine, Dick Evans, told me. "When the company president called me into his office to ask for my opinion, I was so proud I couldn't get my hat on my head for a week!"

Not only do you make a person feel proud and important when you ask for his ideas and recommendations on how to do something, but you also satisfy these additional desires of his:

1. Recognition of efforts, reassurance of worth
2. Social or group approval, acceptance by others
3. The desire to excel, to be the best
4. The feeling of belonging, being a team member
5. The opportunity for creative expression
6. The accomplishment of something worthwhile
7. A sense of personal power
8. A feeling of self-esteem and self-respect
9. Emotional security

When you can do all this for an employee just by asking for his ideas and opinions, you know full well he will be persuaded to back you to the hilt and support you in whatever you ask him to do. His cooperation will be automatic.

A Specific Example of How to Use Participatory Management in Business

As Jimmy Durante always used to say, "Everybody wants to get into the act!" Employees are no different. They want to have some say in how things are done, too.

You can make them feel it's *their* company, department, or section by giving them a say-so in the planning, decision-making formulation of rules and regulations, policies and procedures. You can use any number of ways to let people participate in the management process. Let me give you one of the best ones:

One of the biggest personnel problems in companies and corporations is that executives and administrators at the top make up *all* the rules and regulations for people at the bottom.

But most people—and that includes me, too—don't like being told what to or what not to do. They rebel automatically. After all, rules and regulations are restrictions on their personal and individual liberties. So people tend to resist those rules or disobey them altogether.

If that's your problem, let me suggest that you use the method Pamela Clark, a personnel manager, recommends. Here's what she says about how her company uses the participatory management technique to get results.

"One of the best ways we've found to cooperate with our people is to let them make up their own rules and regulations to govern themselves," Pamela says. "After all, no two departments have the same functions or identical tasks so it's difficult for top management to work out rules that apply to everyone.

"Not only that, we've found that when employees are allowed to set up their own rules for their departments, they are usually a lot stricter on themselves than we are. And since those rules are their own, the ones they personally made up, they'll be much more likely to follow them than when management tells them what to or what not to do. It's an excellent way of using participatory management to persuade people to cooperate with us and we like the results we get."

Other Places You Can Use Participatory Management

Participatory management doesn't apply only to business and earning a living. You can use this method on others to persuade them to do what you want them to do. You can use it in all your personal relationships, your church and social activities, civic groups, school and community affairs. This technique also works on your friends and neighbors, too.

For instance, I have a neighbor two doors down the street from me, a retired electrical contractor, who's a regular handyman around the house. I'm all thumbs when it comes to sharpening knives or lawnmower blades, fixing a dripping faucet, repairing a faulty window latch or doorknob—that sort of thing.

All I have to do is ask Hal for his opinion or his advice on the subject, and out comes his tool chest. He has helped me install my ceiling fans and my garage door opener, assemble my bookcases and microwave cabinet, and Heaven only knows what else. He even made me a half-dozen fishing leaders complete with hooks, sinkers, and all the trimmings when I merely mentioned that I wished I could catch fish the way he did!

You might ask what I'm giving Hal first to get all this cooperation and help from him. Fair enough. That's a good question and I'll answer it for you.

I'm fulfilling Hal's need for recognition of efforts; I'm offering him reassurance of his worth. I'm letting him know he's still wanted and appreciated—something that people especially need after retirement to keep from feeling useless. I'm feeding his ego and making him feel important by asking for his advice and his opinion. I give him a sense of personal power when he can do certain things far better than I can. And finally, I give him dignity and a sense of self-esteem by showing my respect for his abilities.

All in all, I think it's a fair trade. I'm giving Hal something he needs and wants. I'm getting advice, help, cooperation, and support from him in return.

Another good place to use participatory management is in your own family relationships. Marriage counselors tell me that the divorce rate is much lower with couples who use this technique.

I've also learned from educational authorities that teen-agers coming from families that practice this method in the home cause far fewer discipline problems for their teachers. They also get along much better with their fellow students.

So what it all comes down to is this: You can best succeed in life—financially, professionally, and personally—when you can persuade others to cooperate with you and support you; to back you to the hilt. And participatory management is one of the best ways you can do that.

So if you're looking for a reliable technique that you can use to get to the top quickly, then use this method in everything you do. It's a real key to your successful persuasion of people to do what you want them to do every time.

How to Use the Buffer Technique to Get Cooperation and Support

The buffer technique is one of the best methods you can use to get people to cooperate with you, support you, and back you to the hilt. Let me show you what it is and how well it works.

A company controller, Earl R., was having all sorts of trouble with the people under him. Late payrolls were an especially sore point with him for they were a constantly recurring problem.

When one of the department heads would take him to task for this, Earl would snap back testily, and say, "That's not my fault. I don't make up the blasted payrolls myself." He would then pass the buck to one of his subordinates. That person would then catch it from both Earl and the complaining department head.

"Earl, you're taking the wrong approach to solving this problem," I said to him one day. "As long as you pass the blame down to someone else, you're going to have this difficulty. You're never going to solve your problem this way.

"But as soon as you accept the responsibility for the mistakes of your subordinates and act as a buffer between them and those complaining department heads, you'll find that your people will back you to the hilt. They'll get the job done right and on time. If you protect them, they'll protect you."

Earl was doubtful about this solution to his problem, but he decided to try it, more or less as a last resort. Naturally, this method worked just as I knew it would.

I learned a long time ago that you must always accept complete responsibility and take the blame for the failures of those who work for you if you want them to support you 100 percent, cooperate with you, and back you to the hilt.

When you do this, you'll find people will go all out to keep mistakes from happening. When you keep them out of trouble, they are anxious to keep you out of trouble, too. The buffer technique, properly used, is a great persuader.

Three Magic Words That Will Get People to Support You

There are very few words that can work magic for you, but "I need you" are three you can always use to gain cooperation and support. They build up a person's ego and make him feel important as well as being wanted and needed. I must admit that I've had others use these three words on me with devastating effect more times than I care to admit. You see, I'm susceptible, too!

People always want to feel they are needed, no matter who they are or what they do. Earlier, I mentioned my next-door neighbor, who knows more about botany than most professional botanists do. I'm always asking him for advice about some plant or shrub or tree.

When Bill tells me what to do, I thank him and apologize for bothering him and taking up his time. "Bother, my eye," he says. "When you're retired, you begin to feel completely unnecessary and unwanted. It's good to feel needed again."

If you want your wife to be happy that she married you, let her know she is both wanted and needed, not only in words, but also by your actions. And this same philosophy applies to the wife as well, so let your husband know that you need and want him, too.

If you want to get better cooperation and support from your employees, let them know you need them . . . tell them how important they are . . . how valuable their work is to you.

If you've never used this phrase, "I need you," before, do so for the next several weeks. You'll be absolutely astounded at the good results you'll get. This technique, as well as the others I've given you in this chapter, will literally work wonders for you. And that's the truth.

In conclusion, here are the techniques you can use to gain people's complete cooperation and full support:

1. If you want to gain the complete cooperation and full support of others, give them your cooperation and support first. As you give, so shall you get.

2. Five ways to win and hold the confidence of others:
   a. Practice absolute honesty and truthfulness at all times.
   b. Make your word your bond.
   c. Be accurate and truthful in all your written statements
   d. Stand for what you believe to be right.
   e. Be ready to accept the blame if you are wrong.

3. To win a person's trust and confidence, prove your point by bringing on your witnesses.

4. A good way to gain cooperation and support from your subordinates is to help them do the job. However, remember that when the boss gets too involved in the actual work, he's no longer the boss.

5. The best way to get people to support you even when you're the boss is to ask for their ideas on how to get the job done. This is often called *participatory management*. It can be used effectively in both business and the home.

6. Use the buffer technique to get cooperation and support from your subordinates. When you protect and defend your people and keep them out of trouble, they will be anxious to keep you out of trouble, too.

7. Three little words that can work magic for you are "I need you." Use them; they'll literally work miracles for you.

PART V

Special Conversational Situations

Part V, Special Conversational Situations, *includes Chapters Sixteen through Nineteen and shows you how to use your conversational expertise in certain specific circumstances.*

For instance, I'm sure that at one time or another you'll be asked to give a talk or make a speech. Chapter Sixteen will show you exactly how to do that. And you'll also learn the trade secrets of professional platform speakers in Chapter Seventeen.

In Chapter Eighteen, you will see how you can use your conversational abilities in important business situations to gain your goals. In Chapter Nineteen, you'll discover the techniques of talking with all sorts of people at different business and social levels.

chapter 16

How to Give a Talk
or Make a Speech
Like a Professional:
A 7-Point Checklist

When you know how to give a talk or make a speech like a professional, you can literally talk your way to success. One of the best ways to become prominent and well-known in your community is to speak at various business and social functions whenever you have the opportunity to do so.

If you're going to become a household name in your city, you must become well-known. People should recognize your name immediately. Becoming a good speaker who is always in demand is not the only way to gain recognition, but it is one of the best. Another way is to be your own press agent.

Get your name in the newspaper whenever possible. Offer to speak to church or civic groups without any sort of reimbursement just as long as they promise to send notices to local papers to publicize the event.

If you're an authority on any subject, you can get on local radio and television talk shows. Local program directors develop ulcers trying to find the right people and get enough interesting material to fill their own programming requirements. They'll welcome you with open arms if your subject is timely and you really know what you're talking about.

To sum up this idea of being your own press agent or your own public relations person, let me say this: If you don't blow your own horn, no one else will, so toot away and enjoy it!

SIX SPECTACULAR BENEFITS THAT YOU'LL GAIN

When you know how to give a talk or make a speech like a professional,

1. You'll become prominent and well-known in your community. People will recognize your name immediately.

2. You'll become a powerful and influential person. You can easily be the leader in all the social, political, and civic affairs in which you participate.

3. If you're in business for yourself, such recognition and prominence will bring you an increased number of customers.

4. If you're working for a company or a large corporation, you'll attract the favorable attention of your boss.

5. You'll be regarded as an authority in your own particular field. People will turn to you for advice, for your suggestions and recommendations.

6. You'll also develop these 5 desirable character traits:
   a. A winning, positive, and outgoing personality
   b. Greater inner security and self-confidence
   c. The ability to think clearly and to express yourself precisely
   d. The skill to get others to think and act favorably toward you
   e. The power to motivate others to do your will

TECHNIQUES YOU CAN USE TO GAIN THESE MARVELOUS BENEFITS

How to Overcome Your Fear of Giving a Talk or Making a Speech

I suppose that speaking in public strikes fear in the heart of nearly everyone at first. I know I nearly panicked the first time I stood up in front of a large audience. My throat was dry; my voice was raspy. My palms were sweaty and my heart was pounding wildly.

But when I got the first sentence out, I immediately felt better. As I continued to speak, my fears quickly faded away. Confidence came to me for as soon as I did the thing I feared to do, I gained the power to do it.

Marjorie Reynolds, an author of self-improvement books and a popular lecturer, says she used to suffer untold agonies before every one of her talks. But gradually her fear lessened as she kept on speaking until she completely overcame it, simply by doing the thing she was so afraid to do. Last year she spoke more than 100 times to large audiences all across the country. She said her only regret was that a year was only 365 days long.

Doing the thing you fear to do so you will gain the power to do it is such an important idea, I want to give you some other examples to illustrate its use. If you were to gain only this one thought out of the entire book, it would be worth more to you than ten times the price you paid.

For instance, if you want to become a painter, then you must paint. There simply is no other way to become an artist. You can dream all day long about how famous and how successful you are as a painter, but until you actually pick up the brush and start painting, you will never gain the power to do it.

If you want to become a writer, then you must write. If you want to become a concert pianist, then you must practice and play the piano day after day after day. The same principle applies to golf, baseball, swimming, science, medicine, business, salesmanship, and so on. You must make the first move yourself. Until you do that, you will never gain the power to do anything.

So, if you want to be able to talk to large groups of people or give a speech to a big audience, but are afraid to do so, start with a smaller group, say a Sunday school class, for example, so you can gain some confidence in yourself and in your own abilities. However you do it, just remember this one idea: *When you do the thing you fear to do, you will gain the power to do it and your fear will disappear.* Honestly now, it's just that simple.

Understanding the Difference Between Nervousness and Fear

I've already told you how you can get rid of your fear in speaking to a large audience, but you must also realize that the person who isn't nervous about speaking in public is as rare as a blacksmith or a good cribbage player. St. Louis University conducted a survey of its speech classes and found that 95 percent of their students suffered from nervousness both at the beginning and the end of the course.

But a certain amount of nervousness is actually useful. This is how your body prepares itself for this strange, new, and unknown situation. More adrenalin is pumped into your bloodstream. Your pulse beats faster, your breathing speeds up, your muscles tense. Don't become alarmed at this. It's just nature's way of doing things.

By understanding the basic physiological functions of your own body, you can keep this normal preparatory nervous tension from developing into uncontrollable fear. That extra shot of adrenalin will help you to think faster, to talk more easily, and to speak with greater emphasis and intensity than under ordinary normal circumstances. So don't worry about this kind of nervous tension. It's quite normal and to be expected, even in experienced professional speakers.

Why You Should Know the Purpose of Your Talk or Speech

Every speech or talk must have a worthwhile purpose or it should remain unspoken. If you don't yet know what you want to achieve by speaking to a group, then you are definitely not ready to go before your audience. Is your general purpose to order or direct—to inform— to persuade? Chances are if it's not a talk given to your employees or your subordinates as a part of your regular work in directing their activities, it'll be to inform, to persuade, or a combination of these two general purposes.

Every talk requires not only a general purpose, but also a specific objective to attain. Together they will make your speech more direct, forceful, and concise. They furnish a road map for you to follow. Once you have determined the general purpose of your talk—whether to direct, inform, or persuade—your next step will be to fix in your mind the specific objective you want to attain. Keeping your general purpose in mind will help you find clear explanations or convincing reasons to support your specific objective.

The answer to "What is my specific objective in giving this talk?" may be obvious or it may require long study. But if your specific objective is clear and distinct to you, then your talk will be effective. If you find it hard to isolate and define your exact objective, then your talk cannot possibly be effective. If it is not clear to you what you want to gain by speaking, it cannot be clear to anyone else either.

How to Identify and Pinpoint Your Main Ideas

"Successful speakers know that deciding what to leave out is just as important, if not more so, than what to leave in," says Allen Gannon. Allen teaches a class in public speaking in the adult education division of a university.

"Words, ideas, and facts that might be interesting as such, but that are not essential to the understanding or the acceptance of your specific objective can only weaken your talk or hide its main purpose " Mr. Gannon says.

"It doesn't really matter whether your talk is going to be based on your personal knowledge, reading and research, or both. The problem you usually face is too much material rather than not enough.

"So preparing your speech is primarily a process of defining, sifting, and discarding until you have left only one clear purpose or objective in mind and the main ideas necessary to either support it or reach it."

I can vouch for the truth of what Mr. Gannon says. I find that in writing a book, my biggest problem is not what to say, but what *not* to say.

Organizing Your Talk or Speech

Once you know your general purpose, after you've determined your specific objective, and pinpointed your main ideas to support it, you're ready to outline and organize your talk so you'll know exactly what you're going to say. If you don't organize your talk, you could sound like the speaker I once heard at a convention in Miami.

This gentleman rambled and wandered for five minutes or so without coming to any point whatever. His audience grew nervous and restless. Realizing this, he stopped, and said, "Please be patient with me. When I get through talking here, I'm going to say something." Only his sense of humor saved his speech from being a total failure. You might not be that lucky.

The best way to organize your talk is to make up a written outline. There isn't a single idea in the whole world that can't be expressed in writing. Even Einstein was able to reduce his complicated theory of relativity to a simple mathematical formula.

By the same token, if you can't get your proposition down in black and white, you're not ready to give a talk yet for you don't have a completely developed idea. You must know the details of your own idea if you expect to be able to put it across to someone else. The very act of finding the right words to express yourself will force you to make your thoughts and ideas clean, clear, and concise.

There are no doubt many good ways to make up an outline for your talk or speech, but in my own experience, I've found the following one to be most useful to me:

1. The opening
2. The benefits to be gained
3. Techniques to be used to gain those benefits
4. Examples of others who've gained the benefits by using those techniques
5. Conclusion

1. *The opening* sets the theme of your talk. It is always best to use a "grabber" to gain the immediate attention of your listeners. You can use any one of the following 5 methods to do that:

    a.   A startling statement

    b.   An unusual anecdote

    c.   A strong example

    d.   An authoritative quotation

    e.   An arresting question

As a professional platform speaker once told me, "Your opening sentences must shock your audience, startle them, or get their attention in some way. If you don't catch them with your first few sentences, you can resign yourself to talking to the wall." He also recommends you forget opening with a joke. "Leave that to someone like Bob Hope or David Brenner who has spent a lifetime learning to perfect that technique," he says.

2. *The benefits to be gained* are stressed to keep your listeners interested and to show them how your talk will be helpful to them. If I'm giving a talk to persuade my audience to do something, I will often combine steps one and two and open immediately with the benefits to be gained.

3. *Techniques to be used.* In the third step, you tell your listeners the methods they can use to gain the benefits you've offered them or told them about.

4. *Give them examples of others who've succeeded.* In this step you prove that what you say is true. You give your listeners concrete examples that show that the techniques you've offered really do work to gain the benefits. Your examples must be specific and give names, dates, places, and so on, as applicable.

5. *Your conclusion.* If your talk has been meant to persuade, then your conclusion would probably be an appeal for action of some sort. If your talk has been primarily to inform, then your conclusion should be a summary of your main points.

Twelve Ways to Make Your Talk Sound Forceful and Convincing

Force makes your speech powerful and convincing. It gives strength and vigor to what you say. Force creates movement and movement creates force. Force and movement make things happen; they bring life to your words. Here are twelve guidelines you can use to make what you say positive and powerful, forceful and convincing:

1. *Speak with the voice of authority.* To be able to do this, you must really know your stuff. The more you know about your subject, the better off you'll be when you're giving a talk or making a speech. If you know more than your audience knows, no one will be able to trip you up.

2. *Use simple words and short sentences.* The simple things last longest and wear best. The simplest writing is always the best because it's the easiest to understand. The same can be said about speeches.

3. *Use active verbs or motion for force.* Verbs that denote actual physical movement make what you say move and come to life. Nouns and abstract verbs made out of nouns do not. They are dead words. Verbs of physical movement act as a stimulus and motivate people to take the action you want them to take.

4. *Use concrete and specific words and phrases.* As I've said before, the absolute master of this art was Jesus Christ. The words He used when He said, "Follow me," were simple, concise, to the point, and easy to understand.

5. *Give your listener only one idea at a time.* Too many ideas at once confuse and muddle your listeners' thinking. When you come to the end of one idea, stop. Take a breath. Then go on to your next thought.

6. *Specify; use illustrations and examples.* If you want to sound convincing when you talk, use many illustrations and examples. Use such personal words as *you, me, we, us, John, Mary.* Avoid such terms as "They said" or "They want." These two phrases completely destroy the force and power of what you're saying.

7. *Avoid needless words and useless information.* Don't talk as if you were in love with the sound of your own voice. The person who talks constantly and never listens to others usually has very little worthwhile to say. Don't clutter up your listeners' minds with unimportant trivia and worthless details.

8. *Be direct and to the point.* Stick to your subject. Don't wander off and talk about anything else. You'll completely lose the attention of your audience if you do that. Not only that, some sharpshooter in the group will shoot you down if you get into an area where you're not the expert.

9. *Don't exaggerate.* Not only should you never exaggerate or stretch the truth, but you would also be wise to understate your case. Then you need have no worry about any repercussions. At any rate, never make any statements that you cannot prove.

10. *Don't talk down to your listeners* by using pompous and pretentious words. Even though you're the authority on the subject, that's still no reason for you to talk down to your listeners. I've never yet met a person who wasn't more knowledgeable in some area than I was.

11. *Present the proposition that is best for your listeners,* not the one that is best for you. Do that and no one will ever be able to cut the ground out from under you. Your defenses will be impenetrable.

12. *Answer all questions frankly and openly,* but if you don't know, then say so. Don't try to bluff your way through. The technique I've always used to good advantage is simply to say, "I don't know, but if it's important to you, I'll find out and let you know."

Five Ways to Develop Confidence in Your Ability to Speak to an Audience

Before I end this chapter, I want to give you five simple secrets that professional speakers use to develop confidence in their own abilities to speak to an audience:

1. *Don't memorize your talk word for word.* There is nothing wrong with memorizing certain key phrases, but to memorize your entire talk is to invite disaster. If you forget where you are for one split second, you're dead!

The best way to memorize is to commit certain key points to memory. However, let me say that if your talk has a natural continuity, even that will become unnecessary since you can easily move from one idea to the next. All you need do is arrange your ideas in a logical sequence before you start.

2. *Rehearse your talk first.* This one point often marks the major difference between the professional public speaker and the amateur. By the same token, it can separate the successful performance from the unsatisfactory one, too.

One extremely successful and colorful speaker, Harvey Freeland, who's in the advertising business, is constantly in demand to speak at Kiwanis luncheons, Rotary Club breakfasts, Chamber of Commerce meetings, and the like. I asked Harvey why. Here's what he told me:

"I test my ideas for a new talk in everyday normal conversation with my friends. Instead of wasting time on the weather or politics or gossiping about my neighbors, I use my coffee break or lunch period to say something like this: 'Sam, I had a funny thing happen to me the other day. I'd like to tell you about it.'

"I watch his reactions closely as I tell the story. If it registers well, I know I have the nucleus for a new talk. He never realizes I've been rehearsing with him. As far as he's concerned, we've just had a pleasant conversation with each other."

You can test your new ideas the same way Harvey does. And you can rehearse your talk in front of a mirror or give it to your wife or son. It's always good to get a reaction from both sexes before you firm up your speech in its final format.

I personally like to dictate my speeches into my tape recorder. A lot of mistakes I didn't hear when I spoke come back to me magnified when I listen to myself on tape.

3. *Know your subject and stick to it.* Be thoroughly prepared. Know your subject from top to bottom. Be the final authority. But don't try to know everything about everything. It can't be done. Learn your own subject and then stick to it. Then you can be an expert, too. Remember that you're an expert only as long as you stick to your own line.

4. *Concentrate only on the job to be done.* "It is impossible for a man to lose all his fear of battle," says Colonel Edward Gann, "but he'll tend to forget it if he gets his mind off himself and concentrates only on his job."

The same thing is true of speaking in public. Forget yourself and concentrate only on your subject. If you start worrying about errors of grammar or the possibility that you might run out of time before you've covered all your material, you can destroy your self-confidence even before you start. Just concentrate on your message and you'll make it through in fine shape.

5. *When you've achieved your objective, stop talking!* A poor salesman often loses a sale because he keeps on talking after the sale has been made. He gives the customer a chance to change his mind. So when you're through, quit. Don't be like that preacher who always says more than he has to talk about. In fact, the smartest thing you can do is to quit even before you're through. Then your audience will want to come back the next time to hear you for they'll want to learn more.

The major points I'd like you to remember from this chapter are these:

1. You can overcome your fear of giving a talk or making a speech by giving a talk or making a speech. When you do the thing you fear to do, you'll gain the power to do it, and your fear will disappear.

2. Fear and nervousness are not the same thing at all. It's perfectly normal to have a few butterflies in the stomach before a performance. Even the most experienced professional speakers have them, but they know how to control them

3. Know the specific purpose of your speech or talk.

4. Identify and pinpoint your main ideas.

5. Outline and organize your speech or your talk. The outline I recommend is this one:

   (a) Your opening

   (b) The benefits to be gained

   (c) Techniques to be used to gain those benefits

   (d) Examples of others who've gained those benefits by using these techniques

   (e) Your conclusion

6. Twelve ways to make your talk forceful and convincing:

   (a) Speak with the voice of authority.

   (b) Use simple words and short sentences.

   (c) Use active verbs of motion for force.

   (d) Use concrete and specific words and phrases.

   (e) Give your listeners only one idea at a time.

   (f) Specify: Use illustrations and examples.

   (g) Avoid needless words and useless information.

   (h) Be direct and to the point.

   (i) Don't exaggerate.

   (j) Don't talk down to your listeners.

   (k) Present the proposition that is best for your listeners.

   (l) Answer all questions frankly and openly.

7. Five ways to develop confidence in your ability to speak to an audience are these:

   (a) Don't memorize your talk word for word.

   (b) Rehearse your talk first.

   (c) Know your subject and stick to it.

   (d) Concentrate only on the job to be done.

   (e) When you've achieved your objective, stop talking.

And I'm going to practice that last technique myself right now. I'm going to quit before I'm through so I can save some important material for the next chapter: "Eight Important Trade Secrets of Professional Platform Speakers."

chapter 17

Eight Important
Trade Secrets
of Professional
Platform Speakers

The successful people from whom I gathered the information for this chapter are all professionals in the art of conversation and public speaking. Their professions and occupations include professional platform speakers, politicians, television and stage personalities, sales managers, ministers, college professors, and many others. When you learn the trade secrets of these highly skilled people,

YOU CAN GAIN THE FOLLOWING MAGNIFICENT BENEFITS FOR YOURSELF

1. You'll be able to stand up in front of a large audience and give a talk, make a speech, or voice your ideas and opinions without fear.

2. You'll know how to hold your own in a conversation with anyone. You'll be capable of handling yourself successfully in any business or social situation.

3. You'll have no trouble at all in getting people to accept your idea or your point of view.

4. You'll have the power to control the emotions and actions of your audience.

5. You'll gain the respect of your friends and be the envy of your associates.

6. You'll be able to think clearly and to express yourself precisely even when you're under heavy pressure.

7. A winning, positive, and outgoing personality will be yours. As your skills in public speaking improve, your confidence in yourself and your own abilities will expand and increase immeasureably.

8. The ability to speak without fear in public will give you a sense of personal power and fulfillment unlike anything you've ever experienced before. You'll have a tremendous feeling of self-accomplishment.

TECHNIQUES YOU CAN USE TO GAIN THESE VALUABLE BENEFITS

How to Develop Your Own Distinctive Speaking Style

The style of your talking, the way you speak to others, makes a vital contribution to your reputation and to your success. For example, if you talk down to people, they will resent you. If you are too deferential to your superiors, say your supervisor or employer, they may look at you as weak and spineless and not worthy of advancement or promotion. Your conversational style is not only a matter of the words you use, but also your way of using them, as well as your attitude and bearing.

The best way to develop your own distinctive and personal speaking style is to be natural, to be yourself. Don't try to imitate someone else or be something you're not. Develop a style that is distinctively yours, not someone else's.

For instance, I was born and raised on an Iowa farm. Except for the last fifteen years, I have made my home in the midwest most of my life. I still sound like a midwesterner when I talk, but I've never tried to change that way of speaking. Why should I? What's wrong with being from the midwest?

If you have a southern accent, don't try to get rid of it, unless it's so thick you can't be understood. As long as people understand you, leave it alone. The same goes for the long Texas drawl of the southwest or the clipped abrupt New England way of speaking. Where you come from is a part of your heritage. This helps make you a unique person and an individual different from all others.

It's far more important for you to get rid of such voice problems as nasality, stridency, shrillness, breathiness, and lack of projection, than it is to worry too much about a regional accent.

If you could make only one improvement in your voice, it should be to lower the pitch of your voice, for all those problems I have just mentioned go hand in hand with a high-pitched voice. This is especially important for a woman to correct, for a woman's high-pitched voice can be disturbing to men and really turn them off. The more you can develop a low-pitched, strong, firm voice, the better, since it is that relatively higher pitch of a woman's voice that causes men to be wary and on guard. Such a voice can wreck a woman's chances for advancement in the business world.

I have always been fortunate in having a deep and resonant baritone voice that people remember easily. Two years ago I saw a lady whom I had met for only a few hours nearly 40 years before. "I wouldn't have remembered your face, for then you didn't wear a mustache, and, of course, we were both much younger," she said, "but the moment you spoke, I remembered you. Your voice is so distinctive no one could possibly forget it."

How to Control the Emotions of Your Audience

A top-notch preacher knows how to control the emotions of his audience. Watch some of those television ministers work. You may not approve of their methods or their constant clamor for pledges and contributions, but you must admit, they do know how to control the emotions of their studio audiences.

One of the greatest masters of all time of this technique was John Wesley, the founder of the Methodist faith. He enjoyed an enormous success as an English evangelist. He had a shrewd and intuitive understanding of the inner workings of the human mind.

Wesley would open his sermon with a long and vivid description of the agonies and torture to which his listeners would be condemned for all eternity unless they became converted to the faith. Then after a sense of terror, guilt, and extreme anxiety had brought his audience to the brink of a complete nervous breakdown, he would offer eternal salvation to those who accepted Christ and repented of their sins.

By this kind of preaching, Wesley converted hundreds and thousands of people. Intense prolonged fear exhausted his listeners' nervous systems and produced a state of greatly intensified suggestibility in their subconscious minds. In this highly vulnerable condition, they accepted the preacher's theological message without question. They emerged from this religious ordeal with new behavior patterns firmly planted in their subconscious minds.

I'm not proposing that you use such extreme measures to control the emotions and behavior patterns of your audience. I would suggest, however, that you find a suitable method that fits your own style and personality. I would also recommend that you keep one of my previous thoughts in mind while searching for such a technique. That idea is simply that the head never hears 'til the heart has listened, for that's the quickest shortcut I know of to control the emotions and actions of others.

Five Methods You Can Use to Overcome Your Nervousness

As I told you before, nervousness is a perfectly normal physiological reaction to a new or strange situation. However, although it's normal, you must make sure you don't let it take over completely. Here are 5 simple methods you can use to control your nervousness and keep it from getting out of hand.

1. *Be thoroughly prepared.* Master your subject completely. Be the authority. This is the biggest confidence builder you can use. By the same token, a lack of professional knowledge about your subject is the deadliest confidence killer of all.

2. *Have a positive mental attitude.* Be confident in yourself and have faith in your own abilities. Act as if it were impossible to fail and you will always succeed.

3. *Have your initial remarks well in mind.* The first few moments are always the most critical, for the first impression will usually be the lasting one. Knowing exactly what you are going to say when you start to speak will get rid of those butterflies in your stomach.

4. *Tell a story on yourself, Jack Benny style.* Although telling a joke is not recommended by most public speakers, telling a story on yourself makes you human. It releases tension and endears you to your audience.

5. *Be deliberate . . . slow down.* Don't hurry. Force yourself to speak more slowly. Take a breath and pause slightly after each sentence. Your normal poise and bearing will quickly return to you.

Four Ways to Physically Project Your Personality While Speaking

Your audience will respond to what they see as well as to what they hear. Your movements and gestures can be highly expressive and extremely influential in helping you make your point. They can make the difference between an excellent enthusiastic talk and a dull and lifeless one.

Any physical attitude you assume, any body movement, or any gesture that attracts attention to itself rather than emphasizing or complementing what you are saying is distracting to your listeners. It then becomes a hindrance, not a help. To be helpful, your movements and gestures should appear free and natural.

Bert Flanders, an expert in training people to speak in public, says that there are four main methods you can use to physically project your personality to an audience.

"You must maintain an erect posture," Bert says. "Take a position where your entire audience can see you. Stand erect with one foot slightly ahead of the other. Put most of your weight on that leading foot. Lean forward slightly toward your audience. Don't slouch and never lean on the lectern. You don't have to stand rigidly at attention as if you were in the army, but you should look physically and mentally alert. The key to correct posture is to think tall.

"Next, be vital and enthusiastic. Vitality comes easily when you are enthusiastic about your subject. If you believe in what you are saying, then the sincerity, warmth, and positive feeling that guarantees a good talk and an excellent audience response will come through loud and clear. Enthusiasm is contagious. Of course, your enthusiasm has to be based on a thorough knowledge of your subject and an understanding of how your talk will benefit your listeners.

"You should use gestures to emphasize your point," Bert says. "If you're making a strong point, don't be afraid to bang your fist on the lectern—once—or to hold out your arms to your audience in a bold closing call for action. Your gestures should come spontaneously from your enthusiasm, your convictions, your emotions. Don't try to emphasize every single sentence with a gesture. If you did that, you'd look more like a windmill than a good speaker and you could actually defeat the purpose of your talk.

"My last point about how to physically project your personality is this: Since your message comes from your face, leave loud clothes like prints, checks, and plaids at home. The more simple the design of your clothes, the more effective you'll be as a speaker. The most effective public speakers wear subdued clothes with only one striking point of interest in either color or design near the face. With a man, that's usually a tie—not a busy one, please—and with a woman, it can be a necklace. As far as colors go, navy and white have been proven to inspire the most confidence in the speaker, although black and white run a close second."

How to Be the Final Authority on Your Subject

There's absolutely no substitute for knowledge, but there is also a slick stage technique you can use to let your audience know that you are the absolute master of your subject. I learned this secret from an enterprising young minister many years ago. I've used it to good advantage ever since.

I used to marvel at the way Paul could move swiftly and uner-ringly from one reference to another in his Bible during his sermon. I'd have sworn he knew the entire Bible by heart.

Paul would start off by reading some scripture. Then he would say, for example, "And in Matthew, the Eighth Chapter, the first through the fourth verses, we find . . ." Then he would turn to that scripture. After reading it, he would say, "We also find confirmation of this principle in the Fifth Chapter of Luke, the twelfth through the sixteenth verses." And he would turn to that scripture. And so it went.

One day I asked Paul how he could retain such a tremendous number of scriptures in his memory, know the material each one contained, and be able to cross-reference the way he did.

Paul smiled and then, with my promise not to reveal his secret, told me how he did it. "I know the first reference," he said. "I have to know that one, but it's the only one I need know. Let's say the subject of my sermon is "Love Your Neighbor As Yourself." I want to establish a scriptural basis for my theme, so I'll start with the twenty-second Chapter of Matthew, the thirty-ninth verse, where Christ says, 'Thou shalt love thy neighbor as thyself.'

"Now on that page I have a tiny card inserted that says, *Turn to Mark 12:31 on page 39.* Inserted there will be still another small card that says, *Turn to Romans 13:9 on page 124.* Each one of these references will have to do with loving your neighbor as yourself. Of course, since I have no visible notes in front of me, it appears that I have a pro-digious memory. And that's how it's done."

I haven't broken my promise to Paul in revealing his secret to you. He's now retired and said he didn't object if I passed it on.

Seven Irritating Mannerisms to Avoid

I know you've listened to people who had some irritating habits that distracted you and caused you to view those speakers unfavorably. I went to a doctor once, who, when explaining my physical condition to me, had the habit of constantly asking, "Do you follow me?" with every third or fourth sentence. After a few minutes, this really got on my nerves. I found myself betting mentally when he would say it again, rather than actually listening to what he was telling me.

Others will use such phrases as "you know" over and over again. Tape yourself on a recorder and see if you pick up any repetitive phrases when you play it back. And have someone else—your wife, your children, or a friend—listen to your tape, too. They'll hear words or phrases that you use too often. You'll miss them because you're so used to hearing them.

Physical mannerisms can include cracking your knuckles, drumming your fingers on a desk, excessive gum chewing, rubbing your nose, stroking your mustache, pulling your ear, adjusting your glasses. By themselves they're nothing, but when your listener sees them constantly, he's distracted by them. He loses interest in what you're saying. Here, now, are seven specific distracting mannerisms to avoid when you're making a speech or giving a talk to a large audience:

1. *The dying warrior*. In this position, the speaker leans heavily on the lectern. He wears an air of total exhaustion and never moves. All he needs to complete this picture is a feather drooping down over his forehead from an Indian headband.

2. *The fig leaf* is favored by the speaker who has no lectern to lean on. He stands solidly with both hands clasped in front below the waist, feet 18 inches apart and completely immovable, his body solid as a rock.

3. *The walkie-talkie* is a descriptive term in itself. This one is the pacer who never holds still for a single moment. Most "walkie-talkies" seem to be would-be lawyers who imagine themselves pacing back and forth in front of the jury.

4. *The chained elephant* stands with his weight first on one foot, then on the other. He goes nowhere, but constantly moves his feet in position, shuffling back and forth.

5. *The change counter* constantly counts the money in his pocket. Soon the audience hears only the jingle of coins rather than what he's saying.

6. *The swordsman* works with a pointer and a chart. He has the bad habit of fighting imaginary duels with his pointer as if he were holding a sword.

7. *The baton twirler* also uses a chart and a pointer, but he is more advanced in his techniques than the "swordsman." He uses his pointer as if he were entertaining the crowd at half time.

Seven Important Don'ts to Remember

I normally do not like to discuss techniques from a negative viewpoint, but this time I feel it's justified, so here goes:

1. *Don't bluff*. Never bluff to cover up a lack of knowledge. If you

don't know the answer, say so. Then find the answer and let the person know as soon as you can.

2. *Don't use profanity or obscenities.* Not even a tiny "Damn!" or "Hell!" is ever permissible. The moment you use profanity, you run the risk of losing the respect and attention of some of your listeners.

3. *Don't use sarcasm or ridicule.* This is especially true if you have a captive audience. Your listeners will resent it if they can't respond in the same sarcastic manner. If a person resents you, he won't listen to you.

4. *Don't talk down to your listeners.* You might be smarter than your listeners, but only in one subject, and you selected that one. Never treat your listeners as ignorant people if you want them to keep listening to you.

5. *Don't lose your patience.* If a listener asks you to cover a point again, don't get upset. His inability to understand might be your failure to explain it properly. Repeat the information or use a different approach to make your point clear to him.

6. *Don't hide behind the lectern.* You must be clearly visible to the audience. If the lectern doesn't show you at least from the waist up, be brave and step out to the side.

7. *Don't make excuses.* Don't start off by saying, "Ill-prepared as I am . . . I didn't have a chance to go over this material . . . I'm not really qualified to speak on this . . . I wouldn't be here, but . . ." I've heard these comments and so have you. You were turned off immediately, right? Well, if you use them, your listeners will be turned off too. Never apologize or make excuses. Only amateurs do that; profes sionals never do. Be a pro.

The Professional Way to Use Visual Aids: Eight Guidelines

First, let me tell you the advantages of using visual aids: One, they can be powerful tools to help get your message across to your audience. They can add interest and vitality to your presentation. They will help focus your listeners' attention on the point you're making.

Two, visual aids make it easier for your audience to understand a complicated point. Your listeners will more easily grasp your idea when they can see as well as hear what you're talking about.

Three, visual aids save time for your listeners can learn more rapidly. And time is always valuable. The older you get, the more you'll realize that. For instance, I used to joke saying I had more time than money when I was doing my best to keep from losing my patience while standing in a long checkout line at the supermarket. Unfortunately, I've reached the age where that statement is no longer true.

To be usable and worthwhile to you, a visual aid should have these seven specific characteristics:

1. A good visual aid should be appropriate. It should help you illustrate a point or stress a feature.

2. It should be simple and easy to understand. The best way to keep it simple is to have it emphasize only the point you want to get across; nothing more.

3. Your visual aid must be accurate. Be sure your facts and figures are correct and up-to-date. Any inaccuracy will destroy your credibility.

4. Your aid should be portable and durable. It must be lightweight for easy handling, or constructed in quickly assembled parts. Don't end up with something that requires several people to move it.

5. Your visual aid must be easy to use. Aids that are intricate, complicated, and require a great deal of time to use make an audience nervous, edgy, and impatient with you.

6. Your aid must be attractive. Dirty and grimy visual aids turn off your listeners immediately. If you're using charts and some of them have become smudged, replace them.

7. Your visual aid should be necessary. It should illustrate an essential point so you can give a better presentation. Never fit your talk to your visual aid; always fit your visual aid to your talk.

Now I want to give you the eight guidelines for using visual aids effectively that I promised you earlier:

1. *Prepare time-consuming drawings in advance.* This guideline is applicable if you're using a blackboard. If you spend half your time writing on the blackboard instead of talking to your audience, you'll irritate your listeners. In fact, unless you have a captive audience, some of them will have disappeared by the time you're ready to talk. To keep that from happening, put your material on the board before your audience arrives.

2. *Prepare yourself in advance for using the visual aid.* Know your visual aid thoroughly so you can answer any questions about it.

Rehearse your presentation several times using the aid exactly as it will be used later in your live performance.

3. *Introduce your aid at the proper time.* If your aid is on stage, keep it covered. If you can keep it offstage and have an assistant bring it on, that's better yet. But either way, don't expose your visual aid until you're actually ready to use it. If you expose it too early, your audience will spend its time looking at it rather than listening to you.

4. *Explain your visual aid.* Elaborate visual aids are often used to illustrate highly complicated and technical subjects. When you first show this kind of aid, briefly explain its purpose. Otherwise your audience will be trying to figure out what it's for and miss some of what you're saying.

5. *Show the aid so all can see it.* Display your visual aid so everybody can see it. If it's a chart, view it from the back of the room yourself to make sure it can be read. If necessary, change the seating arrangement so all can see. The best visual aid is of no value if everyone cannot see it.

6. *Talk to your listeners, not to the aid.* Amateurs tend to talk to the aid and not to the audience. When you're explaining a chart or drawing, keep your eye on your listeners.

7. *Use a pointer.* A pointer can be used to focus your listeners' eyes on a particular part of your visual aid. It also keeps you from walking in front of the aid. Always put the pointer away when you're not using it so you won't be playing with it.

8. *Use an assistant if you can.* If you have a clerk or secretary who can help you, have him do so. Make sure he's been rehearsed, too. He must know exactly what he is to do and when to do it. An assistant can make things go much more smoothly for you when you're using visual aids. However, keep him offstage, too, when he's not helping you.

Let me summarize these 8 important trade secrets of professional platform speakers now so you'll have them in one place for ready reference.

1. Develop your own distinctive speaking style. Don't try to copy or imitate someone else. Be yourself.

2. Learn to control the emotions of your audience. To capture your listeners, aim for their hearts as well as their heads.

3. Use these 5 simple methods to overcome and control your nervousness:

   (a) Be thoroughly prepared.

   (b) Have a positive mental attitude. Act as if it were impossible to fail.

   (c) Have your initial remarks well in mind.

   (d) Tell a story on yourself, Jack Benny style.

   (e) Be deliberate; slow down.

4. Physically project your personality to your audience by standing erect, using gestures to emphasize your points, being enthusiastic about your subject, and by wearing quiet subdued colors that do not distract your audience.

5. Be the final authority on your subject and only your subject. Don't try to know everything about everything.

6. Avoid these 7 irritating mannerisms:

   (a) The dying warrior

   (b) The fig leaf

   (c) The walkie-talkie

   (d) The chained elephant

   (e) The change counter

   (f) The swordsman

   (g) The baton twirler

7. Seven important don'ts to remember are these:

   (a) Don't bluff.

   (b) Don't use profanity or obscenities.

   (c) Don't use sarcasm or ridicule.

   (d) Don't talk down to your listeners.

   (e) Don't lose your patience.

   (f) Don't hide behind the lectern.

   (g) Don't make excuses.

8. Eight professional guidelines for using visual aids:

   (a) You should prepare time-consuming drawings in advance.

   (b) Prepare yourself in advance for using your visual aid.

   (c) Introduce your aid at the proper time.

(d) Explain your visual aid to your audience.

(e) Display the aid so all can see it.

(f) Talk to your listeners, not to the aid.

(g) Use a pointer.

(h) Use an assistant if you can.

To wrap up this chapter, I want to say that speaking in public will expand your life and its meaning. It will give you a sense of personal power and fulfillment unlike anything you've ever experienced before. And the more you express your ideas and feeling to an audience, the more you'll want to do so, for you'll find that you really do enjoy doing it. You'll have a tremendous feeling of self-accomplishment that nothing else can ever give you.

And now on to the next chapter where I'll give you some tips on how to use your conversational expertise to succeed in business.

chapter 18

Using Your
Conversational Expertise
to Succeed in Business:
A 7-Step Program

In this chapter, I want to show you how to put all your conversational expertise to work so you can succeed in business. *What* you say and *how* you say it will be two of the major factors in how far you can go in your business and professional career. When you know how to speak effectively to influence others, you can literally talk your way to success. Before I get into the techniques you can use to do that, I want to first tell you about . . .

THE FABULOUS BENEFITS YOU CAN GAIN

1. *You'll make much money.* Ever since the Phoenicians invented money several thousand years ago, the primary aim of every person has been to accumulate as much of it as possible. This chapter will show you how to use your conversational expertise to get ahead in the business world so you can amass even more of it.

2. *You'll gain great personal power over others* when you become successful in business. You'll find that your influence will expand and spread and you can become the leader not only in business activities, but also in social, political, and community matters as well.

3. *Personal power, prestige, respect, and recognition will all be yours* along with your financial gain when you become a successful business person.

4. *You can go clear to the very top.* When you know how to use your verbal skills to handle the top-level people in the power structure, there is absolutely no limit as to how far you can go. You can become president of the company or even chairman of the board if that's what you really want and are willing to pay the price in time and effort. It's all up to you, for you can reach whatever goal you want to achieve if you really have your heart set on it.

TECHNIQUES YOU CAN USE TO GAIN THESE TREMENDOUS BENEFITS

How You Can Talk Your Way to Success

A famous and well-known psychologist made a detailed study of hundreds of successful men and women to determine the reasons for their success. She found that all these people had one thing in common:

their skill in using words. She also discovered that their earning power was closely linked to their skill with words. You, too, can expect your own earnings to increase tremendously when you improve your skills in the use of language to deal with people.

If you want to be a successful person in your business and in your community, you must know how to use words to control people's actions. Since you cannot use force to get what you want, you must learn how to use language that will achieve your desired results.

I can say without any hesitation whatever that when you can command words to serve your thoughts and feelings, you are well on your way to commanding people to do your will and serve your purposes.

If you want to be able to talk your way to success, then, you must first master the language. And language is ever so important, for if you will analyze your day, you'll find that not less than 75 percent of it is spent in oral communication with someone: explaining, persuading, advising, ordering, influencing, asking and answering questions. In short, you'll spend most of your time putting your proposals and ideas across to others so you can get them to do what you want. When you can do that, you'll be successful no matter what kind of business you're in or what you do for a living.

How to Sound Like a Top-Level Executive

There's an old cliché that says if you want to be a top-level executive, then you must dress like one and look like one. I could also add that you must talk like a top-level executive as well.

Howard Meadows, personnel director for a large corporation, says that what you say and how you say it can mark you unmistakably as a prime candidate for upper management, or it can tag you permanently as a low-level manager or a permanent resident of the office typing pool. I've already covered the "how" of what you say in the last chapter where I discussed such voice problems as nasality, stridency, breathiness, high pitch, and the like. In this chapter, then, I want to tell you how to solve some of the problems in *what* you say.

Howard told me that one of the biggest stumbling blocks to a person's upward progress in management is improper grammar. Let me give you a quick example here so you can see if this might be a problem to you:

> Mom don't feel good. I would of gone to see her, only I had to work. I sent her a card from Sally and myself. If you and me ain't heard from her by Saturday, we better call.

How many errors did you spot? There are a total of seven mistakes. In the following version, I have indicated by italics where corrections were made.

Mom *doesn't* feel good. I would *have* gone to see her, *but* I had to work. I sent her a card from Sally and *me*. If you and *I haven't* heard from her by Saturday, we *had* better call.

Misused pronouns, lack of agreement between the noun and its verb, mixed-up tenses, slang words such as *ain't* are the most common grammatical errors. If you suspect your own grammar might be holding you back, you can resolve that problem in one or more of several ways.

You can take an adult education course in English by attending night school, you can buy a book on grammar and study it, or you can listen carefully to the conversation of someone who does use proper English.

Aside from grammatical errors, there are other mistakes that can tag you as the nonexecutive type; for instance, misused words.

People who misuse words are usually trying to impress others by using fancy words that they don't actually know the meaning of. A few examples are these: *Irregardless* (there's no such word; I know for I lost a ten dollar bet on it when I was in college); *Firstly* (pretentious, just say first)—*simplistic* (means simple). There are many others. *Lie* and *lay* often cause problems for many people.

Careless diction indicates laziness to the people who count. Sloppy pronunciation like "I'm *gonna* . . . do you *wanna* . . . *whaddya* think?" can quickly lead your boss to suspect the quality of your work.

So if you want to sound like a top-level executive or a manager who's on the way up, watch what you say and how you say it. Be on guard constantly to prevent grammatical errors from creeping in. If you're not sure, find out from someone who can give you the correct answer. I'm the author of more than a dozen books, but to this day when I encounter a grammatical problem where I'm not sure of the right answer, I pick up the phone and call the high school English teacher. She's never told me yet to stop bothering her. After all, when I ask for her advice, I'm making her feel important; I'm feeding her ego. That makes her happy.

Making That First Good Impression in a Job Interview

All sorts of books have been written on how to act in a job interview, the clothes to wear, that sort of thing. Here, however, I will approach the situation strictly from a conversational viewpoint

There are four specific points I consider to be extremely important for a successful job interview. The first one is to always wear a great big smile. Let it be a real one, not a phony one. If you have trouble doing this, think of one of the happiest times in your life and you can put a sincere smile on your face with no trouble at all.

A big smile implies many things to the other person. It means you're a happy, enthusiastic person who is not a pessimistic sourpuss. It shows that you're the kind of person others like to associate with and enjoy having around. A smile can mean you'd be a real asset to the company.

Second, when the interviewer says something, don't just sit there like a block of wood. Give some verbal feedback. Nod your head; say, "Oh, yes, I see . . . Oh no, of course not," or whatever is appropriate.

Third, wear an attentive look. Appear alert and interested in what's going on. This will show the interviewer that you are an alert and aware person. I've known brilliant people to lose out on a good position simply because they appeared bored with life and wore a jaded look.

Fourth, look at the speaker's face. This shows a definite interest on your part in the other person and in what he's saying. And everybody likes attention, remember? Make that person feel important and he'll think that you're important, too.

These four points are not only useful for making a good first impression in a job interview, but they can also be helpful when you're being interviewed for promotion or advancement to a higher management position in your company.

How to Get That Raise You Deserve So Much: Seven Guidelines

Preparation for your raise begins long before you actually ask for it. I talked at length with a career management specialist who teaches people how to get ahead and be happy at their jobs. Her clients include corporate vice presidents, managers, supervisors, executives, bankers, secretaries, and many others—all of whom pay her quite handsomely for her advice.

You're fortunate. You're going to get the same information free. Ms. Darby says that there are seven vital steps to be taken in preparation for your raise, which are . . .

1. *Become the authority in your chosen field.* It is important, first of all, to know your business and keep on knowing it. Progress is perpetual. If you don't keep up with developments in your own profession,

you'll soon be passed over for promotion. But at the same time, don't think you're indispensable. No one is. I have a cousin who retired from the army as a three-star general. He thought the service would fold up without him, but to his chagrin, it continued to do quite well.

·2. *Establish a cordial working relationship with your boss.* No manager or supervisor will go out of his way to give a raise or a promotion to a person he doesn't like. The average boss likes people who praise him sincerely and make him feel important.

Smart employees appreciate their bosses and show them that appreciation. You can do that, too, without polishing the apple or using flattery. The best way to praise a person is to compliment him for what he *does*, not for what he *is*. Praise the act, not the person.

3. *Learn to blow your own horn.* The idea that if you just do a good job, promotions and raises will come automatically is a myth. Just doing good work alone is not where recognition comes from. The boss expects you to do acceptable work without making mistakes. After all, that's what he's paying you for. But that alone is not enough. You must make yourself noticed by calling favorable attention to yourself by blowing your own horn.

Often your boss just doesn't realize how good you really are. Let him know that—without being obnoxious or overbearing about it—in the office, at a business lunch, at an office party or some other social function, or anywhere else you can.

I've told you before that it also helps to become well-known in the community, for this brings credit and recognition to your company. So don't be bashful. Speak to church groups or civic clubs in your field of expertise whenever possible.

Do anything you can to keep your name uppermost in your superior's mind. This is precisely the way the most effective advertising works. As one executive told me, "The most important thing about advertising is repetition. It takes constant repetition to build a reputation. We don't care whether people remember exactly what we say *about* the product. We just want them to remember the *name* of it. That's enough."

Remember, then, it's your reputation that's being negotiated when you blow your own horn. If other people think that you're the best, you'll win the game. You must project a winning reputation so others will believe it.

4. *Don't hesitate to delegate the work.* When you're in a management position, don't hesitate to delegate the work to your subordinates.

Every time you let something go, you free yourself to accept additional responsibilities.

Top managers always feel much more at ease when they know a competent person is available to take care of new assignments and new developments. Be smart; let them know that person is you.

5. *Keep your superiors informed and up-to-date.* Without constantly breathing down their necks, let them know that your assignment is under control and proceeding on schedule. This shows you are a dependable person who's getting the job done.

6. *Psych yourself up for the actual raise negotiation.* Don't be backward about this or sell yourself short. In our system we equate value with cost. Your value to your company has a direct relationship to how much you're being paid.

Let your boss know the benefits he will receive when he grants your raise. One of the biggest benefits he'll gain is retaining your valuable services.

But before you issue any ultimatums, be sure you have a concrete job offer somewhere else. As a far wiser man than I once said, "The biggest fool in the world is the person who quits one job before he has another."

7. *How to time your request for your raise.* I've found the best time to nail your boss for a raise is just after you've done a really outstanding job on an extraordinarily difficult assignment, and he tells you that himself.

Praise for a job well done is much appreciated. It is one of the basic desires we all have, but you can't eat words alone. The object of working is to make money. The more you make, the more important you feel, and the better you can live.

So if your boss won't come across with a raise right after you've done an excellent job for him, it could be that he never will, so it might be high time for you to move on to where your talents and efforts will be more appreciated, not only psychologically, but also financially as well.

Seven Techniques You Can Use to Talk Your Way to the Top in the Big Company

The seven guidelines I've just given you for getting that raise you deserve so much can also be used to gain a promotion so you can work your way to the top in the big company. However, in addition to those seven techniques, I also want to give you seven more methods that will show you how to establish good cordial relationships with people to help yourself get ahead.

1. *Never make an issue of small matters.* Always go along with minor or insignificant points when you can do so without causing damage to yourself or to your own position. When you do have to make an issue of something, be sure it's a major point. Then your objection will stand out and you'll be remembered and well thought of for your professional conduct and attitude.

2. *State your objection calmly and courteously.* If you disagree with a major point, back up that disagreement with logic, reason, and facts. Objections based on emotion or how you "feel" about something won't carry much weight. If the final decision goes against your recommendation, don't carry a chip on your shoulder. Do your best to support the selected course of action of your superior. You'll be highly respected as a team player when you do.

3. *Develop the "golden touch" in human relationships.* The ability to get along with others is an absolute must if you want to get ahead in the big corporation. You cannot move up the ladder of success if you make an enemy out of everyone. In fact, knowing how to handle people is one of the hallmarks of executive leadership. If you can't get along well with your associates, if you are constantly involved in verbal warfare with someone, you'll be let go, no matter what your qualifications and abilities are.

4. *Be highly enthusiastic about your job.* Don't expect to move up the management ladder to the top if you don't really have your heart in your work. Your boss can tell, for your attitude will be reflected on your face and in your actions.

If you can't go to work smiling because you love your job and enjoy the people with whom you work, then I really feel sorry for you. I would suggest you quickly get enthusiastic or that you change jobs before it's too late.

5. *Don't be afraid to take a reasonable risk.* Top-level executives expect their subordinates to have the courage to take reasonable risks. If you always play it safe, you'll never get anywhere. Good prior planning will prevent most major problems and greatly reduce the risks for you.

6. *Always look for more responsibility.* The person who ducks responsibility will never reach the top. Upper-level executives are always looking for those who can accept more and more responsibility. The person who can is always labeled a "comer."

Remember that every time you delegate a job to someone else to do, you're not passing the buck. Instead, you're freeing yourself to accept additional responsibility. Top management is always happy to find a competent individual who is available to take care of new projects. If you want to climb the management ladder and achieve success, then let that person be you.

7. *Dream up your own technique for advancement.* Dwight L. used one of the cleverest techniques I've ever seen to quickly climb the executive ladder to success. Shortly after he went to work for a large corporation, Dwight realized that promotion was going to be a slow tedious process unless ne did something drastic. Then he had a brilliant flash of inspiration.

One of his college friends had gone to work for an executive recruiting firm. He, too, was anxious to succeed. Dwight gave his boss's name to his friend who was able to lure him away from the firm. Dwight then moved into his boss's slot. He used the same procedure several times to reach his present position in top-level management, leaving behind others with more seniority and experience, but with far less initiative and ingenuity.

How to Attract the Favorable Attention of the Upper Hierarchy

Although you do want to keep your boss happy with you and your work, your primary objective must be to get ahead. The first thing you must realize is that no one is interested in your success but you. To tell you the straight unvarnished truth, your own boss is the last person in the company who wants to see you get ahead. Do you know why? Because if he loses you, he has to train someone else all over again to take your place.

One of the best ways to move up the ladder to the top is to become known as a knowledgeable and competent individual who really knows the working of the organization inside out. The more information you gain about the company, that much more will your boss depend on you for answers. It can reach the point where he won't even go to a staff meeting without you. When he turns to you for an answer when the president of the company asks him a question, guess whose name is going to be remembered.

Let me tell you how I used this technique so successfully when I was in the army back in World War II. I was a sergeant. My boss was a major. As a regimental staff officer, he attended division staff meetings on a weekly basis. Since he was hard of hearing, he almost always came back with unintelligible notes. I suggested to him that I attend the meetings with him and take notes for him.

High-ranking division officers got used to seeing a sergeant come with a major to take notes and answer questions. One day, the Commanding General attended the meeting. I saw that he watched me intently and that he asked several other officers why I was there. After the meeting was over, I was directed to report to his office.

"You shouldn't be an enlisted man," the General told me. "You should be an officer. You're already performing the duties of a major, but you're only receiving the pay of a sergeant. I'm recommending you immediately for a field promotion to first lieutenant."

Sixty days later I was commissioned an officer in the United States Army without having to endure the physical and mental stresses of 13 weeks of Infantry Officers Candidate School.

You may not be able to use that specific technique, but one simple way you can attract the attention of the upper hierarchy is to time your departure from work with that of your boss's boss. The more he sees of you, the more he will remember you. Carry some trade journals under your arm so he can see how interested you are in your profession. But don't carry anything that suggests you're doing your office work at home. This gives the impression you're not efficient enough to get your work done during normal working hours. Take whatever other action is necessary to make sure your boss's superior knows your name and exactly what you do.

Eight Ways to Let Your Business Do Your Talking for You

In the small amount of space and time we have left, I want to give you eight methods you can use to let your business talk for you even when you're home and sound asleep in bed.

1. *Have a big sign—a gigantic one—the biggest one in the town* that can be seen and read 24 hours a day. This is the most effective and inexpensive advertising you can use. Remember, as that advertising executive said, "We just want people to remember the *name* of our product, that's all." This is the best way you can do that. After the initial cost, the maintenance is negligible.

2. *Use your windows as salesmen.* Your window displays can pay for 25 percent of your overhead if you use them as silent salesmen. Let them work for you 24 hours a day, just as your sign does.

3. *Let your store shelves sell for you, too.* Well-displayed goods are

already half-sold. This is the key to success in the supermarket. If people can't see what you have to sell, then they can't buy it.

4. *Friendly and cheerful employees sell for you.* A cheerful and friendly face attracts customers. A sour face drives people away. A smile is one of the biggest assets your employees can have.

5. *Tie a slogan to your business.* Give people something to remember you by. For instance, people always associate the slogan, "You're in good hands with ALLSTATE" with Sears Roebuck.

6. *Use color to promote sales.* Brighten up your place. Bright colors are cheerful and attract customers. Paint the door red and let people know you're alive and kicking.

7. *Advertise . . . advertise . . . advertise,* if only a few lines in the newspaper, on a billboard, or mail promotion. Remember that doing business without advertising is like winking at a girl in the dark. You know what you're doing, but no one else does.

8. *When something new comes out, get it for your customers. New* is the greatest word of all in merchandising. People always want the latest thing, so give it to them. The two most used words in television advertising are *new and improved,* but they must work, for advertisers use them over and over.

Before going on to the next chapter, I want to recap the major points from this one for you.

1. You can talk your way to success in the business world when you develop your skill in using words. When you can command words to serve your thoughts and feelings, you are well on your way to commanding people to do your will and serve your purposes.

2. If you want to be a top-level executive, you must look the part, dress the part, and speak the part.

3. If you want to make a good first impression in a job interview, always wear a big smile, give some verbal feedback, wear an attentive look, and look at the speaker's face.

4. To get that raise you so richly deserve, follow these 7 guidelines:

   (a) Become the authority in your chosen field.
   (b) Establish a cordial working relationship with your boss.
   (c) Learn to blow your own horn.
   (d) Don't hesitate to delegate the work.
   (e) Keep your superiors informed and up-to-date.

(f) Psych yourself up for the actual raise negotiation.

(g) Proper timing is a key element in your request for a raise.

5. Seven techniques you can use to talk your way to the top in a big company:

(a) Never make an issue of small matters.

(b) State your objection calmly and courteously.

(c) Develop the "golden touch" in human relationships.

(d) Be highly enthusiastic about your job.

(e) Don't be afraid to take a reasonable risk.

(f) Always look for more responsibility.

(g) Dream up your own technique for advancement.

6. To get ahead in a big company, figure out ways to attract the favorable attention of the upper hierarchy.

7. Eight ways to let your business do your talking for you.

(a) Have the biggest sign in town.

(b) Use your windows as silent salesmen.

(c) Let your store shelves sell for you.

(d) Friendly and cheerful employees are a must.

(e) Tie a slogan to your business.

(f) Use color to promote sales.

(g) Advertise . . . advertise . . . advertise.

(h) When something new comes out, get it for your customers.

If you've been discouraged or you've felt stalemated in your upward movement in your profession, use the techniques I've given you in this chapter and things will get better and better for you. Don't expect any overnight miracles; but you should be prepared for them. Sometimes they really do happen.

chapter 19

Making
Your Conversation Count
with the Most Important
People in Your Life

There are a lot of people in your life, besides your family, who really count: your boss, your employees, your associates at work, your friends in the neighborhood and community. I've already discussed your family and friends in Part I. In this chapter, I want to talk about how you can converse with your boss, how to give a briefing to very important people (VIPs), how to talk at employees' affairs, how to talk easily with your business associates, and how to talk to members of the opposite sex without feeling ill at ease. First, however, let me tell you about . . .

THE HUGE BENEFITS YOU CAN GAIN FROM THIS CHAPTER

1. When you practice the first technique, learning how to get along with your boss, you'll better your chances for advancement and promotion.

2. When you practice the second technique, how to put your ideas across to your boss, you'll easily get him to accept your suggestions and recommendations.

3. The third technique will gain you the benefits of establishing good employee relations in your company.

4. The fourth technique gives you the ways you can benefit when you have the savvy of briefing some visiting VIPs. This is an excellent way to impress your boss with your capabilities of handling yourself in front of very important people. It's also a good way to display your vast knowledge of the company to those who really count.

5. The fifth technique shows you the advantages to be gained by friendly small talk with your business associates.

6. The sixth and last technique will show you the dividends to be gained by being comfortable and at ease in conversation with members of the opposite sex.

THE 6 TECHNIQUES YOU CAN USE
TO GAIN THESE BENEFITS

How to Get Along with Your Boss

In the last chapter, I said that if you wanted to get ahead in the business world, you should establish a cordial and warm working relationship with your boss. No doubt about it, if you want to get to the top and stay there, you must get along with your superior. No one is more important to you and your career than the person who can get you promoted or who can raise your pay.

You'll also get along much better with your boss if you're known as a hard worker. Nothing makes an employer happier than the sight of an employee toiling away at the job. Looking busy, sounding busy, and being busy, are not only smart office politics, but also simply good business, period.

Being a good worker is not enough. Another important way of getting along with your boss is to reinforce and build up his self-image, while doing the best job you can for him. To do that, let your style mesh with his. If he works at a rapid-fire pace, then give him short and concise answers—bare facts stated briefly without embellishment. If he enjoys hearing a lot of detail, then give him that. Always follow his lead; after all, he is the boss.

If you're a woman and your boss is a man, he might want to establish too warm and cordial a relationship with you. If that does happen, you must know how to rebuff his advances without destroying either him or yourself while doing so. If your boss does make a serious pass at you, you want to turn him off without destroying his ego or yourself at the same time. Don't be like the young female executive who said, "To hell with his ego and his feelings! He's the one who made the pass—not I!" She then proceeded to ridicule him to every woman in the entire company. You can guess how long she lasted.

The best way to let your boss down easily is simply to say, "I'm sorry, but I'm already committed . . . there's someone else I care for very much." This allows him to withdraw gracefully without hurt pride or anger for you haven't really rejected him as such.

If this should fail, tell him that your husband or your boy friend is insanely, even murderously, jealous. It's amazing to see how quickly a man will lose interest in an office romance when he finds out that the results could be deadly dangerous to himself.

How to Put Your Ideas Across to Your Boss

Presenting an idea to your boss successfully depends not only upon the specific words you use, but also on the preparation and research you do before you ever start talking. So you must know *what* you are going to talk about and *how* you're going to put your ideas across to him.

What you are going to talk about should follow these three specific guidelines:

1. *You must know your subject* inside out, backwards and forwards, from top to bottom. Be prepared to make decisions when your boss asks for your recommendations. Don't ask him to make your decisions for you. He has enough problems of his own to solve. He will appreciate you much more if you'll take some of the load off his shoulders by making some decisions that he can support.

2. *Know all the details of your proposition,* so you can answer any possible questions your boss might ask you, but don't drown him with all those details in your presentation. Give him only the basic points he needs to understand your idea unless he asks for more information. He will assume that you have all the details of your plan worked out. A sharp boss will check you on a few of them at least just to keep you alert and on your toes.

3. *Make your presentation brief, coherent, complete, and salesworthy.* Save time for your boss by having your idea outlined in writing so he can review it later on if he so desires. A written outline of your plan will also help him if he wants to present your idea to his superior for approval.

Now let's discuss how you're going to *physically* put your ideas across to your boss. There are five guidelines you should follow:

1. *You must know and understand your boss's personality* and have the intelligence and adaptability to go along with it. To be able to psych your boss to your way of thinking is just as important as being super-capable in your job. This is not polishing the apple. It is using applied psychology, applied where it will do the most good for you—on your own boss.

2. *Pay your boss the respect and deference he is due* when putting your idea across to him. Even if you don't really care for him, his position alone entitles him to some respect. As they used to tell me when I was in the army many years ago, "You salute the uniform, not the person wearing it."

3. *Adopt a "nothing sacred" attitude about your idea.* Don't act as if your idea is a God-given revelation, and, thus, immune from criticism. It must be able to stand on its own merits because it's a good idea, not just because it's your idea.

4. *Be courteous when presenting your idea.* Develop insight and understanding of your boss's problems. Consider his feelings when offering your idea to him.

5. *Let your boss set the mood for your presentation.* After all, he is the boss so you must have the ability to roll with the punches and adopt whatever attitude the occasion dictates: flexible or firm . . . friendly or aloof . . . humorous or serious. In short, you must be able to play it by ear.

How to Talk at Employees' Affairs

In Parts II and III, I discussed many of the aspects of how to talk with your employees in your daily work. Here I want to show you how to turn special occasions for your employees to your own advantage.

Good employee relations are important in every company. Satisfactory human relations must be established inside the company before you can ever expect to have good public relations outside.

Every company has the opportunity to hold special affairs or celebrations that can be attended by most or all of the employees. It could be an annual company picnic or party. It might be the banquet for presentation of trophies to the company bowling league. You may be invited to speak on these or other special occasions. Talks like these give you perfect opportunities to put yourself across favorably to both your superior and the company's employees. Everything you can do to promote better employee-management relations makes you a more valuable asset to your company.

"If need be, you can invent opportunities to improve human relations in your company," says Michael Justice, Director of Public Relations for a Kansas City, Missouri, company. "The number of affairs you hold throughout the year will depend entirely upon you.

"For instance, you could honor employees for length of service, using five-year periods as a basis. You don't have to limit such special occasions only to celebrating a person's years of service. You can hold the appropriate ceremony if a person has performed some especially meritorious act—either inside or outside the company—that is worthy of public acclaim and recognition. You can even hold a special function when someone gets married.

"Whatever the reason for the special occasion, you can make it an affair that brings everyone closer together. It can help establish a feeling of unity, harmony, and teamwork between you and your employees."

Japanese companies do things like this for their employees all the time to bring management and labor closer together, and look at how successful they've become in the world's economy. Let me give you a sample outline now that you can use for celebrating a person's years of service in the company:

1. Offer your own personal congratulations to the individual.
2. Emphasize that he has come up through the ranks; mention some of his previous jobs and responsibilities.
3. Recall some of his earlier days with the company.
4. Stress his personal development: industry, reliability, resourcefulness, cooperation.
5. Tell some aspect of his work that is worthy of special praise and recognition.
6. Mention how the company has benefited from his long years of faithful service.
7. Tell some of the good things his co-workers say about him.
8. Offer him congratulations on behalf of both the company and all the employees.
9. Present him with a suitable gift or appropriate reward.
10. Express your personal wishes for many happy and useful years ahead, whether he's retiring from the company or staying on with you.

This outline is not a final format, by any means. It is only a guide. You can make up your personalized one to fit the specific occasion by adding or deleting items as you see fit.

When presenting awards during an employee's earlier years, you can honor groups of people and speak in more general terms about all of them at the same time. However, when a faithful employee has given many years of loyal service, it would be far wiser to honor that person on an individual basis.

How to Give a Briefing for a Group of VIPs

It used to be that only heads of state, high-ranking government officials, generals, admirals, presidents of corporations, and chairmen of boards of directors rated VIP briefings.

However, today, because of the enormous volume of technical information and statistical reports he has to cope with to keep up with current developments, the average company executive and business-person has to depend on briefings by his subordinates—junior executives, middle managers, foremen, supervisors—to keep fully informed and up-to-date.

So, no matter how junior you might be in your organization, sooner or later you'll have to give a briefing to someone, so it's best to be prepared now. VIP briefings are here to stay.

Let me first tell you several things that a VIP briefing should *not* be used for. It should not be used to persuade or sell or get a person to take action or make a decision. It should not be used to impress or convince your listener of anything; nor should it be meant to entertain. *A VIP briefing should be used only to inform.* That is all it's meant for. It has no other legitimate purpose.

You can look at a VIP briefing as a method of giving up-to-date information about your own operation to someone who is either your senior or your superior.

GUIDELINES FOR A VIP BRIEFING

1. *Restrict your subject to fit your time.* If you've been given only 15 minutes to talk, and you think you need half an hour to tell about your entire operation, then something has to give, either your time or your subject.

Since the time of your VIP is usually limited—that's why he has to depend on briefings in the first place—chances are you'll have to condense your material and cover only the major points of interest about your operation.

You'd be better off sticking to a few salient points and covering them well than trying to cover everything and leaving a blurred and confused impression in your listener's mind. Later on, although he may not remember your face, he'll think of you as "that fellow who was so confused he didn't seem to know what was really going on in his own department."

2. *Arrange your ideas in a logical sequence.* Almost all ideas can be developed logically by using a time or procedure sequence. In a time sequence, for instance, you simply treat your subject from a past, present, and future viewpoint. Or you can begin at a specific date and move forward from there.

"A procedure sequence is especially useful in industrial briefings," says Tim Kelly, a factory production superintendent. "It begins with the raw materials stage and moves through each step of the manufacturing process until the finished product is reached.

"If you were in charge of a production line, for example, you could brief your VIPs by starting with the smaller component parts and move down the line to the final assembly point."

3. *Number your points as you make them.* One of the best ways to keep your briefing neat and clean and show you really know what you're talking about is to enumerate your principal points. Simply say it this way: "Today, I want to cover six points of interest for you. My first point is . . . The second point I want to talk about is . . . Third, I want to tell you . . . Sixth and last, I want to say . . ." You'll be remembered as a person who really knows his business.

4. *Avoid technical terms.* You might be briefing the chairman of the board, but that doesn't mean that he understands all the exact technical terms of your department. So use short simple words that are easy to understand.

"I once watched a smart young chemist in the research department of a large cosmetics firm brief the corporation president," says Donald Larson, an executive from Chicago, Illinois. "He wanted to show his boss how much he knew and how important his job was.

"So he used every technical term he could think of to show off his vast knowledge, although he usually translated his highly scientific terminology into ordinary common words for the men who worked in the compound room and on the mixing tanks.

"Unfortunately, the president took a dim view of his briefing, and summarily fired him, for he felt the young man was a pompous egotistical showoff. 'We can't afford to have smart alecks like him around,' he said. 'No one can understand what he says. Plenty more chemists where he came from!'"

5. *Use audio-visual aids.* Even VIPs enjoy audio-visual aids. It's the fastest way to transmit information and it saves valuable time for them. So use them whenever you can. Your listeners will appreciate you and your efforts when you do.

Five Don'ts to Keep in Mind When Giving a VIP Briefing

A VIP briefing is different from any other kind of talk or speech you might give. Being unique, it has five specific don'ts to keep in mind:

1. *Don't summarize a VIP briefing.* A VIP briefing is already a summary in itself. It should give a synopsis or an abridgement of your operation. Your listener assumes that you've included only the major points of interest he should know. It makes no sense to summarize a summary.

2. *Don't ask questions.* The technique of using questions to check on audience understanding is entirely out of place here. Whatever you do, don't insult the intelligence of your listeners by asking them questions. If *they* have questions, they'll ask them; you can be sure of that.

3. *Don't emotionalize.* Remember the specific purpose of a VIP briefing. You are not giving a talk to persuade or get action or a decision. You are not trying to impress or entertain. The sole purpose of a VIP briefing is to inform, nothing else, so be factual.

4. *Don't use the phrase, "As you know . . ."* Don't tell your listener something he already knows. This can irritate him no end. The purpose of your briefing is to tell him something he doesn't know.

5. *Don't use a strong closing statement.* Since you are giving a briefing only to inform, a strong closing statement to get your listener to take action of some sort is not in order here. The best way to close is simply to say, "Ladies and gentlemen, this concludes my briefing. Thank you."

How to Talk with Your Associates and Fellow Workers

"If you don't know how to relax and make small talk with your business associates, you can ruin your chances for advancement and promotion," says Norman Haines, a top-level company executive. "If you haven't been promoted lately, despite your obvious professional abilities, this could well be your problem.

"Instead of making others feel comfortable and at ease when casual conversation is called for, you could be making people feel uptight and tense. A few moments of conversation like this will make people want to avoid you at all costs. You'll be unwelcome wherever you go."

Businesspeople and executives place great confidence and trust in individuals who can get along well with others in the organization. If you're in management, no matter what your field, you'd better be able to deal with people at all levels. And that includes, among other things, the ability to engage in lighthearted chit-chat in all sorts of quasi-business, quasi-social situations.

Some people, for example, see every conversation as a battle—someone has to win, someone has to lose. They insist on having the last word on the subject, no matter what it is. An open exchange of views and ideas is not what a person like this has in mind in conversation with his associates.

Others feel that unless a conversation is serious, there should be no discussion at all. When this sort of person talks, his sense of humor vanishes, his voice becomes loud and forceful, and he insists that he is right. He will usually use pompous and pretentious words, all in a vain effort to sound important to his listeners.

If you want to be able to handle small talk gracefully with your associates, keep these four don'ts in mind:

1. *Don't spout statistics* as if you were a walking encyclopedia. Most people cannot absorb a barrage of technical data. Not only that, it's tiresome and boring to them. Keep your statistics and figures for your charts and written reports.

2. *Don't use technical jargon* except when you're in the company of those who understand it. Even then, if it's a quasi-business, quasi-social occasion, avoid it when possible. Keep office business where it belongs—in the office.

3. *Don't talk in clichés* or constantly say, "Do you understand?" "Do you get it?" "Do you follow me?" This will drive even your best friend up the wall in short order.

4. *Don't tell stories in which you are always the hero.* If you want people to like you and to enjoy talking with you, always use the small "i" and the great big "YOU."

All in all, good relations with your colleagues are most important to your career. The better relations you can establish with the individuals you encounter every day, the greater your chances are for building a successful reputation. If you can build your friendships on the basis of benefit, profit, and interest to your associates, they will be glad to reciprocate by doing what they can to advance your interests, too.

How to Talk Successfully with Members of the Opposite Sex

The best way to show you how to talk successfully with members of the opposite sex is to show you some of the conversational problems that men and women have at work. When you know the pitfalls, then you can easily avoid them.

For instance, in conversations with men—particularly those who are strangers—some women tend to revert to "weaker sex" role. Instead of speaking up, they let the man dominate the conversation completely. They let him decide what to talk about and how the subject will be discussed. Instead of participating actively in the conversation and contributing their own thoughts, they limit their comments to "please tell me more" or "please go on."

Women who carry on a so-called conversation like this are showing a lack of self-respect as well as a lack of self-confidence. They are also afraid that if they state their own point of view, they will be looked as too pushy, an ERA proponent, or even a potential troublemaker.

Some men tend to seize control of the conversation even when the woman does not offer them that opportunity. They also often add a sexual connotation to these encounters with their female business associates, especially when they're talking with an attractive young woman. Their conversation is sprinkled with sexual innuendos—even offers—at every opportunity.

If the woman is old enough to be their mother, they often adopt a condescending attitude toward her with such remarks as "And how are you today, *young* lady?"

But as Rex Hunter, a corporation executive, says, "If a businessman thinks the average woman, either in or out of the business world, wants to be treated in a patronizing way or a flirtatious manner just because she is a female, he is out of date and behind the times. This sort of attitude can get an otherwise capable executive into a lot of hot water. It's not wise to risk offending a woman, no matter what her job or her position might be."

The best way, then, to talk successfully with members of the opposite sex is to follow a guideline I've given you before: "Treat every woman like a lady and every man like a gentleman." Do that, and you'll never go wrong

In a nutshell, the major points to remember from this chapter are these:

1. Learn how to get along with your boss. No one is more important to you than the person who can get you promoted or who can raise your pay.

2. Know how to put your ideas across to your boss. You can do that if you follow these guidelines:

    (a) Know your subject inside out.

    (b) Know all the details of your proposition.

    (c) Make your presentation brief, coherent, complete, and salesworthy.

    (e) Know and understand your boss's personality.

    (e) Pay him the respect and deference he is due.

    (f) Adopt a "nothing sacred" attitude about your idea.

    (g) Be courteous when presenting your idea.

    (h) Let your boss set the mood for your presentation.

3. Volunteer to speak at employees' affairs. This brings you to the attention of those who really count.

4. How to give a briefing for a group of VIPs: five guidelines:

    (a) Restrict your subject to fit the time available.

    (b) Arrange your ideas in a logical time or procedure sequence.

    (c) Number your points as you make them.

    (d) Avoid technical terms.

    (e) Use audio-visual aids.

5. Five don'ts to keep in mind when giving a VIP briefing are these:

    (a) Don't summarize a VIP briefing. It is already a summary in itself.

    (b) Don't ask questions to check on audience understanding

    (c) Don't emotionalize.

    (d) Don't use the phrase, "As you know . . ."

    (e) Don't use a strong closing statement.

6. To talk successfully with your associates and fellow workers,

    (a) Don't spout statistics continually.

    (b) Don't use technical jargon.

    (c) Don't talk in clichés.

    (d) Don't tell stories in which you are always the hero.

    7. To talk successfully with members of the opposite sex, follow this one simple guideline and you'll never go wrong: "Treat every woman like a lady and every man like a gentleman."

PART VI

Conversational Problem Areas

Part VI includes Chapters Twenty through Twenty-two and in it I discuss the major problems you can encounter in both your oral and written relationships with people.

I want to give you the methods and the techniques you can use to solve your problems when they do come up, or better yet, show you how to keep them from happening.

chapter 20

How to Write
as You Talk:
The Master Formula
for Powerful and
Persuasive Writing

One of the best ways to put yourself across with the people who really count is to write clear and concise, strong and forceful letters, memoranda, and reports. It doesn't matter who you are or what you do—salesman, manager, executive, supervisor, businessman, preacher, teacher—if you can make yourself understood in your writing, you'll greatly increase your chances of becoming successful and getting ahead. In this chapter I want to show you how you can gain these goals.

How you write can bring you prestige, respect, influence, promotion and advancement, or the complete opposite of these. It can mark the difference between a low-paying menial job the rest of your life, or advancement to an important and prestigious executive position. Your ability to write persuasive letters can give you great power over others, for it is as true today as it was many years ago when Disraeli said it: "Men govern with words."

If writing presents a problem for you as it does for so many people, then the techniques in this chapter are just right for you. I'm not saying they will turn you into a professional writer, but they will make your writing clear, concise, to the point, and easy to understand. They'll help you streamline your correspondence so you can say what you really want to say. Along with that big dividend,

YOU'LL ALSO GAIN THESE 6 OUTSTANDING BENEFITS

1. *You will be able to put yourself across to others.* Every letter you write is a personal contact with another person. To people who've never met you, your letters are you. They tell your reader what kind of person you are. So express yourself clearly, make what you write easy to understand, and you'll put yourself across to your reader with no trouble at all.

2. *People will cooperate with you and do as you want them to do* when you write masterful letters that express your message with clarity and power.

3. *There will be a genuine meeting of the minds* when you know how to write masterful letters to gain clear communication and definite understanding.

4. *You will achieve your purposes.* With powerfully written letters, goals can be reached, missions accomplished, objectives obtained.

5. *You will succeed in getting what you want from others,* for it's a proven fact that 'successful individuals know how to communicate their orders, commands, and desires to people.

6. *You will definitely better your chances for getting ahead.* If you work for a big company, you'll improve your chances of getting ahead if you handle yourself well on paper. Learn to write clear and forceful letters and you'll attract the attention of the people upstairs who really count. Without a doubt, you'll be promoted long before the person who cannot express himself forcefully and clearly in writing.

EIGHT TECHNIQUES YOU CAN USE TO ACHIEVE THESE BENEFITS

Six Ways to Make Sure You're Understood

Unless your letters, memos, directives, and reports say exactly what you want them to say, they can become real troublemakers for you. Your job is to make your writing crystal-clear. Here are six ways you can do that:

1. *Make your writing brief.* "Say what you have to say and be done with it," says Bill Mallory, managing editor of a large daily newspaper. "If you can tell your story in one paragraph, then don't use three or four to do the job. And don't worry if there's a lot of white space left on the page. If it bothers you that much, take a pair of scissors and cut it off!"

Being brief doesn't mean you should make your letters read like telegrams. You can't get the kind of brevity you want by leaving out the articles *a, an,* and *the.*

But you can gain brevity by leaving out unnecessary details, by dividing complex ideas into short sentences, and by steering clear of deadhead words and phrases, repetition, and pompous elaboration. The next four techniques are also useful in achieving brevity so you can make your meaning clean and clear.

2. *Use the active voice of the verb.* Don't rob your writing of its strength by using the passive voice of the verb. When you use the

passive voice, it means the subject has had something done to it by someone. For instance: The ball was hit *by* Tom.

But the active voice means that the subject has done something to the object. *Tom hit the ball.*

The key word to watch for so you can get rid of the passive voice of the verb is the preposition *by,* either spoken or *implied.* The use of the active voice makes for clear brief writing for it says succinctly *who* does *what.*

Ninety-five percent of the time your writing will be simpler, shorter, stronger, and to the point when you use the active voice of the verb.

3. *Take a direct approach.* Learn to express your ideas directly. Starting your sentences with the unnecessary phrases *it is, there is,* or *there are* weaken them and slow down your reader's understanding. They also tend to put your sentences into the passive voice.

"*It is* the recommendation of the supervisor that this progress report be forwarded to the main office immediately by us," would be much better said this way: "The supervisor recommended that we send the progress report to the main office at once." Instead of saying "*There is* a standing rule in this company," say "This company has a standing rule."

4. *Change long modifiers to short ones.* This is another way to achieve both brevity and clarity in your writing. "Mr. Prescott, *who is* the chairman of the board, will preside at the meeting," could be made shorter and clearer by saying, "Mr. Prescott, chairman of the board, will preside . . ."

"Equipment *that is* deadlined" can be shortened to "Deadlined equipment." "They gave us a month *for accomplishment of the mission*" can be simplified and shortened by saying, "They gave us a month *to do the job.*"

5. *Break up long sentences into short ones.* The other day I read this sentence in a leading national business magazine: "There is not enough time available for the average corporation executive to do everything that needs to be done so it is necessary for him to determine judiciously the essential tasks and do them first, and then, to spend his remaining time on those that are of secondary importance."

Now let me show you how the author could have broken this monstrosity up into three short, simple, and intelligible sentences:

"The average corporation executive does not have enough time to do everything he needs to do. He must decide what is essential and do that first. Then he can spend his remaining time on things that are of secondary importance."

6. *Get rid of deadheads.* In railroading, deadheads are nonpaying passengers or empty box cars. In writing, deadheads are useless words or phrases that add no meaning to your sentences and actually get in the way of what you want to say. Here are a few examples of useless deadheads:

a. *Take steps.* Telling someone to take the appropriate steps to do something simply means he should be ready to do it. *Take steps to be ready* means to *get ready.*

b. *In the case of.* This phrase is almost always a deadhead. For instance, don't say, *In the case of* Smith's accident, a report must be made to the safety officer. Say instead, Report Smith's accident to the safety officer.

c. *In the event that* means *if. Due to the fact that* means *since* or *because.*

d. *The importance of this cannot be overemphasized* usually means the chances are its importance can very easily be overemphasized.

e. *Every effort will be made* usually means no effort at all will be made. If you do intend to make an effort, say what effort, when, and by whom.

f. *Numerous instances have been reported* is a well-worn favorite to evade the real issue. Tell what instances apply to whom, when, where, and in violation of what.

g. *Interpose no objection* means I do not object.

h. *An intensive search of the files of this office was made* usually means we looked in a couple of file cabinets.

What to Do About Big Words

If you use simple words of one, two, or three syllables, people will be sure to understand you. That's the sole purpose of communicating with someone: to be understood, not to show how smart you are.

It is important to be familiar with pompous and ostentatious words for only one reason: to understand people who use these words when they write or speak to you. An extensive vocabulary of pretentious words is an asset only if you use these words for catching, not for pitching.

You'll be able to grasp quickly the ideas thrown at you, but these words will not help you put your thoughts across to others. Whenever you stop your reader with a word that forces him to the dictionary, you've broken his stream of thought. Do that often enough, and you'll lose him completely. Your letter will end up in the waste basket.

A minister once complained to me about religious writers using unnecessarily complex language and complicated words. But the next Sunday he spoke about the unfortunate *dichotomization* of the church in his sermon.

My pew neighbor nudged me and whispered, "What does *dichotomization* mean, Jim?"

"It means to break into two branches or split into two parts, Joe," I whispered back.

"My God!" Joe said aloud, forgetting where he was. "Why didn't he just say that?"

Government writers and federal bureaucrats seem to have a special gift for making simple things complicated and hard to understand. Frankly, I can think of no excuse for using big words if small ones will do the job just as well, but most government writers don't agree with me.

For instance, take the government author who said, "Heavy equipment operators must wear *sound attenuators*," when all he really meant to say was *ear plugs*. That same writer went on to say that "Sound attenuators eliminate the heavy equipment operator's ability to detect audible danger signals or apprehend vocalized instructions." You can't correct this kind of writing. The only thing to do is throw it away and start all over.

The Best Way to Get Rid of Big and Useless Words

What big words should you cut out of your writing? Abstract nouns made out of verbs ought to be the first to go.

How can you get rid of them? Simply use two or three smaller words for the big one like this: *falling apart* for *disintegration* . . . *breakthrough* for *penetration* . . . *look down on* for *condescension* . . . *coming between* for *intervention*.

Abstract nouns made out of verbs need weaker passive verbs to support and carry them. A simple sentence like *He decided to go to town* becomes *The decision to go to town was made by him*.

If you learn nothing more from this chapter than how to cut out most of the words that end in *-ion* and *-tion* when you write, you'll do wonders for your style. You'll be saying what you want to say with force and clarity.

How Using Small Words Can Improve Your Writing Style 100 Percent

Now that you know how to get rid of abstract nouns made out of verbs, I want to show you how to use small words so you can completely revamp your writing style. When you write with strong action verbs and specific concrete nouns, your writing will improve 100 percent. I guarantee it.

To help you get rid of those abstract nouns and passive verbs, I've made up a list of simple verbs you can use to describe nearly any action you can think of. When you use these simple but powerful verbs, it is almost impossible to make their subjects a vague and abstract noun.

Ache	Call	Go	Keep	Mark	Press	Shake	Stick	Tie
Act	Can	Happen	Kick	May	Pull	Show	Stir	Touch
Add	Carry	Handle	Know	Mean	Push	Shut	Stop	Try
Aim	Cast	Hang	Lay	Mind	Put	Sit	Strike	Turn
Ask	Catch	Hate	Lean	Move	Raise	Skip	Take	Twist
Bear	Check	Have	Leave	Owe	Reach	Slip	Talk	Upset
Begin	Claim	Hear	Let	Pick	Run	Smell	Tear	Use
Bind	Close	Help	Lie	Pitch	Say	Split	Tell	Walk
Blow	Come	Hide	Like	Pin	See	Stab	Test	Want
Break	Cover	Hold	Look	Plan	Sell	Stand	Think	Watch
Bring	Crawl	Hunt	Lose	Play	Seem	Start	Throb	Wear
Buy	Cut	Hurt	Make	Poke	Set	Stay	Throw	Whirl
								Work

Don't look at this list as final or all-inclusive. Use it instead as a foundation for your own verb vocabulary. Add other simple one- and two-syllable verbs as you run across them.

When you use these simple verbs, it is impossible to write abstract sentences. You're forced to be direct, concrete, and to the point whether you want to or not. Try as you may, you can't be vague and abstract with such verbs as *make, do, hit, walk, run, strike.* Your writing will become powerful, strong, and vigorous when you use these simple verbs.

What to Do About Your Grammar

You do not have to be a grammarian or an English teacher to write a good sentence. The primary reason for all those grammar rules you learned back in school was to help you focus your reader's attention on the meaning you wanted him to get. If you take care to make your meaning clear by using one sentence for each idea, your grammar will usually take care of itself.

When you get right down to it, grammar is simply the arrangement of words together in a way that gives them meaning. The rules of grammar are quite flexible. They leave plenty of room for individual style. All those old grammar school rules of *don't split an infinitive . . . never end a sentence with a preposition . . . every sentence must contain a subject and a predicate* don't stand up in actual everyday usage.

For example, an editor once criticized Winston Churchill's English in his book manuscript when he ended a sentence with a preposition. The editor's letter to Mr. Churchill came back with this brief note which said, "This is the kind of nonsense up with which I cannot put."

Only a fanatic insists that rules can't be broken. When you use short simple sentences, you'll find that good grammar becomes a natural subconscious part of your writing, so that it's really nothing at all for you to worry about.

How to Use Power Words to Get Your Reader to Take Action

By carefully observing people, you can learn which words are the most potent in creating a favorable reaction. But that takes time, so let me give you a head start.

For example, some words cause people to think rationally, using logic and reason. Other words cause them to react emotionally. Let me give you a specific example.

A sharp real estate agent will tell the owner he'll be glad to sell his *house*. He doesn't use the word *home* when talking with the owner. Home is an emotional word and the seller can become reluctant to part with his *home* even though he's perfectly willing to get rid of his *house*. By the same token, the real estate agent never sells the buyer a *house*. He always offers him a *home*.

These two words represent two entirely different ideas for the same object. A house is not a home, it's only a house. It's made of bricks, wood, and concrete. It's a very nonemotional idea. But a home is where your heart is, where your family lives, where your kids grow up. It is an extremely emotional power word.

Emotional words are power words, and people are ruled more by emotion than by logic and reason. Salespeople always like to use emotional words because they cause people to buy. A top salesperson will never ask a person what he *thinks* about a product. Instead, he'll always ask his potential buyer how he *feels* about it.

Think is a nonemotional word that requires a person to use logic and reason. But *feel* is an emotional word that goes straight to the heart, and if you'll remember, *the head never hears 'til the heart has listened.* That one sentence alone tells you more about the human psyche than all the books on applied psychology in the library ever will.

Another point well worth mentioning about power words is this: You should learn which words turn your boss on and which ones turn him off, for no matter what they are, they are power words, too. Everyone has certain likes and dislikes when it comes to language, so you'd be smart to use the "pet" words your boss likes to hear. People like to hear *their* favorite words and phrases played back to them. Emulation of a person is still one of the highest forms of praise when it is subtly done.

The 6 Basic Rules for Writing Powerful and Masterful Letters

1. *Know exactly what it is you want to get done.* Many people fire off letters without having a clear idea of what it is they want to accomplish. I'm sure you've been on the receiving end of letters like that. When you get through reading them, you don't really know what it was the writer actually wanted from you.

If you know your purpose in writing, if the objective you want to gain is clear in your mind, then your letter can be clear and easy to understand. However, if your objective is vague and abstract, your writing will also be vague and abstract. So, before you start any letter, know *exactly why* you are writing it. Figure out what it is you want to say.

Writing, just as speaking, can normally be divided into three general categories:

1. *To order or command* someone to do something.

2. *To inform* someone of something.

3. *To persuade* someone to do something.

All three kinds of letters will be concerned with *who, what, when, where, why,* and *how,* but the emphasis will be different in each case depending on the purpose.

A letter directing action indicates *what* has to be done. An informative letter tells a person *how* to do something. A persuasive letter explains *why* some action must be taken.

These purposes can often overlap, as when you make a directive more palatable by explaining the *how* and *why* as well as the *what*. If you were writing a persuasive memo to your boss asking him to approve some new office procedure, you would emphasize *why* it should be used; that is, you would *stress the benefits to be gained*, as well as explaining *how* the new system would work.

So, even though you might have some overlapping in your letters, keeping these three fundamental purposes in mind will help you find clear explanations or convincing reasons to back up your arguments so you can attain the specific objectives you're after.

2. *Know who your reader is going to be.* Who is going to read your letter? A person with a college degree or one with an eighth grade education? You'll get your point across better when you use words and ideas that your reader can easily understand. Whether a person reads you loud and clear depends on his training and knowledge—not on yours.

"A lot of directives here at the plant are written at college levels of comprehension," says Keith Moore, the office manager for a rubber and tire company. "The writer forgets that people of modest education must read them. I do my best to get everyone to keep their memos simple enough for everyone to understand."

3. *Lay the proper foundation.* Masterful and powerful letter writing is based on proper preparation—the selection, analysis, and organization of your ideas.

Many people write ineffective letters because they start writing before they are actually ready to do so. That's why their letters aren't satisfactory and don't get results.

Before you pick up a pencil or sit down at your typewriter, think your problem through thoroughly. Get the answers to *who, what, when, where, why* and *how* first. Then you can start on your actual job of writing.

4. *Identify and pinpoint your main ideas.* Successful writers of powerful and masterful letters know that deciding what to leave out is just as important as what to put in, if not more so. Words, ideas, and facts not essential to the understanding of your specific idea only hide and weaken it.

It doesn't matter whether your writing is based on your personal knowledge, reading and research, or both. The problem you face is usually having too much material rather than not enough.

So, preparing to write is a process of defining, sifting, and discarding until you have only one clear goal in mind and the main ideas necessary to reach it.

5. *Write from an outline.* Any piece of writing, no matter what, can be done logically and quickly from an outline. An outline makes your writing plan easy to see and helps you keep your specific objective clearly in mind. But it is worthless unless you stick to it and work from it. This is not to say you should not change your outline here and there if better ideas occur to you. You should. Your outline should be a working sketch, not a final blueprint.

6. *Review your writing for objectivity.* Unless you're writing a chatty personal family letter or a love letter, chances are you won't have a finished product ready to go on your first attempt. When you've completed your first draft, you should review and revise your work.

As you do this, concentrate on the objectivity of your writing. Business letters in particular should be objective whether they're informative, persuasive, or directive in nature. When you present a decision or a recommendation to your boss, he will assume that your letter or your memorandum is the result of careful thinking.

How to Use the Hook Technique in Your Letters

To get your reader to take action and do what you want, especially in the persuasive type of letter, you must use the *hook technique*. No persuasive letter is ever complete without the *hook*. You may have written a wonderfully interesting letter. It could be that you've aroused your reader's attention, captured his interest, and sparked his desire. But if you don't hook him, he won't take the action you want him to take.

Your reader will do what you want for one of two reasons. The first is that you've made him so anxious to get what you've offered, he'll take the required action immediately. But most people tend to procrastinate. They want to think it over so they put things off for a while. You must give him another reason to take action. This is where the hook comes in.

You must make this kind of reader understand how he's going to lose out if he doesn't immediately do what you ask. The hook provides a penalty if he fails to take action. That is the second reason the reader will do as you ask—*fear*. Unless your hook arouses the fear in him that he will lose something worthwhile if he doesn't act at once, you won't get the results you want.

Fear is on the opposite side of the coin of desire. If you can't move a person to action by arousing his desire, then you turn the coin over and move him to action by arousing his fear.

For example, I have a letter in front of me right now from the savings and loan association that holds the mortgage on my house. Since my home was bought before skyrocketing interest rates, the bank is anxious for me to pay off my loan so they can lend the money out again at nearly twice the interest that I'm paying.

They are so anxious for me to do that, they are offering me a discount of several thousand dollars on my present loan if I will pay it off. Their letter says my discount may be as high as 25 percent! That's a healthy saving for me and I'm interested, for I'm as anxious to save money as anyone else is.

But to make sure that I will take action without delay, they closed their letter with a *hook*. Their hook says, "Act now! This offer is for a limited time only and may be withdrawn without any prior notice."

Since the hook technique is usually used in a letter where you're persuading someone to do something, I want to give you an excellent format you can use for it.

A 5-Point Format for a Persuasive Letter Using the Hook

1. *The opening.* Here you grab your reader's attention by fitting in with his train of thought (one or more of the fourteen basic desires all people have). You establish your point of contact with your reader's self-interests to excite and arouse his curiosity so he will read further into your letter.

2. *You cover the benefits to be gained.* As soon as you have your reader's attention, tell him how he's going to benefit by doing as you ask. Give him a reason to take action. Do this, not only by describing what your product or your proposition is, but also by letting him know what it will do for him. Tell him about the profit, pleasure, convenience, saving in time and labor, and so on, that he will gain.

3. *Offer proof of what you say.* The best proof you can offer that your proposition will give him the benefits you've promised is to tell him of others who've benefited. Let him check with Sam Jones, Sally Brown, or Joe Gray so he can find out for himself that you're telling him the truth.

If you're going to bring in your witnesses, you must use real people who are willing to let you use their names, addresses, and phone numbers. This requires some extra effort on your part, but there is absolutely no better way to gain a person's confidence and trust in you and in what you say.

4. *Tell him how he can gain those benefits.* This is usually done in the next-to-last paragraph. Here you give your reader his exact instructions. You tell him exactly what he must do to gain the benefits you've offered him.

5. *Close with the hook.* This is the snapper, or the penalty you hold over your reluctant reader's head. You hook him and force him to take action by telling him about the loss in money or prestige or opportunity that will be his if he does not act at once. You normally place the hook in the last paragraph of your letter.

A time penalty is one of the best ways to get the action you want. For example: This offer expires in 5 days . . . Good only until the 15th of March . . . Prices go up in February . . . Limited supply, first come, first served . . . Act now. This offer is for a limited time and may be withdrawn without any prior notice. Four-percent discount good only through the month of November.

Since writing can be so important to your conversational expertise, I want to summarize the main points of this chapter for you here.

1. Six ways to make sure your writing is understood by your reader are these:

    (a) Make your writing brief. Leave out all unnecessary details that can cause confusion.

    (b) Use the active voice of the verb.

    (c) Take a direct approach.

    (d) Change long modifiers to short ones.

    (e) Break up long sentences into short ones.

    (f) Get rid of all deadheads.

2. If you use simple words of one, two, or three syllables instead of big and cumbersome ones, people will be sure to understand you.

3. The best way to get rid of big and useless words is to eliminate all abstract nouns made out of verbs.

4. The best way to handle grammar is to use short simple sentences. Simply focus your reader's attention on the meaning you want him to get.

5. Use power words to get your reader to take action. Power words are emotional words that aim for the heart instead of the head.

6. The 6 basic rules for writing powerful and masterful letters are these:

(a) Know exactly what it is you want to get done.

(b) Know who your reader is going to be.

(c) Lay the proper foundation. Get the answers to who, what, when, where, why, and how.

(d) Identify and pinpoint your main ideas.

(e) Write from an outline.

(f) Review your writing for objectivity.

7. How to use the "hook" in a persuasive letter: a five-point format.

(a) The opening is used to grab your reader's attention.

(b) Next, you cover the benefits to be gained.

(c) Offer proof that what you say is true.

(d) Tell him how he, too, can gain these benefits.

(e) Close with the hook. The hook is the snapper or penalty you use to get your reluctant reader to take the action you want. A time penalty is one of the best hooks you can use.

In conclusion, then, let me say that simple action verbs, concrete nouns, the precise use of words, clear thinking, and careful construction—that is to say, one sentence for each idea—are the elements that make for clear and effective, powerful and persuasive writing.

Admittedly, it is much easier to be lazy and write otherwise, but it is better to write with care. Then, you can be sure of getting the results that you want.

chapter 21

The 7 Cardinal Sins
of Conversation and
How to Avoid Them

As I've mentioned before, I normally do not like to discuss the negative aspects of any subjects. I always prefer to concentrate on the positive rather than the negative, for it is usually better to learn what to do rather than what not to do. However, sometimes it is appropriate to identify certain mistakes and discuss how to avoid them or correct them.

Then, too, I feel that your *Lifetime Conversation Guide* would not be complete without the information in this chapter, for you could be committing one of the cardinal sins of conversation and not even know it, although everyone else would. Moreover, I have followed up each conversational mistake with the correct technique to use, so the right way of doing things will be the last thought in your mind. Now let me tell you about . . .

THE ENORMOUS BENEFITS THAT YOU CAN GAIN

When you know how to avoid the seven cardinal sins of conversation,

1. You'll be regarded as the person "with the golden tongue." You'll be popular and well-liked wherever you go.

2. You'll prevent misunderstandings and hard feelings.

3. You'll keep from making enemies, even accidentally.

4. You'll improve your abilities to get along well with others.

5. You'll be well thought of by your friends and neighbors. Everyone will have a good word for you.

THE TECHNIQUES YOU CAN USE TO GAIN THESE FANTASTIC BENEFITS

The format that I've used in this chapter is somewhat different from that in the preceding chapters. Here I will first discuss each cardinal sin of conversation, and, then, how to correct it or how to avoid it.

The First Cardinal Sin of Conversation Is Not to Listen Attentively to the Other Person

Most of the time, if you do not listen attentively to the person who is speaking, it will be for one of several reasons. It could be because you are preoccupied with what you are doing; for example, watching television or reading the newspaper while your wife (or child) is trying to tell you something. A boss is often guilty of this sin, too, when he keeps on reading the papers on his desk while his employee is trying to talk to him.

Another reason for poor attention could be that you have no interest whatever in the subject that is being discussed, so you spend your time trying to figure out ways to change the conversation to a topic you enjoy talking about.

If you are interested in the subject being discussed, you may be impatient to talk so you can present your ideas, so you spend your time mulling over in your mind what you are going to say rather than listening attentively to the other person.

Whatever the reason, the speaker will notice your lack of attention. Failure to pay attention to the other person and to get what he is saying is in a way an insult. It is a form of rejection, and rejection hurts; attention heals.

How to Correct the First Cardinal Sin of Conversation

One of the most distinguished Supreme Court Justices our country has ever had once said, "To be able to listen to others in a sympathetic and understanding manner is the most effective method you can use to get along with people and tie up their friendships for good." This famous Justice went on to say that few people knew how to practice the "white magic" of being a good listener.

Here are five methods you can use to physically show that you are listening and your mind will automatically follow, for as the Biblical saying goes. "Act as if it were so and it will be."

1. *Look directly at the person while he's talking.* Don't be disturbed by anything else or let your eyes wander. The person speaking will notice that immediately and be upset or hurt by your lack of attention.

2. *Show a deep interest in what he is saying.* You can do this easily without ever saying a single word. Just nod your head and smile or frown whenever it's called for. That's all you need do.

3. *Lean toward the person physically.* Sitting up on the edge of your

chair and leaning forward evidences a deep interest on your part in what the other person is saying.

4. *Ask questions if necessary.* If the conversation founders, all you need do is say something along this line: "And then what did you do? And then what did you say?" This is enough to keep the other person going indefinitely.

5. *Don't interrupt.* Except to ask questions as I've just indicated, don't interrupt the speaker. No one likes to be interrupted. Interrupting others is another one of the cardinal sins of conversation all by itself so I'll discuss that point next in more detail.

The Second Cardinal Sin of Conversation Is Interrupting Others

The second cardinal sin of interrupting others is an offshoot of the first cardinal sin of not listening attentively to the other person. It stems from a person's ego, his desire to be important, to be heard and to be recognized. Interrupting others is also a quick way, not only to become unpopular, but also to be highly disliked. It can be one of the main causes of never being invited anywhere.

I know of no quicker way to insult a person or to hurt his feelings than to interrupt him when he's trying to tell you something. How many times have you been right in the middle of a good story only to have one of your listeners interrupt you and start talking on a brand-new subject? You'd have liked to strangle him with your bare hands, right?

I know exactly how you feel, for one of my close friends did this to me once in front of a large group of people and embarrassed me greatly by doing so. It took me longer than I care to admit to get over my resentment toward him for what he'd done to me.

How to Correct the Second Cardinal Sin of Interrupting Others

I want to give you four easy steps you can use to pay attention to the other person and keep from interrupting him.

1. *Learn to listen with everything you've got.* Concentrate completely on what the other person is saying. Don't let anything distract you. Focus your attention on him with all the intensity and awareness you can possible command.

2. *Teach your ego to hold its breath.* All of us are self-centered most of the time. To me, the world revolves around me; as far as you are concerned, it revolves around you. Each one of us is trying to stand under the spotlight on center stage.

But if you want to pay close attention to the other person and not interrupt him, that is precisely what you must not do. For a few moments of time, make your attention-hungry ego take a back seat. Let the spotlight fall on the other person for a change.

3. *Practice patience.* Be courteous enough to hear the other person out. If you listen closely enough, you might even learn something of value.

4. *Be concerned.* This is the final technique and the most important of all. There's no use paying attention to a person or listening to him unless you honestly care about the feelings of other people. If you pretend, you'll be spotted at once; sincerity can't be faked.

Admittedly, old habits are hard to break, so if this cardinal sin of interrupting others is one of your conversational problems, and you do catch yourself breaking in while someone else is speaking, stop and apologize for doing so and ask the other person to continue. This at least shows courtesy on your part and your rudeness can be forgiven.

The Third Cardinal Sin of Conversation Is Criticizing the Other Person in Public

This third cardinal sin of conversation is most often a bad habit of managers, supervisors, teachers, or anyone in charge of others. If you get right down to it, criticism is what we say about other people who don't have the same faults that we have. Or as the old Chinese proverb says, "Those who have free seats always hiss first."

No one likes to be criticized. No one wants to be told that he is wrong or that he has made a mistake, especially in front of others. Criticism is one of man's deadliest weapons. Let me show you how criticizing others will always work against you.

Psychological studies conducted by a midwestern university of hundreds of persons in all walks of life showed that when people were criticized in public for a mistake, only 30 percent improved their performance the next time. However, if they were praised in public, 90 percent did a better job the next time. In other words, praise works three times better than criticism to get the results you want.

How to Correct a Person's Mistakes Without Criticism

If you're in a management position of any sort where you have people under you, I know you will need to correct a person's mistakes at times. But if you follow two basic principles I'm going to give you, you can easily correct a person's mistakes without arousing this anger or resentment, and without making an enemy out of him.

First of all, you should never correct a person's mistakes in front of others unless a genuine emergency exists that threatens loss of life, bodily injury, or harm or loss of valuable equipment or property.

Second, the only way to criticize is to correct the mistake, not the person. If you want to get the most mileage out of your criticism, be specific about the error that is to be corrected. Tell the person exactly what he is doing that is wrong and then show him how he can correct his mistake. Most people are anxious and willing to do the right thing when they know what the right thing is.

Here is another point worth mentioning about criticism. If one of your employees asks you to look at his work and let him know where he's making his mistakes, don't be misled by that. That isn't what he wants at all. He wants you to tell him what a good job he's doing. He wants you to pat him on the back and tell him he's not making any mistakes. He wants to be praised, not criticized. Read between the lines; listen to what he's really saying. Remember the basic desires that every person has; to be criticized is not one of them.

The Fourth Cardinal Sin of Conversation Is to Use Sarcasm and Ridicule

People who make sarcastic remarks often do so from a desire to be humorous. Unfortunately, this kind of conversation usually backfires, for most people do not like sarcasm, especially when they're the target.

Far worse than sarcasm is ridicule. Those same university studies I mentioned a moment ago proved that when people were ridiculed in public, only one out of ten improved his performance and did a better job the next time around. Nine out of ten did worse.

You see, if you make fun of a person, if you belittle and ridicule him, or if you make a fool out of him—especially in front of others—you'll have an enemy for the rest of your life. He'll never forget and he'll never forgive you, for you've destroyed his sense of self-respect, dignity, and self-esteem as well as deflated his ego and injured his pride.

Besides that, you've also denied him the opportunity to fulfill no less than four more of his basic desires. You've taken away his chance to be recognized for his efforts by ridiculing him instead of praising him . . . you've destroyed him in front of his peers and prevented the group from approving of him . . . you've ruined his desire and motivation to accomplish something worthwhile . . . you've taken away his feeling of emotional security. Can you blame him now for utterly despising you? Look at the amount of harm you've done to him just by ridiculing him and making fun of him.

So, if you do ridicule someone and make a fool of him in public, you'd better load your shotgun, bolt the doors, and bar all the windows. He'll come after you for sure. The basic desire for revenge or vengeance, an eye for an eye and a tooth for a tooth, can be a greater driving force than even the desire for importance or the desire for sexual fulfillment.

How to Correct the Fourth Cardinal Sin of Conversation

The best way to overcome the problem of using sarcasm in your conversation is to substitute other kinds of humor. Develop one-liners or memorize some jokes to tell instead of being sarcastic. Many helpful books are available in libraries and bookstores.

Ridicule, however, is quite another matter. If you've been prone to cutting people to pieces in front of others, you'll simply have to change your attitude completely and take a brand-new approach. I would suggest that instead of looking for reasons to ridicule a person, you look for ways to praise him.

Public praise is the most powerful technique you can use to feed a person's ego and make him feel important. This can be especially helpful to you if the person is your employee, for praise releases energy; it acts as an energizer. Praise causes a person to work harder, more efficiently, and with greater enthusiasm—all the things you want from your employee.

Praise does the exact opposite of ridicule. Where ridicule destroys a person's opportunity to achieve no less than six of his basic needs, praise not only feeds his ego and fulfills his desire to be important, it also satisfies seven more of his fundamental desires, namely:

1. Recognition of efforts, reassurance of worth.
2. Social or group approval, acceptance by one's peers
3. A sense of roots, belonging somewhere
4. The accomplishment of something worthwhile

5. A sense of self-esteem, dignity, and self-respect
6. The desire to win, to be first, to excel
7. Emotional security

The Fifth Cardinal Sin of Conversation Is Talking Down to People

You can usually recognize this kind of personality quite easily. First of all, he'll want you to think that he's the final authority on the subject, no matter what it is. He might not know exactly what you're talking about, but he'll have an opinion on it, you can bet on that.

His assertions will usually be made in a loud, arrogant, and overbearing voice. This kind of person is almost always involved in an argument. People often attack his ideas, not necessarily because his statements are wrong, but because they can't stand his arrogant and haughty attitude.

Another way of talking down to people is by using big and pompous words to show off, or actually, to show how ignorant the other person is.

How to Correct or Avoid the Fifth Cardinal Sin of Conversation

First, never make comparisons. Don't try to show how much smarter you are than other people. You'll never win, for sooner or later you'll encounter someone who knows much more than you do, even about your own pet subject.

Next, I would recommend that you learn the value of the three simple words, "I don't know." Even if you do know all the answers to the subject being discussed, give someone else a chance to shine. And who knows, you might actually learn something new. As President Harry S. Truman once said, "It's what you learn after you know it all that really counts."

Last, learn to talk *with* a person rather than *to* him. When you talk with a person instead of to him, it's extremely difficult to talk down to him. If you adopt this simple attitude, you'll be able to solve this problem even before it happens.

The Sixth Cardinal Sin of Conversation Is Participating in Idle and Malicious Gossip

If you constantly talk about others and blacken their names with idle and malicious gossip behind their backs, you'll quickly lose all your friends and end up with nothing but enemies. Let me give you a specific example of exactly what might happen to you:

"We have a neighborhood gossip who was squelched by ignoring her completely," Sally J. told me. "Three of us were so tired of listening to her slanderous tongue, we made a solemn pact never to speak to her again. Soon our avoidance of her spread throughout the entire neighborhood until she was completely isolated from the whole community. No one would even say as much as 'Hello' to her.

"How effective is this 'silent treatment' technique? It will work much better than getting angry and trying to fight back. Just a few days ago I saw a 'For Sale' sign go up in front of her house."

How to Keep from Committing This Sixth Cardinal Sin of Conversation

First, you need to keep in mind that when the neighborhood "motor mouth" tells you some juicy tidbit about Henry or Mabel behind their backs, or who's sleeping with whom, that you are not immune from this kind of slander yourself. That same person will talk to Henry or Mabel about you behind your back.

The best way to deal with this neighborhood gossip and keep from getting involved is to tell him you are not interested in what he's saying and then refuse to listen. Tell him to take his garbage somewhere else, preferably to the city trash dump. It that doesn't work, then use the silent treatment I told you about just a few moments ago.

Whether you run into the person at social activities, in business, in church, or in the supermarket, put yourself above his vicious level. Don't even say "Hello" to him. Ignore him utterly and completely. Nothing shuts off a rumor monger's tongue more quickly than your refusal to talk with him or to even listen to him. And if you refuse to listen, he can no longer spread malicious gossip and ugly rumors.

The Seventh Cardinal Sin of Conversation Is Using the Big "I" and the Little "You"

In a sense, all the previous cardinal sins of conversation—not listening attentively to the other person; interrupting others while they are speaking; criticizing the other person in public; using sarcasm and ridicule; talking down to people; participating in gossip—all these stem from the seventh cardinal sin, that is, making yourself the big "I" and the other person the little "you."

Now don't get me wrong here. The desire to be important is one of the 14 basic desires I discussed in detail in the first chapter. In fact, some psychologists feel that the desire to be important is the greatest motivational force of all, and one of the major differences between man and animals.

So, it is not wrong to want to be important. It's perfectly normal. It's only when you try to attain this feeling of importance at the expense of others that the problem of the big "I" and the little "you" gets into the picture.

To tell the truth, there is no faster way of driving people away from you than by constantly talking about yourself and your own *great* accomplishments. Not even your best friend can put up with never-ending stories of how important you are. Even he will eventually reach the limits of his endurance.

If you believe that you can win friends by getting them interested in you and your affairs, then I must tell you quite bluntly: you are dead wrong. The only way you can ever win lasting friends is to become truly interested in people and in their problems.

It is the person who has no interest in his fellow human being and his problems who always has the greatest difficulties in life and ends up causing the most harm to others. That person will always fail until he changes his basic attitude toward people.

How to Correct the Seventh Cardinal Sin of Conversation

If you're having a problem with this cardinal sin, here are two giant steps you can take to solve it.

1. *Forget yourself completely.* As I've said before, all of us are self-centered most of the time. We are always busy trying to impress someone else. Most of our waking moments are spent in trying to gain status of some sort.

But if you really want to gain friends and get along with people, you should forget yourself completely for a change. You'll find it's a tremendous relief to get the world off your shoulders and let others carry the load for a while. It'll give you a chance to relax and rest.

2. *Think that other people are important.* Simply tell yourself once and for all that other people and their problems are just as important as you and your problems are. When you adopt this attitude, it'll come through clear as a bell to the other fellow. You won't have to put on a phony face and butter him up to make it work.

With this new approach you can stop looking for gimmicks to make the other person feel important. You won't need any, for you'll have put your dealings with other people on a firm, sound, sincere, and honest basis. Sincerity and honesty are better than a gimmick every day of the week, for you can't make the other person feel important if deep inside you really feel he's a worthless nobody.

The beauty of this technique is that you no longer have to participate in the games that people play to impress each other. All you need to do to make it work is just to think that the other person is important. Pretend that it is so, and it will be.

Let me list these seven cardinal sins of conversation along with the techniques you can use to correct them or avoid them in one place for your ready reference before moving on to the next chapter.

1. The first cardinal sin of conversation is not to listen attentively to the other person. You can use these five techniques to correct or avoid that deadly sin.

    (a) Look directly at the person who is speaking.

    (b) Show a deep interest in what he is saying.

    (c) Lean toward the person physically.

    (d) Ask questions if necessary.

    (e) Don't interrupt.

2. The second cardinal sin of conversation is interrupting others. You can correct this bad habit if you will:

    (a) Learn to listen with everything you've got.

    (b) Teach your ego to hold its breath.

    (c) Practice patience.

    (d) Be concerned.

3. The third cardinal sin of conversation is criticizing the other person in public. To correct this sin, never correct a person's mistakes in front of others unless a genuine emergency exists. The second point to remember is to correct the mistake, not the person.

4. The fourth cardinal sin of conversation is to use sarcasm and ridicule. The best way to overcome the problem of using sarcasm in your conversation is to substitute some other kind of humor. Ridicule is quite another matter. To correct that requires a complete change in attitude. The best way to overcome this bad habit is to praise a

person instead of ridiculing him. This causes you to look for a person's good points instead of his bad ones.

5. The fifth cardinal sin of conversation is talking down to people. To correct that sin, first of all, never make comparisons. Next, learn the value of the simple phrase, "I don't know." Last, learn to talk *with* a person instead of *to* him.

6. The sixth cardinal sin of conversation is participating in gossip. To correct this problem, simply turn your back on the gossip and give him (or her) the silent treatment.

7. The seventh cardinal sin of conversation is using the big "I" and the little "you." You can correct that easily if you will (1) forget yourself completely, and (2) think that other people are more important than you are.

You may have other problems of conversation to contend with, but these seven I've given you in this chapter are the cardinal sins. If you will take care to correct them, you will be well on your way to becoming an interesting and well-liked conversationalist.

chapter 22

A Magic List
of Successful Openers
and Closers
for a Conversation,
a Talk, or a Speech

In this last chapter, I want to give you some practical tips on how to open and close a conversation, a talk, or a speech. The point is, the first impression people have of you will probably be a lasting one, so you want to make your opening the best you possibly can.

By the same token, how you end your conversation or talk will also become an indelible part of your listeners' memories, so you want that final impression to be the best possible one, too.

Even if you drop the ball in the main body of your talk or your conversation, excellent first and last impressions can help you overcome any weaknesses in the middle. Just as a saleman might make a poor presentation, if he can end with a strong closing statement, he can often make the sale, and the end result is what really counts.

Before I discuss the techniques that you can use to gain the benefits I've just mentioned, I want to give you one *never*, which is this: *Never open a conversation by just saying "Hello."* It's a deadly opening for it's not interesting, so the conversation goes absolutely nowhere. The magic key to a successful opening is to get the other person's interest immediately if you want your conversation or your talk to be successful and beneficial to you. Now for the techniques you can use to do exactly that:

The Magic Method You Can Use to Strike Up a Conversation with a Complete Stranger

One of the best ways to strike up a conversation with a stranger and make him feel completely at ease talking with you is to pay him some sort of compliment . . . appeal to his ego . . . make him feel as if he were the most important person in all the world. Do that and you'll have him eating out of your hand in no time at all. Here are some examples of how to use this technique:

1. I've always been interested in computers, but I really don't understand how they work. I know you're an expert in the field. Could you tell me more about them? (This opening can be used for any kind of work.)

2. I've often wished I knew more about the stock market and how it works. Would you tell me more about your position as a stock broker and the kind of work you do? (This opening can also be used for any occupation or profession.)

3. I've never seen such good-looking shoes. Could you tell me what kind of leather they're made of?

4. Your name absolutely fascinates me. Won't you tell me something about its origin and meaning?

5. I've never met an educator I didn't enjoy talking with for I always learn something new. Could you tell me more about your particular specialty?

6. You really have a gorgeous tan. I'd love to look like that, but I always turn as red as a boiled lobster. What's your secret?

Although you can use other conversation starters, I've found that using a leading question to get the person to talk about himself and his own self-interests is the most reliable way to get a person to open up and talk with you.

Simply concentrate your attention on what he's most interested in, not on what you're interested in. If you know nothing at all about the other person's background, you can always compliment a man on his jacket, his shoes, his wavy hair, whatever is striking about him. If the individual is a woman, you can compliment her on her choice of jewelry, her clothing, her hairdo, her beauty.

It doesn't matter how you do it or what you say as long as you feed the other person's ego. Make him or her feel important and you'll never go wrong. It's one of the best ways in the world to strike up a conversation with a stranger. You'll always be remembered as a most interesting person who was a brilliant and scintillating conversationalist.

How to Talk with a Woman If You're a Man

Some men find it extremely difficult to talk with a woman. They are overly worried about saying the wrong thing and having it misinterpreted as either a chauvinistic remark or a pass. Married men are often uncomfortable talking to a single woman, especially if their wives are present.

This will present no problem at all if you stay on safe ground by selecting an appropriate and suitable subject. Surveys of over 1,000 women about their favorite subjects for discussion revealed that the following subjects were at the top:

1. Family and home (including children and grandchildren)
2. Good health
3. Work or job (if a working woman)
4. Promotion and advancement (if employed)
5. Personal growth
6. Clothes and shopping
7. Recreation
8. Travel
9. Men (especially single women)

Subjects that were least liked by women were sports such as baseball, football, and boxing, politics, and religion.

How to Talk with Men If You're a Woman

The topics men most like to talk about are strikingly similar to those women like, according to surveys of 1,000 men. They like to talk about the following subjects:

1. Family and home, including children and grandchildren
2. Good health
3. Work or job
4. Promotion and advancement
5. Personal growth
6. Recreation
7. Travel
8. The opposite sex (especially young single men)

Subjects also preferred by men were sports and politics. They disliked discussions of religion; nor did they care to discuss clothes, fashions, or shopping.

How to Use Topic Teasers to Stimulate Immediate Interest

One of the major problems of opening a conversation is that many people can't get beyond "How are you? How's the wife? How's business? Beautiful weather we're having, isn't it?" If you want to get out of this conversational rut that leads nowhere, and project your own personality at the same time, start off with a *topic teaser*. Let me give you an example.

I watched a friend of mine, Al J., as he used this technique perfectly the other night at a social get-together. When he was introduced to an especially gorgeous woman, instead of saying, "Hello . . . how are you . . . it's nice to meet you," as everyone else had done, he said, "You're really going to be a problem to me tonight."

Startled by his remark, the lady asked, "Why do you say that?"

"Because you're so beautiful, I'll never be able to take my eyes off you," Al said. "I hope you don't mind."

"Mind?" she asked. "Of course not. How could I mind?"

With just that one little sentence, Al was off and running far ahead of the rest of the pack.

You, too, can use a topic teaser to open a conversation. You can arouse interest with it and head off meaningless and boring conversations. Look through your newspaper or a current news magazine. I know you can find some more interesting topics to discuss than the weather, politics, religion, or the state of your health.

To best project your individuality and to make sure you're on safe ground, choose a topic in which you're well versed so you won't get caught short. Avoid controversial subjects that can create enemies for you. Abortion, for example, is hardly a subject for parties or social gatherings. No matter which side you choose, you'll always be in trouble. If you're for abortion, some will view you as a person who advocates murder. If you're against abortion, others will view you as being out of touch with reality. Either way, you'll lose, so don't use such controversial subjects for topic teasers. You do want a subject that's interesting enough to stimulate a spirited conversation, but not one that creates enemies and hard feelings.

A Magic Way to Open and Close a Telephone Conversation

To answer your telephone with just a dull and lifeless "Hello" is a poor start for any conversation. One imaginative businessman of Scottish ancestry I know answers his phone with a "Top of the morning to you! This is McCampbell speaking. And how can I be of service to you?" It's always a pleasure to call him just to hear his happy greeting. No matter how down you might be, he always makes you feel better.

You can let the person calling you *feel* how happy you are to hear from him, too, by the happy sound of your voice. It's so easy to say, "Rick! It's good to hear from you. I'm so happy you called. What can I do for you?"

Equally important is the tactful way to close a long-winded telephone call that's eating away at your working day. You can pleasantly say, "George, I'm so sorry to rush away, but I have no choice. I simply have to go. My secretary's standing in the door right now giving me a dirty look. Let's pick this matter up again as soon as we can," or "If I didn't have to meet my boss in five minutes, Mary, I'd love to discuss the subject in more detail with you. How about getting together some day at lunch where we can talk this over without any interruption?"

Seven Ways to Open a Talk or a Speech

If you're giving a talk or a speech, you want to establish contact, gain attention, arouse interest, and get into your subject quickly and easily. To do that, you can use any one of the following techniques:

1. *Use an effective opening statement* that will show your audience immediately how they will *benefit* by listening to you. Make your opening statement a *grabber*.

2. *Make reference to some previous information.* This method is most often used when your contact with your listener is of a recurring nature. It refreshes his memory and reestablishes contact with him on common ground. It's always best to renew that contact with your listener by talking about a benefit he's going to gain.

3. *Use a startling statement.* To get into your subject with a bang, find some eye-opening statement that can be used to punch home a benefit immediately. Be sure you can back up your startling statement with proof and facts when you use one.

4. *Ask a leading question* that offers an immediate benefit to your listeners. A leading question that promises a benefit is one of the best ways to open a business conversation or a talk. Your listeners have to respond in some way to you. When they do, you've established contact with them. This method is so important I will discuss it under a separate heading in a few moments.

5. *Use an anecdote, a story, an illustration, or an example* to show your listener how he can also gain the benefit you're talking about. People are always more interested in people than in things. To prove your point, tell your listener how it worked for Jim Brown, Sam Green, or Susie Black. Tell your story or give an illustration for a definite and

specific purpose to benefit yourself. Don't tell a story just for the sake of telling a story.

6. *Quote an authority.* "A testimonial from a satisfied user is still the best way to convince a reluctant prospect," says Carl Williams, president of a prominent advertising agency. "If that satisifed user is also an authority in some field, or if he's a celebrity and well-known to the public, so much the better. People tend to believe they'll receive the same benefit the celebrity received from the product."

7. *Use a demonstration that shows the benefits the listener will receive.* When you use a demonstration that shows the benefits your listeners are going to receive, you'll increase your chances of holding the interest of your audience. The lecture method is the poorest way of presenting a subject. Demonstrations get far better results.

I'm sure you've noticed by now that no matter which method you use to open your speech or your talk, you should always emphasize a benefit immediately. If you do not do that, your listener will turn a deaf ear to your proposal.

Your library or your bookstore should have many useful books that will help you when you're going to give a speech or a talk at the Chamber of Commerce, the Kiwanis breakfast, the Father-Son banquet, the Letterman's Club, the company bowling league's party, or any other occasion you might think of.

If you want to be successful as a public speaker, then tuck away in your memory some anecdotes, jokes, stories, and quotations you can use to open your talk and to liven it up as you go along. Even the most serious speech can be helped with a line of humor here and there. It will help to relax your audience and make them even more receptive to what you are saying.

How to Use Leading Questions to Start Off a Business Conversation or Talk

As I said a few moments ago, I consider the leading question technique so valuable, I wanted to discuss it separately under its own heading. You see, in business conversations or talks, you can use a variety of methods to persuade people to listen and pay attention to you. However, I prefer by far the use of the leading question that promises your listener a benefit, for it is by far the most effective approach you can use. Here are some brief examples of this potent technique:

1. How would you like to make some easy money?
2. How would you like to increase profits 25 percent?
3. How would you like to cut your production costs in half?
4. How would you like to double the number of your customers?
5. How would you like to reduce your utility bills by 20 percent?
6. Do you want a car that offers the best mileage on the road?

No matter what your specific circumstances are, use the kind of question that promises your listener an immediate benefit just for listening to you, and he'll be forced to give you his full and undivided attention.

Not only can you offer your listener a benefit with the leading question technique, but you can also get him saying "Yes" at once, and that's ever so important in persuading him to do what you want him to do.

You see, when he says "Yes" to your opening question, he establishes a friendly positive mood. This makes it much easier for him to continue to agree with you.

Asking leading questions that promise a benefit, then, is the surest way of getting a person to listen to you. Questions, rather than statements, can be the most effective way to make a sale, win a person over to your way of thinking, and persuade him to do as you ask.

How to Know When to Quit Talking

"I don't think I've ever seen a church where people actually wait in line to get inside," I said to John Lawrence, pastor of a large Orlando, Florida, church. "What's your secret? A lot of speakers would give anything to draw the crowds that you do."

"Well, I'd like to think people are anxious to hear my message," John said. "I would hope that's at least part of the reason. But I also believe that one explanation for our large church attendance is that I don't beat a dead horse to death over and over from the pulpit. I never take more time than my subject is worth. I leave my congregation anxious to hear more for I always quit before I'm through."

Maybe you can't follow this principle to the letter when you're issuing an order to a subordinate or giving detailed instructions on how to do a certain job. Other than that, though, this rule is good to follow at all times that I can think of. Besides, most orders and directives, rules and regulations, always use more words than are usually necessary to get the job done.

So, don't muddle and confuse your listener with information he doesn't need. Don't drown him in details. Unnecessary trivia can cause confusion, loss of attention, and misunderstanding. Remember that attention is always lost when understanding is gone.

To keep the full attention and interest of your listener, and to gain his complete understanding, don't talk too much. Make your sentences short. Don't use unnecessary words. Stay on course. Stick to your point.

To sum up this idea, let me put it this way: Don't wait too long to finish. Be sure that you stop speaking before your audience stops listening. Do as George M. Cohan advised, "Always leave them wanting more." Then you know they'll always come back.

Why I Try Not to Talk Too Much

Like a great many other people, I tend to keep on talking once I get started. Someone asks me a question about a subject that interests me or on which I'm knowledgeable, and I soon find that I'm spinning away like a phonograph record. I become hypnotized by the sound of my own words. When I discover this is happening, I try to turn myself off, for I'm always reminded of what a famous Hollywood and Broadway character actor once said.

"When I was very young, I was auditioning for a part in a play in New York," this actor said. "I was quite impressed with my speaking abilities and really got carried away during the audition. Right at the climax, a deep voice boomed out of the darkened theater seats and said, 'Young man, you're in love with the sound of your own voice!' That really taught me a valuable lesson I've always remembered through all my acting years."

Let me summarize for you now the major points I'd like you to remember from this chapter.

1. The magic method you can use to strike up a conversation with a complete stranger is to pay him some sort of compliment . . . appeal to his ego . . . make him feel as if he were the most important person in all the world.

2. If you're a man, you can easily talk to a woman if you will select an appropriate and suitable subject. Women normally do not care to discuss sports, politics, and religion.

3. If you're a woman, you can easily talk to a man if you avoid such subjects as clothes, fashion, or shopping. Almost any other subject is suitable.

4. Start a conversation off with a "topic teaser" to capture a listener's attention and stimulate interest.

5. A magic way to open a telephone conversation is to let the other person know how happy you are to hear his voice.

6. Seven ways to open a talk or a speech are these:

(a) Show your listener immediately how he will benefit by listening to you. Make your opening statement a "grabber."

(b) Make reference to some previous information to reestablish contact with your listener.

(c) Use a startling statement.

(d) Ask a leading question that promises an immediate benefit.

(e) Use an anecdote, a story, an illustration, or an example.

(f) Quote an authority.

(g) Use a demonstration that shows the benefits the listener will receive.

7. The best speakers learn to quit before they're through. They know that it's wise to always leave the person wanting more.

8. Don't fall in love with the sound of your own voice.

How to Get the Most Out of Your *Lifetime Conversation Guide*

The title of my book means exactly what it says. It is truly a lifetime conversation guide. It is not meant to be read only once and then placed on a shelf to gather dust, for you could not possibly retain all the valuable information that it contains with only one reading. After all, it has taken me a lifetime to collect the material that has gone into this book.

You'll want to refer to it time and time again, for the instant benefits and help that it will give you to solve your conversational problems, build your expertise, and sharpen your techniques. If you will use your *Lifetime Conversation Guide* in this way, there is absolutely no doubt in my mind that you will become a much better speaker as well as a much better writer. That, I guarantee.

Index

A

Abdominal muscles, 142
Ability:
    above-average, 114–115
    listening, 131–33 (*see also* Listening)
Advancement (promotion), 233–235
Advertising, 236–237
Aids:
    audio-visual, 246
    visual, 221–223, 224–225
Anger, 37–38, 133–135
Anxiety, 142
Argument:
    compromise on trifles, 172, 173
    force is waste of time, 170–171
    help other save face, 172, 173
    knowing when to take action, 172, 173
    let him state his first, 171
    probe and explore his, 171–172, 173
    retain control, 171
    state your side, 172, 173
    work *with* human nature, 171
Arms, 133
Attitudes, 26–27, 28
Audio-visual aids, 246

B

Benefits, emphasize, 155, 158–160, 161, 180–181, 185
Body language:
    abdominal muscles, 142
    appear relaxed, 141, 147
    arms, 133
    closed discussion, 146
    close physical proximity, 143
    deep thinkers, 140
    don't allow interruptions, 146
    ears, 133
    employee really attentive, 143
    equality, 146
    extremely intelligent people, 140
    eyebrows, 133
    eyes, 133, 142, 143, 147
    fear and anxiety, 142
    fingers, 133
    forced to sit close, 146

Body language: (*cont.*)
    forehead, 133
    freer from deception, 139
    gaze, 140
    gestures, 140, 141–142, 146–147
    hands, 142
    head tilted to one side, 143
    immediate corrective action, 143
    look of power and command, 139–140
    male, 142, 146
    mouth, 142
    neutral facial expression, 142, 146
    nose, 133
    office furniture placement, 141
    phone, 144–145
    positive attitude, 140
    power position, 141
    self-confidence, 147
    shoulders, 133
    smiles, 142, 146
    social activities, 145–146
    space on territory, 141, 144, 147
    staring, 142, 143, 147
    steepling, 140–141
    teacher stops trouble, 143–144
    voice, 140
    why understand, 139
    woman, 141, 144, 146
    words to eliminate, 145
Boss:
    putting ideas across to him, 242–243
    relationship with, 232, 241
Briefings for VIPs:
    audio-visual aids, 246
    avoid technical terms, 246
    don't ask questions, 247
    don't emotionalize, 247
    don't summarize, 247
    ideas in logical sequence, 246
    no "As you know . . .," 247
    no strong closing statement, 247
    number points, 246
    restrict subject to fit time, 245
    used only to inform, 245
Business, friendship and, 39, 41
Business conversations:
    body language, 137–147
    complaints, listening, 126–136

Business conversations: (cont.)
   (see also Complaints, listening)
   correcting mistakes, 87–98
   (see also Correcting mistakes)
   employee suggestions, 114–124
   (see also Employee suggestions)
   getting that raise, 231–233
   grammar, 229–230
   job interview, 230–231
   make employee superior, 101–111
   (see also Informing employees)
   orders and commands, 73–86
   persuasion (see Persuasion)
   promotion, 233–235

C

Calming angry person, 38, 133–135
Changes, planned, 108, 109–110, 111
Children, 47, 49–50, 61, 65–66, 68
Closing:
   letter, 267
   talking, 288–289
   telephone conversation, 286
Color, promote sales, 237
Commands (see Orders and commands)
Communication, keep lines open, 122, 124
Comparisons, 276, 280
Complaints, listening:
   always grant hearing, 135
   asking questions, 129–130
   (see also Questions)
   ask what he wants you to do, 136
   attention heals, 131
   being concerned, 136
   between the lines, 132
   body language, 133
   calm angry person, 133–135
   double-check results, 136
   employees like you, 126–127
   explain grievance procedure, 135
   find what people really want, 127
   get all facts first, 136
   get rid of red tape, 135
   help person voice complaint, 135
   hold your fire, 132
   judge content, not delivery, 132
   know employee better, 126
   let employee know your decision, 136
   let them know you are willing, 130
   make first move, 130–131
   make it easy for them, 135
   no hasty or biased decisions, 136
   open mind, 132
   patience, 132
   practice patience, 135–136
   rejection hurts, 131
   reliable information, 129
   resist distractions, 131–132

Complaints, listening: (cont.)
   show interest, 131
   they know you're interested, 127
   watch for ideas, 132
   wholehearted attention, 131
   work at it, 131
   your responsibility, 128
Compliments:
   feed the ego, 4, 5
   friends, 40
   marriage and home life, 63–65, 67, 68
   strangers, 22–23, 28
Conclusion, talk or speech, 206, 207, 211
Control:
   attitudes and emotions, 26–27, 28
   people, 6
   strangers, 26–27, 28
Cooperation and support, gain:
   accept blame if you are wrong, 190, 197
   be part of team, help them, 191–192, 197
   buffer technique, 196, 198
   honesty and truthfulness, 190, 197
   "I need you," 196–197, 198
   participatory management, 193–196, 197
   stand for what you believe, 190, 197
   witnesses, 190–191, 197
   written statements, 190, 197
   you cooperate first, 188–189, 197
   your word your bond, 190, 197
Correcting mistakes:
   benefits, 88–89
   be specific about how to correct, 95–96, 97
   call attention directly, 89–90, 97
   close on up-beat note, 96, 98
   constant improvement, 96–97, 98
   discuss one mistake per interview, 95, 97
   fit penalty to offense, 96, 98
   further action if necessary, 97, 98
   get all facts first, 90, 97
   good reputation to live up to, 97, 98
   his side of story first, 94, 97
   never lose temper, 92, 97
   only way to begin, 92–93, 97
   right time and place, 91–92, 97
   take your own inventory, 93–94, 97
   weigh evidence and facts, 94–95, 97
Corrective action, 143
Criticism, 37, 40, 55, 61, 62, 63, 67, 68, 69,
   87–98
   (see also Correcting mistakes)
Criticizing, 273–274, 279

D

Deadheads, 259
Delegation, 232–233
Desires, 8, 14
Discipline, 65, 68, 143
Distractions, 131–132

E

Ears, 133
Efficiency experts, 116
Ego, appeal, 20–21, 39, 282
Ego-gratification, 7, 8, 15
Emotions:
    audience, 216, 223
    offer emotional security, 79
    strangers, 26–27, 28
Employees:
    friendly and cheerful, 237
    informing, 101–111
    (*see also* Informing employees)
    talking at their affairs, 243–244
Employee suggestions:
    above-average ability, 114–115
    being able to ask, 115–116, 124
    company saved from ruin, 119–121
    feeling of importance, 115
    follow through on idea, 123, 124
    imagination, ingenuity, 115
    initiative, 115, 121–122, 124
    keep communication lines open, 122, 124
    make your problem their problem, 118–119, 124
    needs of employee satisfied, 120–121
    part of team, feeling, 114
    reward, 123, 124
    stop wasting money, 116–118
    worthwhile conversation, 124
Enthusiasm, 103
Equality, 146
Eyebrows, 133
Eyes, 133, 142, 143, 147

F

Facial expressions, 142, 146
Fear, 142, 265–266
Feedback, job interview, 231
Fingers, 133
First impressions, 18–19
Forehead, 133
Friends:
    accept person as he is, 30, 36–37, 40
    angry with you, 37–38
    art of human relations, 31
    associates at work, 40
    benefits, 30–31, 41
    business, 39, 41
    common interest, 35–36, 40
    compliments, 40
    courtesy, 40
    don't lose your temper, 38
    don't show him up, 37
    don't take problems to work, 40
    ego, 39
    Golden Rule, 40

Friends: (*cont.*)
    keep your word, 40
    never criticize, 37, 40
    never speak disparagingly of you, 30–31
    no favorites, 40
    other person's welfare, 40
    praise, 32–35, 40
    (*see also* Praise)
    reliable, dependable, 40
    respect you, 30
    rights of others, 40
    showing how to do something, 37
    sincerity, 40
    stick by you, 30
    treat with dignity and respect, 37, 40
    trust you, 30, 40
    unexpected services, 40
    warm and cordial, 39–40
    you must first give, 31–32, 40
Furniture placement, 141

G

Gestures, 140, 141–142, 146–147
Golden Rule, 40
Gossips, 55, 276–277, 280
Grammar, 229–230, 261–262
Greed, 7
Grievances
    (*see* Complaints, listening)

H

Hands, 142
Hearings, 135
Hobbies, 26, 28
Home life
    (*see* Marriage and home life)
Hook technique, letters, 265–266
Human relationships, 234

I

"I," big, 277–279, 280
Ideas:
    asking person for, 193–196
    (*see also* Participatory management)
    employee (*see* Employee suggestions)
    main one of speech, 205–206, 211
    putting across to boss, 242–243
Imagination, 115
Importance, feeling of, 115
Information from employees, 114–124
    (*see also* Employee suggestions; Questions)
Informing employees:
    benefits, 102–103
    build up value of person's work, 107–108, 111
    eliminate rumors, 103

Informing employees: (*cont.*)
  enthusiasm encouraged, 103
  gain respect and support, 103
  initiative encouraged, 103
  misunderstandings, 108–109, 111
  performance review checklist, 105–106, 110
  planned changes, 108, 109–110, 111
    brief assistants early, 108, 109
    if it affects person, 109, 111
    if it doesn't affect person, 109–110, 111
  praise person for job well done, 106–107, 110
  praise person properly, 107, 111
  well-informed employee is best, 102–103
  when work is unsatisfactory, 106, 110
  where they stand with you, 104, 110
Ingenuity, 115
Initiative, 103, 115, 121–122, 124
Interrupting:
  being concerned, 273
  concentrate completely, 273
  don't allow, 146
  insults or hurts, 272
  practice patience, 273
  stems from person's ego, 272, 273

J

Job interview, 230–231

K

Know-it-all, 51–52, 55

L

Leadership, 21, 28
Leading questions, 10, 155–158, 161, 286, 287–288
Learned needs, 8, 14
Letters:
  benefits to be gained, 266
  close with hook, 267
  hook technique, 265–267
  how to gain benefits, 267
  main ideas, 264–265
  opening, 266
  outline, 265
  proof of what you say, 266–267
  proper foundation, 264
  review for objectivity, 265
  what you want done, 263–264
  who reader is, 2
Listening:
  between the lines, 50, 132
  children, 49–50
  feedback, 51
  gripes and complaints, 126–136
  (*see also* Complaints, listening)

Listening: (*cont.*)
  improve your abilities, 131–133, 271–272
  lean toward person, 51, 271–272
  look at speaker, 51, 271
  nonhearing level, 165
  not, 271
  not interrupting, 272
  questions, 51, 272
  semi-listening level, 165
  show interest, 51, 271
  thinking or comprehension level, 165, 166
  with everything you've got, 49–51, 55

M

Male:
  body language, 142, 146
  talk with opposite sex, 249, 283–284
Management consultants, 116
Mannerisms, irritating, 219–220, 224
Marriage and home life:
  accept people as they are, 61–62, 68
  benefits, 69
  children, 61, 65–66, 68
  choose to be happy, 59–60, 68
  compliments, 63–65, 67, 68
  get up on right side of bed, 60, 68
  irritability problems, 62–63, 68
  no criticism, 61, 62, 63, 67, 68, 69
  only person you can change is yourself, 62, 68
  praise, 63, 65, 66, 67, 68, 69
  say cheerful, pleasant things, 60–61, 68
  spouse, 66–68, 69
  what you say, 58–60, 68
  wife helps husband, 66, 68
Mind:
  open, 132
  right frame, 115–116, 124
Mistakes:
  admitting, 52–53, 55
  correction, 87–98
  (*see also* Correcting mistakes)
Misunderstandings, 108–109, 111
Modifiers, 258
Morale, 103
Motivators:
  accurate information about, 11
  achievement, 8, 15
  approval, 8, 15
  desires or learned needs, 8
  desire to win, 8, 15
  discovering, 9–10
  ego-gratification, 7, 8, 15
  emotional security, 8, 15
  financial success, 8, 15
  greed, 7
  if you help person fulfill, 15
  liberty and freedom, 8, 15

Motivators: (*cont.*)
    list, 8, 15
    love in all forms, 8, 15
    new experiences, 8, 15
    opportunity for creative expression, 8, 15
    physical needs, 7
    privacy from intrusion, 8, 15
    psychological needs, 8
    recognition, 8, 15
    sense of belonging, 8, 15
    sense of personal power, 8, 15
    sense of self-esteem, 8, 15
    use for your own benefit, 13–14
    use to your advantage, 9
Mouth, 142

N

Names, 25, 28
Needs:
    learned, 8, 14
    physical, 7
    psychological, 8
    use for your benefit, 13
Nervousness, speeches, 204, 211, 217, 224
Nose, 133

O

Objections:
    appeal to emotions, 168–169, 173
    find real reason, 166, 173, 178–179, 185
    questions can help, 169–180, 173
    state calmly, 234
    turn into benefit for him, 167–168, 173
Office furniture placement, 141
Openers
    (*see* Strangers)
Opening:
    conversation with stranger, 282–283
    (*see also* Strangers)
    leading questions, 287–288
    (*see also* Leading question technique)
    letter, 266
    man with woman, 283–284
    talk or speech, 206–207, 211, 286–287
    teasers to stimulate interest, 284–285
    telephone conversation, 285–286
    woman with man, 284
Orders and commands:
    aura of command, 84–85
    before issuing, 76–77, 85
    be sure need exists, 75–76, 85
    check for understanding, 82–83, 86
    concentrate on single point, 81
    concise and clear, 74–75, 79–82, 86
    easy to understand, 74
    fit person, 80
    fit to job to be done, 79–80

Orders and commands: (*cont.*)
    get him in mood to obey, 78–79, 86
    get maximum from, 83–84, 86
    give incentive for obedience, 77–78, 86
    how-to, 74–75
    less duplication of effort, 75
    mission-type, 74
    oral, 81
    positive, 79–82, 86
    results you want, 74, 76–77, 85
    simplicity, 75, 80–81
    written, 81–82
Outline:
    any piece of writing, 265
    talk or speech, 206

P

Participatory management:
    cooperation automatic, 193
    desires satisfied, 193
    example of how to use, 194
    person feels proud, 193
    places you can use it, 194–196
    why so effective, 193
Patience, 132, 135–136
Perfectionists, 55
Performance:
    job well done, 106–107, 110
    unsatisfactory, 106, 110
Performance review checklist, 105–106, 110
Persistence, 184, 185, 186
Personality:
    body language projects, 137–147, 217–218,
        224
    new, 6
Persuasion:
    appeal to mind and heart, 152, 161
    benefits, emphasize, 155, 158–160, 161
    concentrate on single point, 181–182, 185
    find out what people want, 153–154, 161
    gain cooperation and support, 187–198
    (*see also* Cooperation and support, gain)
    help him get what he wants, 179–180, 185
    leading question technique, 155–158, 161
    persistence, 184, 185, 186
    reason for not accepting offer, 166, 173,
        178–179, 185
    repeat business, 185
    resistance and objections, 163–173
        arguments, 170–173
        listening, 165–166, 173
        objections, 166–170, 173
        (*see also* Objections)
        questions help, 169–170, 173
    sell benefits, not features, 180–181, 185
    selling right person, 183–184, 185
    signature, 184–185, 186
    take care of old customers, 185, 186

Persuasion: (*cont.*)
    talking too much, 182–183, 185
    "Yes, but . . ." technique, 160, 161
    "yes" answers to questions, 177–178, 185
Phone, projecting personality, 144–145
Physical needs, 7
Popularity:
    accept criticism gracefully, 55
    admit your mistakes, 52–53, 55
    ask questions, 51, 54
    be interested in others, 47, 48–49, 55
    be yourself, 54
    checklist, 54–55
    forget yourself, 47, 48, 55
    gossip, 55
    interesting subjects, 55
    listen, 49–51, 54, 55
    (*see also* Listening)
    mistakes to avoid, 44, 54
    never argue, 55
    not be a perfectionist, 55
    not being *know-it-all*, 51–52, 55
    offer opinion, 54
    pay attention, 45–47, 55
        children, 47
        make person feel important, 45
        wife, 46
    please and thank you, 46–47
    practicing techniques, 53–54
    right and wrong, 55
    sense of humor, 55
    smile, 55
Positive attitude, 140
Power:
    body language
    (*see* Body language)
    when you control conversation, 5–6
Praise:
    different from flattery, 34–35
    getting person in mood to obey, 78–79, 86
    marriage and home life, 64, 65, 66, 67, 68, 69
    person for job well done, 106–107, 110
    properly, 107, 111
    satisfies needs, 33
    sincere, 34
    ways, 33–35
    what person does, 32, 34, 35, 40
Problem areas:
    big "I", little "you," 277–279, 280
    comparisons, 276
    criticizing, 273–274, 279
    gossip, 55, 276–277, 280
    interrupting, 272–273, 279
    not listening
    (*see* Listening)
    sarcasm and ridicule, 274–276, 279–280
    talking down to people, 276, 280
Profession, 26, 28

Promotion (advancement), 233–235
Psychological needs, 8
Purpose, talk or speech, 205, 211

Q

Questions:
    asking, 129–131
    best one asks "Why?", 130
    definite answers required, 129
    discourage guessing, 129
    get honest answers, 10
    leading, 10, 155–158, 161, 287–288
    not at briefings, 247
    one point at time, 129
    popularity, 51, 54
    specific purpose, 129
    subtle techniques, 9
    understood by everyone, 129
    "yes" answers, 177–178, 185

R

Raises, getting:
    become authority in field, 231–232, 238
    blow your own horn, 232, 238
    delegate, 232–233, 238
    keep superiors informed, 233, 238
    psych yourself up, 233, 238
    relationship with boss, 232, 238
    time your request, 233, 238
Recommendations, employee, 114–124
    (*see also* Employee suggestions)
Relationships:
    "golden touch," 234
    with boss, 232, 241, 242–243
Relaxed appearance, 141, 147
Repeat business, 185
Responsibility, look for more, 234–235
Rewards, employee suggestions, 123, 124
Ridicule, 274–276, 279–280
Risk, 234
Rumors, eliminate, 103

S

Sarcasm, 274–276, 279–280
Self-interests, 21, 27
Sentences, written, 258–259
Sexual innuendos, 249
Shelves, store, 236–237
Shoulders, 133
Sign, name of product, 236
Signatures, 184–185, 186
Slogan, 237
Small talk, 247
Smile:
    body language, 142, 146
    job interview, 231

Smile (*Cont.*)
  popularity, 55
Social activities, 145–146
Social conversations:
  friends, 29–41
  marriage and love life, 57–69
  opening with stranger, 17–28
  popularity, 45–55
  use person's motivators, 3–15
Space or territory, 141, 144, 147
Special occasions, 243–244
Speeches:
  benefits to be gained, 206, 207, 211
  conclusion, 206, 207, 211
  confidence, develop, 209–210, 211
  doing thing you fear, 203–204, 210
  examples, 206, 207, 211
  forceful and convincing, 207–209, 211
  how to make, 201–212
  main ideas, 205–206, 211
  nervousness and fear, 204, 211
  opening, 206–207, 211, 286–287
  organizing, 206–207, 211
  outline, 206, 211
  purpose, 205, 211
  secrets of professionals, 213–225
    control emotions of audience, 216, 223
    develop distinctive style, 215–216, 223
    don'ts, 220–221, 224
    irritating mannerisms, 219–220, 224
    overcoming nervousness, 217, 224
    project your personality, 217–218, 224
    visual aids, 221–223, 224–225
  techniques used, 206, 207, 211
Spouse, 66–68, 69
Staring, 142, 143, 147
Steepling, 140–141
Store shelves, 236–237
Strangers:
  appeal to ego, 20–21, 282
  compliments, 22–23, 28, 282
  control attitudes and emotions, 26–27, 28
  conversation openers, 20–21, 24–26, 282–283
  hobby, 26, 28
  make good first impression, 18–19
  man's name, 25, 28
  profession, 26, 28
  recognize superiority, 23–24, 28
  self-interests, 21, 27
  smile wins a smile, 27, 28
  take control immediately, 21–22, 27–28
Style, distinctive, 215–216, 223
Suggestions, employee, 114–124
  (*see also* Employee suggestions)
Superiority, recognize, 23–24, 28
Support
  (*see* Cooperation and support, gain)

T

Talking down to people, 276, 280
Teachers, 143–144
Teamwork, 103, 191–192
Technical terms, 246
Telephone conversation, 285–286
Temper, don't lose, 38
Territory or space, 141, 144, 147

V

Visual aids:
  accurate, 222
  appropriate, 222
  attractive, 222
  complicated points, 221
  easy to understand, 222
  easy to use, 222
  explain, 223
  help get message across, 221.
  introduce at proper time, 223
  portable and durable, 222
  prepare in advance, 222–223
  rapid learning, 221
  simple, 222
  talk to listeners, 223
  time-consuming drawing, 222
  use assistant, 223
  use pointer, 223

W

Wife, 46–47, 66, 68
Windows as salesmen, 236
Women, 141, 144, 146, 249, 283–284
Words:
  big, 259–260
  eliminate, 145
  power, action, 262–263
  skill in using, 229
  small, 261
Writing:
  active voice of verb, 257–258
  big words, 259–260
  brief, 257
  direct approach, 258
  grammar, 261–262
  letters, 263–267 (*see also* Letters)
  modifiers, 258
  power words, 262–263
  rid of deadheads, 259
  short sentences, 258–259
  small words, 261

Y

"Yes, but . . ." technique, 160, 161